THE JOY OF
Christmas

HELEN FEINGOLD AND MARY LEE GRISANTI

BARRON'S

New York • London • Toronto • Sydney

All inquiries should be addressed to:
Barron's Educational Series, Inc.
250 Wireless Boulevard
Hauppauge, New York 11788

Library of Congress Catalog Card No. 88-3483
International Standard Book No. 0-8120-5874-7

Library of Congress
Cataloging in Publication Data

Feingold, Helen
  Joy of Christmas
  Includes index,
  1. Christmas. I. Grisanti, Mary Lee. II. Title.
GT4985.F43 1988   394.2′68282   88-3483
ISBN 0-8120-5874-7

PRINTED IN THE UNITED STATES
OF AMERICA

890 977 987654321

CREDITS:

Prop Stylists: Julie Gong, Linda Cheverton
Food Stylists: Andrea Swenson, Helen Feingold
Photographer: Matthew Klein
Book and Cover Design: Milton Glaser, Inc.

PRATESI: *Linen*
BACCARAT: *Crystal*
BUCCELATI: *Silver*
JAMES II GALLERIES LTD: *Antiques*
THAXTON & CO: *Crystal, silver, china*
CERALENE RAYNAUD: *China*
LENOX CHINA & CRYSTAL: *China*

FRETTE FINE LINEN: *Linen*
D. PORTHAULT & CO.: *Linen*
CARTIER COMPANY: *China*
HUTSCHENREUTHER: *China*
ANICHINI: *Linen*
BARDITH, INC.: *Antique China*
ROYAL COPENHAGEN/GEORG JENSEN SILVERSMITHS: *China*

 # TABLE OF CONTENTS

The Christmas Story—5

Deck the Halls: Festive Decorations for Indoors and Out—20

Decorating the Table for Family and Friends—27

The Crafts of Christmas—34

Let the Children Help: Recipes and Projects the Kids Will Enjoy—52

Gifts from the Kitchen: From Simple to Sophisticated—63

Tempting Holiday Tidbits: Party Snacks and Hors d'oeuvres—84

The Steaming Tureen: Soups Both Hearty and Delicate—111

Christmas Dinner: Dramatic Dishes, Minimal Effort—126

A Christmas Cornucopia: Vegetable Dishes for Every Palate—175

Salads for the Season—196

The Second Time Around: Tempting Treatments for Holiday Leftovers—214

Warm and Wonderful Loaves: Festive Yeast and Quick Breads—235

Sweetmeats from Around the World: Pies and Ice Cream, Cakes, Cookies, Candy—267

For the Holiday Toast: Beverages of All Kinds—349

Conversion Tables—363

Index—365

THE CHRISTMAS STORY

Somewhere we seem to have lost the plain and simple joy of Christmas. Many of us have childhood memories of an old-fashioned holiday, but today it seems hard to recreate the homespun atmosphere, the excitement of tradition and love that have nothing to do with December's wild surges in the Consumer Market Index. Three-fourths of all retail buying takes place during the pre-holiday season, which means that most of us spend a lot of time driving and tramping around stores and shopping centers. But stop—Imagine staying at home quietly and having everything you need readily at hand. Imagine the tranquil, healing, homey feeling of Christmas in a bygone time. It's not necessarily gone forever and it cannot be bought in a store. It's still there waiting for you with a little time, patience and planning. Perhaps you, too, remember an evergreen tree with real candles, red apples weighing down the branches, along with ornaments collected over many years and a fuzzy spun-glass angel, worse for years of wear, on top. In my family, a pail of water was always handy for dousing the tree if the candles set it on fire, but the flickering candles were only one of the rich sights and smells of Christmas in those days. Piny, winy, spicy cooking, baking and roasting odors permeated the house. The closets were stuffed with mysterious packages; my mother and father, like so many others, had worked for months making toys for the children at night when we were safely tucked in bed.

It was a time of gathering together, when the house bulged with family and visitors from afar. Carolers sang, Christmas cards were stuffed into envelopes and there was a sharing of warmth, hospitality and giving that made this time of year different from all the others.

Of course, nostalgia makes it easy to forget the hard times and the back-breaking work that such homemade Christmases once entailed. None of us would want to go back to that but we do want to recapture the exhilarating feeling of anticipation. Our present lifestyle makes it difficult to slow down and take time to really enjoy Christmas; most women work outside the home, and children's after-school hours are fully scheduled. But we squeeze in music lessons, dental appointments, exercise classes. We can also make time for a very special holiday—it won't take as long as you might imagine. And think what you get in return! I'm talking about a loving and sharing that transcends religion. Confidences and conversations in the relaxed atmosphere of a kitchen can bridge many a gap between parents and children.

The pressures of modern living have served to streamline many family traditions. Special dishes can be prepared more easily with such new appliances as microwaves, food processors, electric mixers, ice cream machines, blenders and pasta makers, to name only a few. A lighter, fresher, more natural diet has produced a newly evolving vital cuisine, lower in calories, sugar, salt and fat. Even in the winter months, markets abound with summertime foods from the other side of the globe. Once offering only the most mundane foods, super-markets have exploded with fresh herbs, oriental staples, greens of all kinds, baby vegetables, cheeses, fresh pasta, exotic fruits and berries, fresh poultry and processed foods from all over the world. In the last few years merchants have realized that the quality and flavor of foods are crucial. The good cook knows that the best ingredients give the best results—and busier cooks mean business. When you put your time and attention into a dish, you want to be able to

count on something special. Today the resources available to the serious chef are as never before.

The "frantics" of the holidays can be lessened by planning meals with style but not a lot of extra work. This will leave time for one or two more time-consuming projects or for some fondly remembered traditional family recipe.

Happily, in this country we are a blend of many ethnicities and cultures. Each family can create its own Christmas look—traditional, contemporary, country, high-tech, or just sentimental and heartwarming—anything goes. Every family group is unique, be it a gathering of singles, a young married couple, "golden oldies" or families with children of all sizes and ages. Since most families combine all of these, this book offers suggestions to create a Christmas ambience suitable for all kinds of people and all kinds of homes—from the smallest apartment to the largest family estate.

The recipes in this book have been carefully chosen to provide not only tried-and-true Christmas favorites, but also fresh ideas consistent with the way we tend to eat now, which is more concerned with health and nutrition. You will find recipes both simple and gourmet, to please the cook with little time and the full-time homemaker alike.

After dinner any time during the holiday season, a cassette or record of Christmas music or stories or a Christmas video on the VCR—Frank Capra's classic It's a Wonderful Life has become a tradition across America—will help set the mood. This can be a nice time, too, to really look at that stack of cards and read the messages; think about old friends, and jot notes or call them.

Christmas is not just the sum total of all the activity you've busily engaged in; it is also an indefinable, intangible atmosphere that settles over everyone.

It is a season in which each person should be able to find his own way of giving and expressing himself, his own style of holiday cheer. In that spirit: Merry Christmas and Happy New Year.

THE CHRISTMAS TREE STORY

*N*othing symbolizes Christmas more than the decorated evergreen covered with lights and tinsel. In the 1500s, in Latvia and Estonia, townspeople placed a tree decorated with paper roses in the square, danced around it and then set it afire. It took the ever-practical Germans to admit that freezing outdoors was no fun, so they took the tree inside.

Decorated with apples, the German tree was used at Christmastime in plays to represent the "Paradise tree" of Adam and Eve. Later, paper roses, candies, pieces of sugar and communion wafers were added to adorn the Christbaum (the tree of Christ). Every family had a tree in the parlor, and no matter what the financial status, it was decorated. Jewelry, pieces of mirror, cotton wool, even silver knives and forks were used, as well as handcrafted ornaments. The tree was small and perched on a table covered with cloth; the gifts were arranged on the table.

In some homes, the top of a large tree was cut and hung upside down in the doorway and then decorated. Some trees were not trees at all, but wooden frames onto which boughs were fastened. In the homes of the wealthy, parents decorated several small trees—one for each child in the family—with small toys, mesh bags of gold coins, tops, bells, balls, stuffed animals, small games, flags, drums and puzzles.

Then as now, collections of ornaments were handed down from one generation to another and treasured. One or two items were added to the collection each year. For lights, the trees were hung with candles, carefully placed to avoid burning an upper branch. A pole tied with a wet rag was kept handy for just such an emergency. In the evening, father would light the tree behind closed doors while excited children hopped with anticipation. Doors were flung open

and the tree was admired by all. But dripping wax caused innumerable fires, a problem solved by the invention of electric lights at the turn of the century. As if to make up for bringing a sheltering evergreen indoors, outside sheaves of wheat were bundled and studded with pieces of suet and seeds for the birds.

In Germany, St. Nicholas came on January 6th, and in anticipation of his visit children left their shoes in front of the fireplace. If they were good, the shoes were filled with oranges and dried fruits. If they were naughty, rocks or coals were their reward. When the serious St. Nicholas arrived in America, he became a hearty, chubby Santa Claus, a relative of the Dutch Sinter Klauss.

In the United States, the Christmas tree also underwent a transformation; as is our style in this country, it got bigger. We adopted a hefty floor model complete with stand. Years ago, the tree was decorated only with edibles such as apples, fruits, nuts, Springerle, marzipan, honey cut-out cookies, strings of cranberries, peanuts in the shell, large raisins, and pretzel-shaped cookies to symbolize hands folded in prayer. During Christmas no one was allowed to eat the goodies on the tree, but on January 6th the children shook the tree and made off with the edibles. In this way, the dreary job of dismantling the tree was made considerably more exciting.

Soon, though, edible trees were seen as requiring too much time. In Europe, especially in Germany, ornaments became permanent works of art. They were handcrafted of embossed cardboard, tin, wax and glass—molded, blown and spun. They came in myriad shapes and sizes, silvered inside and with painted decorations outside. Glass bead and tinsel ropes became popular, as well as cotton wool for snow, paper ornaments from Japan, and papier-mâché objects. Glass ornaments and, later, molded light bulbs were made in every shape: Santa Clauses, reindeer, angels, pine cones, grapes, drums, fruits and vegetables, houses, animals, trumpets, bears, violins, birds with hangers or clip-ons for fastening to the tree branches.

Some towns in Germany had cottage industries with families that spent their entire lives making glass ornaments. But time marches on, and now machines blow more ornaments in a minute than could be produced by a glassblower in a day.

Nearly all the traditional symbols of Christmas that we take for granted once had some religious significance. Christmas is, after all, the commemoration of Christ's birth. The evergreen tree is the sign of eternal life brought by Christ. Holly is symbolic of the crown of thorns; its red berries are drops of blood. Ivy represents the soul of mankind and denotes immortality through union with the Lord. Hanging mistletoe is supposed to let everyone know that last year's animosities are forgotten—a good reason for kissing under it. But watch out, it must be burned on Twelfth Night or those who have kissed under it will never marry.

With tinsel comes the legend that a spider wove webs over a tree and, when it was blessed by Christ, the webs were turned to silver. In fact, I remember silver webs on my grandmother's tree. Bells are for rejoicing on this happy occasion. Lights are for joy and faith. The star at the top of the tree represents the Star of Bethlehem, and angels are, of course, the heavenly hosts proclaiming the birth of Christ.

Long ago, the manger, the crêche and the Yule log were more important than the tree. Crude, as well as very artistic, reproductions of the crêche, Mary, Joseph, the Three Kings and the animals were the center of attention. In some homes figures were moved each day to symbolize the drawing near of the Magi, or the homage of the shepherds. A giant Yule log was placed in the fireplace and had to be lighted with a piece saved from last year's log. It burned for 12 hours as pine cones were added to the blaze to create bursts of brilliant color. Shoes as well as stockings were placed in front of the fireplace to dry, and there they remained to be filled by Santa.

A WORLD OF CHRISTMAS CUSTOMS

*A*merica, as John F. Kennedy said, is a nation of immigrants. All of us, whether one generation back or many, have the traditions of another culture calling to us. I'd like to note briefly some of these ethnic traditions in hope that today's families, who often feel disconnected from their roots, might be encouraged to make room for some of these charming and meaningful customs. The observance of Christmas in America today is a hybrid affair with roots in Anglo-Saxon and Germanic practices. Did you know that America adopted the Christmas tree before England did? The custom of lighted trees was brought here during the Revolutionary War by Hessian soldiers.

Many of the customs we follow today are shared by the British Commonwealth (which, as the British Empire, exported such customs as caroling and Christmas trees to places like India and Pakistan) and by West Germany.

It is in England that kissing underneath the mistletoe became a custom. Though its origin was in Druid fertility rites, the practice was very popular in Tudor and Stuart times and in Queen Victoria's day. Many of the lovely sights, smells and songs we associate with Christmas in this country were features of Victorian Christmases (lovingly described by Charles Dickens, and not only in A Christmas Carol). Plum pudding is English, and lighting the pudding is the high point of the substantial English Christmas dinner. Making a pudding is a wonderful project, best done weeks and even months before the holiday.

There are many facsimile editions of 18th- and 19th-century cookbooks with authentic recipes to try (there is also a simpler one in this book). To create a majestic "plummy pudding" is to taste a little bit of English literature and history.

Boxing Day, a traditional day of gift-giving to the poor and to charitable

institutions in English-speaking countries, evolved into the present mad frenzy of giving to everyone. The gifts symbolize gifts from God and the gifts of the Wise Men to the Christ Child.

In Ireland, the "old country" to many, many Americans, a big, thick candle is placed on the sill of the most conspicuous window in the house. The youngest child usually lights it and it stands as a beacon of welcome to any travelers who, like Joseph and Mary, may be in need of shelter. During the long English occupation of what is now the Republic of Ireland, a lighted candle in a window also meant there was a priest within—a sign to persecuted native Catholics to come and hear the forbidden Catholic Mass.

In Ireland, to this day, there is the flamboyant custom of dressing up in costumes on the day after Christmas, St. Stephen's Day, and singing from door to door, soliciting money to feed "the poor, starving wren." The wren in question is now a live little wren carried in a cage atop a pole, but in former years it was a dead wren; called "the Devil's bird," wrens were once thought to have warned sleeping British soldiers of an ambush by pecking on their drums. In any event, the money goes to feed the poor, starving (more likely, thirsty) carolers.

In Scotland, the first person to enter a house on New Year's Day brings either good or bad luck. All women are presumed to bring bad luck (this tradition is not for feminists), as are flat-footed people or people who squint! The best "first foot" is a handsome, dark-haired (in some districts, fair-haired) stranger. Failing a romantic interloper, a friend can "first foot" or a family member can go out and come back in—as long as he brings back the traditional gifts of a piece of coal, some bread, salt and money—all signs of warmth and prosperity for the New Year.

In Germany, where Christmas trees and the melodic "O Tannenbaum" originated, Christmas presents are supposed to be from the Christ Child himself,

usually dressed in long, white robes with golden wings. There are also a number of customs that are related to St. Nicholas, but which focus on catching our naughty behavior. In Bavaria, a little boy dressed as a girl called Nickolo-Weibl arrives with twelve Buttenmandeln—men dressed in straw and animal masks. The little girl gives out presents and the Buttenmandeln drive the people outside the house with shouts and punches! In other areas, a knight named Rupprecht may supplant St. Nick and show a very intimate knowledge of children's misdeeds. He and St. Nick can read thoughts and definitely know if you've been naughty or nice. In the North, Ru-Klass, or Rough Nicholas, examines children to see if they say their prayers correctly and he can be mean if they don't!

In Austria, people throw molten lead into the snow on New Year's Eve. The future can supposedly be foretold in the shapes the lead suddenly assumes.

In Italy, as in most Catholic countries, Christmas includes the Feast of St. Nicholas on December 6th and culminates most impressively on Twelfth Night, the Feast of the Epiphany.

Families set up a presepio, or manger; some are incredibly elaborate and have hundreds of figures. All the churches display them as well, and vie with each other for the grandest.

Generally, Christmas Eve is celebrated with a large meatless meal of fish, shellfish and pasta. At midnight, champagne corks fly and sausage is placed on the fire. Each town has its own variety of Christmas sausage. My grandfather came from a place where the sausage was made of veal and pork, flavored with savory licorice-scented fennel—and had little chunks of mozzarella cheese inside which melted over the meat.

In Italy, it is a witch, La Befana, who brings presents on January 6th. She is a benevolent witch, a survivor of Italy's heady pagan past. In Sicily, it is said that La Befana was a woman who befriended the Three Wise Men on their journey but was too busy cleaning her house to go with them!

France, also, is noted for its beautiful crêches—*mangers filled with exquisite figurines that tell the Christmas story.*

The little figurines, called santons *(little saints), not only show figures from Scripture, but also hometown characters like the mayor, the butcher and the baker! French children put out their shoes to be filled with goodies by* Père Noël—*Father Christmas. After midnight Mass, the family has a meal called* le réveillon—*including ham, vegetables and salads, cakes and wine.*

In Alsace, there is goose; in Brittany, buckwheat pancakes and sour cream; in Paris, oysters are very popular. One French tradition that has taken hold here is the delicious bûche de Noël—a chocolate-iced cake in the shape of the Yule log. Sometimes this cake is so realistically decorated that it is accompanied by little forest mushrooms or meringue dusted with cocoa.

In the Scandinavian countries, there is the saying, "Christmas lasts a month." Here, Christmas begins on St. Lucy's day, when the youngest daughter, dressed as Lucy, the patron saint of the blind, opens her parents' bedroom door at dawn wearing a wreath with burning candles in her hair. She brings them breakfast in bed, a warm assortment of special St. Lucy's buns and cakes. The day is December 13th, coincidentally the day when the days begin imperceptibly to get longer again, so it is a festival of light in the long, dark northern winter. The celebrations last until the 13th of January, St. Knut's Day.

In Sweden, the main family meal begins with a smörgasbord. It is followed by fish, sun-dried cod in cream sauce. Then there's ham, and finally a white pudding, inside of which is hidden a whole almond. Whoever gets the almond will be married before the end of the year!

As in the other Scandinavian countries, people in Sweden love to go to church by sleigh. In Norway, so many cookies are baked for the holidays that the first great thaw following the Christmas snow is called the "cookie thaw"—as though the heat from all the ovens had melted the snow. In Finland, it is traditional to bake gingerbread in every size and shape.

Opposite: Christmas Dinner

In Holland, St. Nick is the man of the hour, and Dutch children put their (formerly wooden) shoes outside their doors or by their beds to be filled with delicious Dutch chocolate and other presents. As we know, this is when Hans Brinker received his famous silver skates! Sinter Klass, as St. Nicholas is known, is accompanied by "Black Peter" (guess who), who keeps his eye out for naughty children.

In Czarist times, Russian Christmases were gay and grand affairs, with parties, feasting and Christmas trees. The Soviets have banned the religious holiday, replacing it with New Year's festivities, but Russians have taken to New Year's with the old gusto and decorate New Year's trees, sing New Year's carols (usually folk songs and not the propagandistic songs created for the occasion), and feast as best they can. The Russian Orthodox also do not eat meat on Christmas Eve, but have borscht (beet soup), cabbage stuffed with buckwheat groats, and wheat cakes dripping with honey. Everyone sends New Year's cards, and more and more people go to the few available church services.

Mexico and South America have wonderful Christmas customs, some Spanish in origin, others Indian and some a mixture of both. It is a religious festival, and, in Mexico, families travel, like Mary and Joseph, to each other's homes. They are welcomed with prayers—and then a party.

The high notes of these parties are the famous piñatas—*papier-mâché animals filled with toys and candies. The piñata is suspended from the ceiling while blindfolded children with bats try to crack it open. When the piñata breaks and all the goodies fall out, the children scramble to scoop up the loot.*

Mangers are popular in Latin America; in Costa Rica the manager may fill a whole room, not just one corner. In Panama, the nacimiento *is very elaborate and includes trees, grass and waterfalls.*

In Brazil, Nativity scenes may include all of modern Brazil's tributes to God—hydroelectric dams, speeding trains and airplanes!

In Argentina, Christmas dinner is outdoors on the veranda and the table is decorated with roses and jasmine. The main course is cold roast turkey or chicken. On Twelfth Night, Argentinians leave fresh water outside their doors for the Wise Men's camels; they've come a long way, and they're no doubt quite thirsty.

In Colombia, Christmas Eve is a night of reveling—everyone goes out dressed in costumes and masks—but if you recognize someone, you can claim a present.

Christmas was brought to Africa by colonizing missionaries—with only one exception, and that is Ethiopia. The Coptic Christians of Ethiopia have celebrated Christ's birth since earliest times. There is a religious procession and the distribution of bread blessed by the priests. In Ghana, as in other Christianized countries in Africa, the celebration is traditional but with an indigenous flavor—there are fireworks and fufu, *a dish of pounded yams. Food is sent to neighbors and presents are exchanged. In Liberia, the Christmas tree is an oil palm decorated with bells.*

These are only a handful of countries and a smattering of the traditions of each. I hope you will feel inspired to learn more about the traditions in your past and incorporate them in your Christmas Present and Christmas Future!

DECK THE HALLS

Festive Decorations for Indoors and Out

*T*he most important outdoor Christmas decorations are the most meaningful ones: those that remember the animals in winter. On a balcony, patio or in the garden, it would be a treat for the birds to have a small tree outdoors tied with seeds and bird food. If you have a bird house, feeder or bath, decorate it with fresh greens and fill it with seed and balls made of suet and seed worked together. (The fat keeps the birds warm.) You can also sprinkle nuts for squirrels and, if you live in the country, hay and salt for deer.

Of course, stringing lights outdoors creates the festive look we associate with the season. Make sure all lights are well insulated and wires are protected against damage by cold and moisture. In areas where winter is warm, wires must also be protected against exposure to the sun.

All lights should be tested before they are hung, not only to see which ones need to be replaced, but to check for worn spots or loose and/or corroded sockets. Be careful not to pierce the wires when you are tacking or stapling them to house and trees. Grounding plugs are a must.

The trees and bushes outdoors can be strung with lights of one or many colors. Tiny "fairy" lights have become so popular that some people use them all year. Just make sure you use a sturdy ladder and ask someone to help. Holidays marred by accidents are no fun.

OUTSIDE THE HOME

Fences and porch or patio railings can be wrapped with red and green plastic ribbons and tied with big bows. Gates should be edged with large plastic candy canes or baskets filled with holly branches. Tie outside stair railings with pine boughs and cones. Add a festive touch to your mailbox by wrapping the post with a spiral of ribbon and topping the box with a holly branch and a big red bow. You could even add a covered clear plastic container filled with candy canes and a sign to "help yourself." A mail slot or apartment mailbox can be decorated with lots of gold stars or Christmas tree cutouts, or paper or real holly leaves.

An apartment door with a simple pine wreath (perhaps framed by a circle of lights) is just as appealing as the most complicated decorations. Other ideas for wreaths might incorporate real fruit, hot red peppers or bay leaves, and anything that children make with pine cones, glitter or what have you.

Keep outside decorations simple and they will set the stage for entrance into your home—your holiday world.

INSIDE THE HOME

The banisters can be candy-striped with ribbon or tied with pine boughs, Christmas balls, candy, pine cones or tiny lights. Colored cellophane mounted in each window pane will make them seem like stained glass (children love to do this). Running a ribbon diagonally across the window with a big bow will create a giant "package" (not for children, as you must lean out the window to attach bows).

Wreaths are the most fun for decorating and the most traditional. Craft shops have all kinds of wreath materials—styrofoam, into which you can pin or toothpick anything, braided straw into which you can stick objects, wooden rings for decorating, as well as dried vines to which you can add dried flowers, fruit and ribbon. Decorating materials are not restricted to ribbons, dried flowers, laces, beading, bulky yarns, artificial flowers and fruits, artificial snow, glue-on glitter—anything is eligible. Try cut-outs of old wallpaper or Christmas

cards, bits of jewelry, small stuffed animals, nuts, even odd shapes of pasta!

Probably the easiest thing to use as a base for a wreath is the lowly wire coat hanger. Using pliers and your hands, bend the body of the hanger into a large circle. For the most traditional look, cut small sprigs of pine; holding several together at the stems, wire them in place using any flexible wire or florist's wire. Repeat until the entire ring is covered. Add a big bow or red ribbon. You might try pine cones, mistletoe, holly (wear gloves—they prick), Christmas balls, dried flowers, bundles of candies, candy canes, cinnamon sticks wrapped with orange peel, tiny pomander balls of clementine or kumquat, pom-poms of yarn, dried wheat stalks, crêpe paper ruffles or anything that reflects your taste and imagination.

Personal touches tucked into the wreath—tiny toys, birds, little hats, mittens, beads, cars, knitting needles or whatever—are wonderful. And of course, use the hanger part to hang the wreath when finished. (If your wreath is going to be heavy, wire two coat hangers together to make the base more rigid.)

If you have grapevines, cut them in the fall and strip off the leaves. While they are moist they can be tied into a wreath and used plain or decorated. Tie on hearts, even heart-shaped cookie cutters; lots of tiny wrapped boxes filled with little gifts for a grab bag; small plastic fruits and vegetables, sprayed white, gold or silver. If you are a chocoholic, tie on chocolate kisses, bars or cordial-filled chocolate bottles. When a wreath is used as a table centerpiece, it can be placed on a piece of mirror and the center filled with candles. A wreath can also be used to surround the punchbowl or a platter holding a special bread or cake.

If you have a fireplace use the mantel for all your candlesticks, tied with ribbons and surrounded by pine or holly sprigs. Choose candles of all sizes, shapes and fragrances, especially bayberry, to give not only light but atmosphere to the room. (Votive candles placed anywhere give a soft, flickering light; they can be combined with pine and flowers to make an individual floral piece at each person's place at the table.)

Fasten a runner of pine around the fireplace opening with ribbon, pine cones or Christmas balls. If you have no fireplace, stockings could be hung at the windowsill. If the children love to draw, let them draw a fireplace on a large sheet of paper and mount that on the wall.

All through December beautiful Christmas cards are arriving, and displaying them makes the home more colorful. Tie big bows of 2-inch-wide red velvet or other ribbon and attach 36-inch lengths to each bow. Using straight pins, attach cards to the lengths of ribbon, and hang on a wall or door. Let children stretch long lengths of bulky yarn across the room or a corner of the room and hang the cards over them. Or pile the cards in a large basket or several small baskets and decorate with ribbon and pine.

One of the most creative holiday decorating challenges is to make use of things you already have and use during the rest of the year for table or buffet decorations. Here are a few suggestions: a large punchbowl or glass salad bowl filled with Christmas balls; large baskets of fruit and gourds, cookies and ornaments; small baskets piled with candies, nuts and dried fruits, or candy and presents; arrangements of assorted goblets and glasses filled with cranberries, popcorn, mints, pretzels, Christmas candies and shelled nuts; a wine cooler displaying poinsettias; empty flowerpots covered with colored foil and filled with candy canes, candied fruits and bonbons; crocks heaped with pine boughs or pine cones; copper molds or unusual baking pans with votive candles and holly; pots of Christmas flowers lined up on a jelly roll board; a small old sled or toy sled filled with pine branches and baskets of nuts, or gaily wrapped presents; a large wooden salad bowl of shiny red and green apples and sprigs of dried flowers or lots of decorated gingerbread boys and girls; tankards filled with peppermint sticks, lollipops and long cinnamon sticks; pitchers and jugs piled with Christmas greens and handles tied with ribbon.

Using straight pins or round toothpicks, spear styrofoam cones (sold in craft stores and in some supermarkets) with decorative elements such as ribbon, tiny

ornaments or gold braid, as well as food like cherry tomatoes, shrimp or meatballs (use florist's clay to fasten cone securely to serving dish). Use styrofoam rings to make tabletop wreaths of molded marzipan, gumdrops of all sizes and colors, green mint leaves and fresh sugared grapes.

The problem of where to put a Christmas tree in a small apartment can be solved by placing a tiny tree on a bridge table covered with a favorite tablecloth, old-fashioned quilt or afghan. Trim with carefully selected small treasures and leave room on the table for piles of presents.

The choice of an artificial or real or rooted tree should depend on your personal preferences. Certainly an artificial tree is appropriate if you hate cleaning up needles and want to pay for a tree only once. It is possible to buy extremely real-looking artificial trees, but you might want to have something fun and glitzy like a silver tree; decorated with, say, tiny blue lights, sumptuous brocade ribbons and pretty paper ornaments (there are many Victorian reproductions marketed now), your tinsel tree could be both tasteful and smashing.

But if you love the smell of a real pine, the long-needled Scotch pine or short-needled Douglas fir or blue spruce is for you. The short-needled trees, also shorter in height, have a lush look that can fill out a low-ceilinged room beautifully; longer-needled variety are also taller and can tend to be sparser. They take more decorations than the short-needled type. Make sure your tree stand has a container for water and that the room in which you keep your tree is not too hot.

A tree skirt makes it easier to get rid of the needles that fall. Use an old circleskirt or make a circle of felt or burlap. The skirt is a terrific place to set up a small circle railroad, a racing car track or a traditional manger.

If you use a rooted and balled tree, you must keep it moist at all times and you will need a container large enough to hold it, such as a washtub. Where the weather is not too cold, it will be easy to dig a hole and plant it after the

holidays. But in very cold areas, digging a hole in frozen ground is a problem. You might have to consider digging the hole earlier in the year, storing the earth removed indoors and covering the hole with boards until you are ready to plant.

Once the tree is positioned, decorating can begin. Check all the lights before they are put on the tree. Repair any damage, taping cracked wires and replacing worn-out bulbs. Place the lights on outside branches to weight them and make them spread. Place the ornament on the top of the tree first, not last, since you will knock other things off if you do it later. Hang the ornaments on the tree, then add the garlands and tinsel last.

If you are a pure traditionalist, the tree will be filled with antiques and handcrafted traditional items collected over many years and from many lands. But it's just as nice to cover a tree with bows of all colors, with natural wood ornaments, decorations all of one color, all kinds of bells or perhaps crystals of all shapes and sizes. With children, it's easy to return to the old-time edible Christmas tree with apples, dried fruits, nuts, low-sugar candy, candy canes, pretzels, bags of gumdrops, jelly beans and chocolate gold coins, and perhaps tiny musical toys—something for children who come to visit, and for those moments when you need a ready treat or distraction for your own little ones.

For the collector, a tree can reflect many interests and hobbies. All kinds of Santa Clauses, miniature animals, bracelets or necklaces, Peruvian bread dolls, Scandinavian wood ornaments, hearts of all materials and sizes, small copper molds, tiny bottles, doll's hats, mittens, in fact any small treasure you collect can be strung and hung on a tree. For a laugh, the tree could be hung with all kinds of whistles, fortune cookies with outrageous fortunes, birthday snappers and paper hats (after all, it is a birthday celebration), funny faces, wax lips and other disguises, joke books or goofy things from the local magic shop. Very young children might arrange their blocks around the base of the tree to spell Merry Christmas!

DECORATING THE TABLE

for Family and Friends

*F*or this occasion, many families have a
special Christmas cloth or family heirloom of lace or
embroidered linen. If not, nothing could be simpler than
making a cloth using several yards of red or green felt, cotton or even velvet.
(If you choose expensive fabric, or one with a nap, Scotchgard it and it will fare
dinner spills quite well.) Felt comes in very wide widths and the edges do not need
to be hemmed but can be cut with pinking shears for a fast, decorative border.
Measure your table and allow a 12-inch overhang on all four sides. Even easier, get
a flat sheet of the right color and size and use it for a tablecloth.
To make life simpler at the last minute, the table should be set the day before. If you
have room, a separate table for the children is usually a hit, both with them and with
the adults—provided the children are close enough in age. Please don't exile
teenagers with toddlers.
In a small apartment, several small tables, or even snack tables, scattered
throughout, make a sit-down dinner feasible. In this case, placemats are easier
to use than tablecloths, and even easier to make. Be sure they are at least
14 x 20 inches. Make disposable paper mats with the large pages of a
decorative calendar, the pages of a discarded wallpaper sample book,
pieces of corrugated cardboard
covered with Christmas wrapping paper and tied with
ribbon to look like packages with name cards

attached, or Mylar cut into decorative shapes. Once you start thinking of materials to use, you will come up with even more ideas. Glue on stars, glitter, ribbons, mirror tiles and other mosaic pieces, even sprigs of fresh holly.

Silverware can also be presented festively. Wrap the service in a folded napkin and tie with ribbon and greens. Or get some inexpensive small Christmas stockings and use them to hold napkins and flatware. Tuck the napkin into a goblet, forming a big ruff, and bundle the silverware with ribbons and bells. A little basket tied with ribbons can also be used for the napkins and silver. Place cards might be attached to big candy canes, little gingerbread men, a branch of mistletoe.

Each table should be decorated with a centerpiece (even snack tables can accommodate a red carnation and a twig of pine in a cordial glass). Make sure centerpieces are not so tall as to interfere with conversation. Flowers are always appropriate, but a wreath of gourds around a bowl of red apples would be colorful on a less formal table, as would a copper kettle filled with fresh vegetables and pine sprigs, or a basket of Christmas balls with fat candy canes. For the more traditional table, try a marble or glass bowl filled with pears and grapes (and decorated with some dark green leaves), or a series of large and small crystal and silver pitchers filled with holly, ivy and mistletoe; these could be studded with tapers (use the dripless kind) or surrounded with votive candles in glasses of various shapes and colors. A grouping of different candlesticks surrounded with a fresh green wreath, or goblets of all sizes and shapes filled with cranberries, nuts, mints and tapers on a bed of Christmas greens, can also be quite special.

SETTING THE TABLE

THE FAMILY TABLE

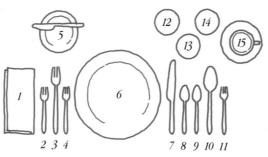

1. *Napkin*
2. *Salad fork*
3. *Dinner fork*
4. *Dessert fork*
5. *Bread and butter plate with spreader*
6. *Dinner plate*
7. *Dinner knife*
8. *Teaspoon*
9. *Teaspoon*
10. *Soup spoon*
11. *Cocktail fork*
12. *Water glass*
13. *Red wine glass*
14. *White wine glass*
15. *Coffee cup and saucer*

For informal service the cup and saucer can be placed on the table. If space is limited, however, put the cup and saucer on the table along with dessert when the main course is cleared.

BUFFET TABLE

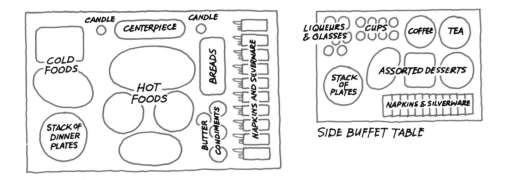

SIDE BUFFET TABLE

Set the buffet table at the side of the room, with the centerpiece and candles at the back of the table. If you have a large group, the buffet should be set in the center of the room with the same food on each side of the table to split the traffic. Start the table with plates, then all the cold foods together, all the hot foods, then the breads, and finally napkins rolled around the silverware. Make sure all the food lends itself to easy eating; juggling a knife and fork while standing is not comfortable. If something requires carving or special service, the host or hostess should do this to speed things up, or better yet, do it in the kitchen beforehand. Beverages should be poured separately. Also, set out dessert and coffee separately; this is a good idea for a sit-down dinner, too, as you can move the guests back to the living room. It's more comfortable than sitting at a possibly crowded and cramped table for a long time, and it creates opportunities to clean up the greater part of the mess before the end of the evening without breaking up the conversation.

BEVERAGE TABLE OR BAR

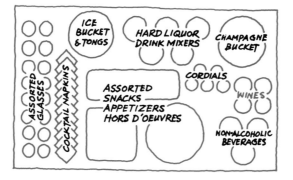

"Beverages" should always mean both alcoholic and nonalcoholic drinks. Low-calorie sodas, mineral waters, such as Perrier, juice and wine are the mainstays. Few people drink much hard liquor these days, and, as there is much traveling from house to house during the holidays, it is wise to discourage heavy drinking. However, you may want to have on hand a bottle each of scotch and vodka—the two most popular spirits. If you are having a big party it's nice to hand your guests a drink when they arrive and get their coats off; the practice is hospitable and prevents a line at the bar. Most people will not refuse a cold glass of champagne!

For friends and neighbors who drop in casually, it is easy to leave a small table, counter or sideboard set up during the entire holiday season. Include wine or cordial glasses and bottles, jars of Christmas cookies, a covered dish with slices of fruitcake, jars of brandied fruit, crocks of crackers, special olives and cornichons. In the refrigerator, stock a small cheese tray or crocks of pâté.

This makes drop-in guests easy on you—you can relax and enjoy the company, confident that you will never be in the position of serving liquor without food to accompany it.

DESSERT AND COFFEE TABLE

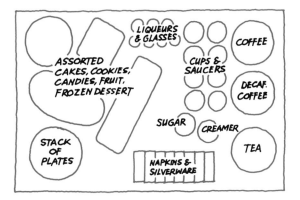

Desserts can, of course, run the gamut from simple to extravagant. Holiday fare tends to be a bit heavy, so it is nice to offer a lighter choice along with the Chocolate Torte and Plum Pudding—a fruit salad or clusters of grapes, for example.

Beverages should include regular and decaffeinated coffee and regular and herbal tea. Liqueurs with glasses can be set on the table as well. After-dinner mints can be placed here, or in small bowls in the areas where the guests are sitting.

THE CRAFTS OF CHRISTMAS

GIFT WRAPPING

*A*fter the fun of selecting just the right gift comes the wrapping. Don't think of it as a chore—it really can be a pleasure. Stores are filled with decorated papers, from plain colored foils to rich prints, gift tags, ribbons (not just paper ribbons, but also satin, velveteen and yarns), seals, bows and artificial flowers. And many other materials can be used for wrapping. Try cloth (you may have just the right extra length languishing in a drawer or closet), vinyl, brown wrapping paper (decorated with fanciful stamps to look as if the package arrived from far away), shelf paper, foil, blueprint paper (children can decorate this by covering the sheet with their hands or other objects in direct sunlight, then washing it in a bath of warm water and peroxide to develop the images), how-to diagrams, sheet music, work aprons (a terrific addition to gifts for cooks, gardeners and craftspersons)—anything goes as long as it is large and sturdy enough.

After the package is wrapped, it can be tied with colored or printed tapes, ribbons, bulky yarn, gold or silver cord or lace. The bows may be decorated with small bells, flowers, pine, holly, wood figures, Christmas ornaments, rings, lollipops, tiny toys and name cards. The gift might be wrapped with a little extra present tucked on top (sometimes these can even serve as original cards; just write on them with an ink marker). You might use a tiny car for

the car lover, a harmonica for the musician, a puzzle for the whiz, a small tool for the craftsman, measuring spoons for the cook, a tiny calculator for the student, any little gift that mirrors the interest of the recipient.

And you can gild the lily! A wrapped package can be decorated with seals, gold stars, all kinds of paper cut-outs attached with rubber cement (and let the children help at this stage; they feel they've done something and the recipient gets the special gift of a child's artwork). Gifts can be varied or wrapped with a color scheme in mind—all white or blue or both, silver or gold touched with red, grid paper with shiny white, anything that suits your taste and decor.

When packing gifts from your kitchen, be inventive. A shoebox covered with colorful paper and lined with paper doilies will hold cookies or a loaf cake. Commercial cookie tins can be sprayed with enamel paints; leave adequate time to dry and always work near an open window. Cover oatmeal boxes with wallpaper; decorate coffee cans with gift paper and gold braid to look like little drums; weave a pretty ribbon through plastic berry baskets, then tie with a bow; prepackaged deli containers or clear plastic can be personalized with paint or telling little touches like hearts, whistles, tiny toys. Plastic toy pails, paint buckets or large plastic tubs can be filled, wrapped with clear plastic or colored cellophane and tied with ribbons and greens.

If you are all thumbs when it comes to tying bows on a package, try this: Tie the cord around the package and make a tight knot, leaving two 6-inch ends. These will be used to tie on the bow. Make two to four loops of ribbon and place on top of knot; bring up knot ends and tie tightly around the loops. Tie on a new piece to cover the knot, allowing ends to hang. Trim. If you are

using a crinkle ribbon, stroke over the ends with a dull knife or the edge of the scissor to make curls. For a pom-pom bow, fold over 3 inches of ribbon and continue folding until you have six thicknesses. Cut a V-shaped section out of both sides of the center of the ribbon. Tie tightly in center. Pull out loops from inside the ribbon, first from one side and then the other, until all are pulled out. Set on package and glue in place.

  Mail packages in plenty of time. Wrap them prettily, then overwrap them with heavy brown paper and mailing tape—not masking tape. Remember that the Post Office will not accept packages tied with cord.

CHRISTMAS STOCKINGS

To make your own, use a firm material such as felt, burlap, any quilted fabric, or corduroy. Fold fabric the wrong side out into two layers and trace a large boot shape, allowing ½ inch for seams, with a piece of chalk. Trim away excess fabric. Sew around boot, leaving the top edge open. Clip curved edges and turn inside out. Turn top raw edge down on outside and cover raw edge with wide ribbon, gold braid or lace, or glue on cotton batting. If you like, paint on a name with glue and sprinkle with glitter, or embroider the name if you are handy with a needle. There are innumerable stocking kits in needlepoint, cross-stitch and appliqué that are featured in catalogs months ahead of Christmas.

  For those of us who just can't find the time, stores that sell work clothes have boot socks in giant sizes that make great Christmas stockings. Decorate with ribbon, lace, felt cut-outs, sequins, bows.

If you are bored with the idea of stockings, have fun with wool stocking hats, tiny shopping bags, small baskets or mesh bags.

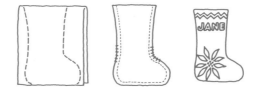

CLOTH CHRISTMAS WREATH

Use 2 yards each of solid-color, calico or small print cotton fabric; you will also need heavy-duty sewing thread and 2-inch-wide velvet or grosgrain ribbon. Crush each material lengthwise into a bulky rope. Secure the ends and wrap the sewing thread loosely around and around the rope to keep the fabric in place. Tie the three ropes together and braid. Tie end of braid and bring ends together, shaping a ring; sew ends. At intervals, clip thread holding fabric in place and remove. Sew back of wreath onto a wire ring or wire coat hanger bent into a ring. Tie a ribbon bow and sew in place over the joining. Dried flowers, small pine cones, artificial berries and other small ornaments can be pushed into the folds of the fabric. Hang wreath on a nail. After the holidays, the wreath can be dismantled and the fabric used for sewing.

HOW TO TIE A PERFECT LARGE BOW FOR A WREATH
Use 2 yards of 2- to 3-inch-wide ribbon. Cut off 16 inches for tying the bow
and set aside. Fold the remainder into eight 7-inch lengths. Fold the free end
of the ribbon under and bring to the first 7-inch marking. Crunch the center
of the ribbon together and twist. Repeat alternating loops from side to side; you
will have eight loops. Wrap with thread in the center to hold loops. Tie the 16-
inch piece around the bow, covering the thread, and allow ends to hang free.
With scissors, cut ends diagonally or into a V-notch.

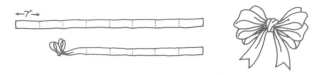

CANDLE HOLDERS FOR CAROLERS
Save large plastic lids from coffee cans or margarine tubs. With a single-edge
razor blade, cut three 2-inch cuts in the center, crisscrossing the lines. Push
candle into center. Plastic can be covered with foil, holly, pine sprigs or ivy

FRILLED CANDLES

Fold 6-inch strips of heavy-duty foil in half lengthwise, dull side out. With scissors, cut into folded edge, cutting ¾ of the way through at ½-inch intervals. Open out carefully and refold shiny side out. Place candle into holder. Place frill ¼ of the way up the candle and pin in place. Wrap frill around and around candle to base. Pin end and fluff frills.

CHRISTMAS TREE ORNAMENTS

CORNSTARCH CLAY ORNAMENTS

In a large saucepan, combine 2 cups cornstarch, 4 cups baking soda and 3 cups water. Cook over medium heat until mixture starts to bubble. Keep cooking until mixture becomes lumpy and then smoothes out. Place on a plate, cover with foil and cool. Dust work surface with cornstarch and knead the clay until smooth. It can be molded with the fingers into desired shapes or rolled to ½-inch thickness and cut with cookie cutters. Place on waxed paper. Open a large metal paper clip so one loop remains and one loop is straightened. Press straight part into ornament, leaving loop for hanging. Let dry for several hours. Decorate ornaments as desired with acrylic paints and let dry. Spray with lacquer or brush with clear nail polish.

PAPIER-MÂCHÉ CHRISTMAS BALLS

Tear newspaper into 1-inch-wide strips (tearing rather than cutting allows paper to be molded more smoothly). Prepare wallpaper paste according to package directions and place in a bowl. Run paper strips through paste until wet and well coated. Stroke off excess glue and place strips over a small orange, rubber ball or styrofoam ball until it is completely covered with a layer ¼ inch thick. Place on a rack in a warm, dry place (a radiator, hot air register or near the furnace is ideal) and let dry several hours. With a single-edge razor blade, cut through the paper around the center of the ball and twist to remove from mold (if using styrofoam, omit this step). Put halves back together, insert a loop for hanging and cover the slash with more strips of wet paper. If you like, paste and apply color pictures from magazines, pretty cut-outs from old Christmas cards, or other colored papers. Let dry for several hours. Paint as desired with acrylic colors, let dry and then brush or spray with lacquer. Abstract patterns, stripes, polka dots, funny faces, Christmas scenes, glitter, flowers, holly leaves, solid colors, words and sayings, anything goes!

YARN POM-POMS AND TASSELS

Cut a 3-inch square of cardboard. Wrap bulky yarn or knitting worsted around and around the cardboard in one direction 48 times. Remove cardboard and tie bundle of yarn tightly in the center several times, leaving ends 8 inches long. With scissors, cut yarn loops open. Trim ends until you have a ball. Knot

8-inch ends together and use to hang on tree. Use yarn of all one color, multicolor or yarns woven with metallic threads.

To make tassels, prepare yarn as above. Remove from cardboard and, using a 12-inch piece of yarn, tie all the loops together at one side of the bundle. Knot the ends together and use this loop for hanging. Tie a piece of yarn around the entire bundle of yarn 1 inch from the first tie. Cut open the opposite end and trim ends straight.

EYE OF GOD

Tie two popsicle sticks, lollipop sticks or skewers together with string to form a cross. Wrap heavy colored yarn around stick and pass yarn in front and back around the next stick. Continue around and around until sticks are covered. Tuck in ends of yarn and attach a string at the top for hanging. Tassels or small bells can be added at the bottom. Vary the colors for striped effect.

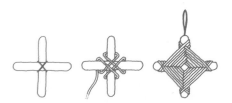

LITTLE GIFT BOXES

Cut a 1-quart milk carton 3 inches from the bottom on three sides. To shape lid, cut 3 inches up on the two sides remaining attached to carton. Cut across carton to release lid. Cover carton with foil or colored paper. Add a loop of thread on lid for hanging. Fill with nuts, dried fruits, candies or tiny Christmas balls.

JEWEL ORNAMENTS

Use cone-shaped or other small paper or plastic drinking cups.
Run a piece of yarn through the point of one cone and make a loop. With thread and a needle, sew together the rimmed edges of one plain cup and one looped cup. They can also be glued together. Brush cones with clear nail polish and sprinkle with colored sugar or glitter. If desired, cover center seam with gold braid and glue in place.

FUNNY FACES

Use styrofoam balls and paint on faces using sets of colored felt markers. Using straight pins, fasten a bow underneath the mouth. Use an orange mesh pot scrubber for the hair; fasten in place with straight pins, adding a loop for

hanging. By the way, styrofoam balls and other shapes are wonderful for decorations.

Their porous texture allows decorations and hangers to be pinned in place. They can be covered with lace, patchwork, fabric pieces, eyelet ruffles or satin. If you decide to use glue or paints on styrofoam, just check the labels to make sure they are made for working with plastic; some petroleum-based glues and paints can melt styrofoam.

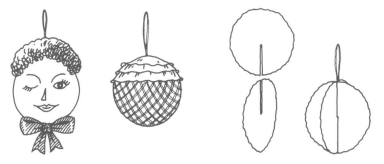

TIN ORNAMENTS

Remove the tops and bottoms from large cans. Using heavy gardening gloves and tinsnips or heavy-duty kitchen shears, cut each circle in half just to the center. Make the cut about ⅛ inch thick. Fit the two circles together, pushing into cuts. Punch a hole and thread a loop for hanging. Edges should be notched with shears to make them less sharp. Circles can also be painted. Cut the side of the can lengthwise and open out. Trim off beaded edges and flatten shiny side up by placing on a heavy board and hammering gently with a ball peen hammer until metal is flat. Cut into desired shapes with shears. If you wish, hammer with a dull nail for texture, or paint the shapes. Use a nail or ice pick on a firm surface to punch through the metal. Thread with a loop for hanging.

ROYAL ICING ORNAMENT

Prepare Royal Icing (see Cookie and Candy House). Place icing into a pastry bag with a 1/4-inch star tip. Lightly mark off 4-inch squares on heavy-duty foil. Pipe desired design onto each square—triangles, stars, webs—and let dry for several hours or until dry to the touch. Carefully remove foil and turn orna-ments upside down to dry thoroughly. Hang with string or yarn. If desired, icing may be sprinkled with colored sugar before drying.

PIPE CLEANER STAR

Use 20 pipe cleaners and colored wool yarn. Pinch pipe cleaners together in the center and tie tightly with yarn. One inch from the center, tie the pipe cleaners together in groups of four; you will have 10 groups. At the ends of the pipe cleaner, tie two pipe cleaners from one group to two pipe cleaners from the

adjacent group. Continue around until you have 10 points. Bend pipe cleaners to shape a star at each side of center. Tie a loop on top for hanging.

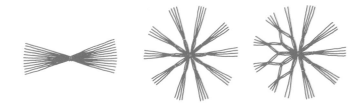

DRUMS

Use empty 12-ounce frozen fruit juice cans made of cardboard.
Using a serrated knife, cut each can in half crosswise (each can will make two drums). Crimp heavy-duty foil over both ends of the drums. Cover sides with a strip of colored paper, glued in place. Glue a zig-zag of gold braid on sides of drum and around the top and bottom edges. Add a loop at top for hanging.

GUMDROP BELLS

Thread small bells at the ends of a string threaded onto a needle. Thread several large gumdrops on top of bell. Tie end into loop for hanging.

TRIPLE BELLS

For two triple bells, cut 3- or 4-inch circle of gold foil or colored paper. Cut each circle in half. Shape each half into a cone and glue edges together. Knot two 12-inch pieces of yarn at end. Thread yarn into a large needle and pass yarn through tip of bell, starting at inside. Make a knot 2 inches above the top of bell and add another bell. Knot again and add third bell. Loop remaining yarn and hang on tree.

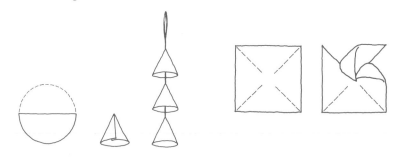

PINWHEELS

Cut 6-inch squares of stiff or foil paper. Make a diagonal cut from each corner to within 1 inch of the center. Turn every other half corner to the center and staple or glue in place. Glue a bow or yarn pom-pom in center and tie a loop on top. Or stick pin through center and attach to small styrofoam cube—that way, the pinwheel will turn in a breeze.

YARN RINGS

Using a serrated knife, cut a cylindrical oatmeal box crosswise into 1-inch-wide rings. Wrap plain paper or multicolored yarn around and around the ring, covering it completely. Fasten end with glue. Tie a loop at top for hanging.

If desired, tie a tassel on the bottom or hang a small toy or tiny Christmas ball in the center of the ring. For smaller rings, use tubes from foil or wax paper.

EMBROIDERED ORNAMENTS

Plastic canvas is sold in sheets and can be cut with scissors into any shape. It is then needlepointed with wool in desired colors and patterns. Add a loop for hanging.

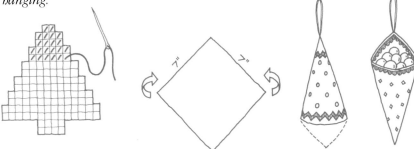

PAPER TREES AND/OR CONES

Cut 7-inch squares of stiff or foil paper. With one corner at the top, roll the paper into a cone and glue edges in place. Trim bottom to allow cone to stand straight. Glue gold braid on bottom of cone like garland; decorate with paste-on dots, stars and seals. Add a loop for hanging.

You can also fill these like little cornucopias--with nuts, candies, Christmas balls, small toys.

ORIGAMI

Birds: Fold 7-inch squares of stiff paper or heavy-duty foil in half on the diagonal. Open out and fold sides diagonally to meet at the center fold. Fold sides again toward center; fold along center line. To make neck, place paper open edge up and push pointed end ⅓ of the way up so it is between flaps. Pull 1 inch of the tip forward to shape the head. To shape tail, push opposite end ⅓ of the way up in the same way as the neck. Flatten bottom, and set birds on branches.

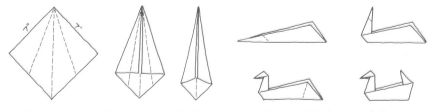

PAPER CHAINS

Children never seem to get tired of this! Cut strips of colored paper ¾ inch wide and 6 inches long. Fasten ends of one strip with glue, tape or staple. Pass second strip through ring and fasten ends in the same way. Repeat until the chain is the desired length. This chain can also be made from pipe cleaners twisted together, or from ropes of crimped foil.

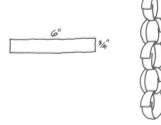

PAPER FANS

Use sheets of colored paper, 8½ x 11 inches. Fold lengthwise into ½-inch-wide accordion pleats. Fold in half and tie with colored yarn 1 inch from bottom. Open out paper at top and add a loop for hanging at the top or bottom of the fan.

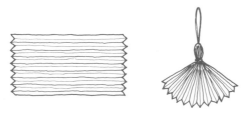

CRANBERRY OR POPCORN STRINGS

Use a needle with a large eye, threaded with heavy-duty thread or waxed dental floss. To make it easier, prepare 24-inch lengths and tie them together until garland is the desired length. Spear the cranberries from top to bottom of the berry. For popcorn, rotate needle and "drill" your way through kernel to prevent splitting. The popcorn and cranberries can be combined in the chain, alternating them in a pretty pattern. This can also be done with peanuts in the shell, large raisins and gumdrops.

LET THE CHILDREN HELP

Recipes and Projects the Kids Will Enjoy

*C*hristmas without children is like the tree
without decorations—the joyousness of the holiday is
irrepressible in children—and we take pains to keep up many of
the traditions just to see the magical effect on their faces. But keeping their little
hands busy with challenging, entertaining projects can make it easier to channel
the sometimes riotous excitement that kids seem to have around this season.
An evening of "do-it-yourselfing" may sound old-fashioned; but to children, nothing
more eloquently underlines the specialness of an occasion than seeing the grownups
set aside time just to be with them. Parents and children working together really do
produce "memory moments" treasured by both in later years. This is how traditions
start: someday when your children are grown they will be making Christmas cookies
with their children, remembering that this is the way you did it together. All the
starred (*) recipes are suitable for shipping.

*CHRISTMAS CUTOUT COOKIES

1 In a large bowl, cream shortening with sugar until fluffy. Gradually stir in honey, eggs and lemon rind. Add remaining ingredients and mix until dough forms a ball.

2 Turn dough out on a floured surface and knead a few times until smooth. Wrap dough in foil and chill for several hours.

3 Roll dough out, a small amount at a time, on a floured surface to ¼-inch thickness. Cut into desired shapes with floured cookie cutters. Place on greased cookie sheets 1 inch apart.

4 Bake in a preheated 375°F oven for 8 to 10 minutes or until no imprint remains when lightly touched. Cool on racks, then decorate as desired.

5 To decorate, buy prepared colored frostings in squeeze tubes. Using the round writing tip, out-

MAKES ABOUT 6 DOZEN, DEPENDING ON SIZE AND SHAPE

INGREDIENTS
1 cup vegetable shortening
1 cup sugar
2 cups honey (for light cookies) or molasses (for dark cookies)
3 eggs
Grated rind of 2 lemons
8 cups (2 pounds) sifted all-purpose flour
1 tablespoon baking soda
1 teaspoon salt
Colored frostings, decorations and/or Egg Yolk Paint (see below)

line the cookies and make faces or other details. Decorate with chocolate chips, nuts, raisins, small gumdrops, jelly beans or candied cherries.

These cookies can be decorated with Egg Yolk Paint. Beat 2 egg yolks with ½ teaspoon water. Divide mixture among several small dishes. Stir desired food coloring into each and mix well. Use small paintbrushes to apply mixture to cooled cookies. If paint thickens, thin with some water.

To make Greeting Card Cookies, roll out dough as above; cut into 3- x 5-inch rectangles. Bake and cool cookies. Use tubes of frosting with plain tip to pipe on names, other tips for flowers and leaves. Makes about 24.

To hang cookies on a tree, cut a small hole in the top of each while still hot. (To do this, remove the metal eraser end of a discarded pencil and push out eraser. The metal tip makes a tiny cookie cutter.) Cool cookies, decorate; hang with a loop of yarn or very narrow ribbon.

*CANDY CANE COOKIES

MAKES 36

INGREDIENTS
3/4 cup vegetable shortening
3/4 cup confectioners' sugar
1 egg
1 teaspoon almond extract
1 teaspoon vanilla
2 cups unsifted
    all-purpose flour
1/2 teaspoon salt
1/2 teaspoon red food coloring
    Additional confectioners'
    sugar (optional)

1 In a medium bowl, mix shortening, sugar, egg and extracts until well blended. Stir in flour and salt. Turn dough out on a floured surface and knead a few times until smooth.

2 Cut dough into 2 equal pieces and blend red food coloring into 1 part. Cut each piece of dough into 36 pieces. Working with 1 cookie at a time and using floured fingers, roll out 1 piece of red dough and 1 piece of white dough each into a 4-inch rope. Twist the red and white ropes together.

3 Place twists on an ungreased cookie sheet and curve one end down to resemble a cane. Repeat with remaining dough.

4 Bake in a preheated 375°F oven for 8 to 10 minutes or until firm to the touch. Cool on racks. If desired, dust very lightly with confectioners' sugar.

Opposite: Christmas Cutout Cookies, page 53

COOKIE AND CANDY HOUSE

1 This house is built of corrugated cardboard and held together with masking tape. Cut pieces of cardboard as follows: 4 pieces, 8 x 10 inches, for long sides and roof of house; 2 pieces, 7 x 12 inches, for narrow ends of the house; and 1 piece, 15 x 18 inches, for base of the house. The narrow ends of the house must be cut to shape a peak for the roof: mark off 8 inches on each 12-inch side. From each mark, draw a diagonal line to center of closest 7-inch side. Cut away corners. Tape the 8-inch sides of the house together, alternating rectangular and peaked pieces; house should measure 7 x 10 inches. Tape roof pieces in place. Set house diagonally on top of base cardboard and tape in place.

2 For Royal Icing, combine unbeaten egg whites and 2 cups confectioners' sugar in a medium bowl and beat until well blended. Gradually add remaining sugar, beating until mixture holds peaks.

MAKES 1 HOUSE
CORRUGATED CARDBOARD
CARTONS OR HEAVY CARDBOARD
SCISSORS
MASKING TAPE

INGREDIENTS

ROYAL ICING

6 egg whites
6 cups sifted confectioners'
  sugar
1 package red licorice strings
2 packages striped, red, round
  peppermint candies
2 packages brown-edge
  wafers or frosted cookies
½ pound small gumdrops
2 packages green decorating
  sugar
1 package pointed ice cream
  sugar cones
1 bag thin pretzel sticks
10 to 12 large candy canes
1 package ginger men cookies

Keep bowl covered as you work to prevent drying.

3 To assemble, spread one side of the house at a time with icing. Press pieces of licorice string into icing to outline windows. Press round peppermint candies into wall. Repeat with remaining walls, marking windows and doors. Spread roof with frosting and place overlapping rows of brown-edge wafers on roof to resemble tiles. Drip icing over sides of roof to imitate icicles. Spread base with icing and outline path from front door with licorice string.

4 Stud path with gumdrops. Sprinkle remaining base with green sugar. Spread outside of ice cream cones with icing and sprinkle with green sugar; stand pointed end up on base to resemble trees. Halve pretzel sticks and stand upright on base to form a fence. Place candy canes at edge of roof, fastening in place with icing. Decorate with ginger man cookies.

Opposite: Cookie and Candy House, page 56

GINGERBREAD HOUSE

1 Build a cardboard house frame on a base as for the Cookie and Candy House. Set aside.

2 In a large kettle, heat honey, molasses, sugar and butter until butter melts. Remove from heat and stir in orange juice, eggs and yolks. When well blended, stir in flour, baking powder, spices and salt.

3 Turn dough out onto a floured surface and knead a few times until smooth. Wrap with foil and chill several hours.

4 Roll out half the dough to ½-inch thickness on a floured surface. Cut out pieces of dough the same size as the pieces of cardboard for the house. Repeat with the remaining dough to cut all the pieces. Gather the trimmings and knead into a smooth ball. Roll out to ½-inch thickness. Cut into 2-inch rounds with a cookie cutter, then cut rounds in half to use as roof tiles.

5 Bake cookies on greased cookie sheets in a preheated 350°F oven 30 to 35 minutes for large cookies and 8 to 10 minutes for the small half-rounds. (If large cookies spread during baking, they can be trimmed with a sharp knife while still hot.) Cool cookies on the sheets.

6 Prepare Royal Icing. Decorate wall cookies with windows, doors and wreaths. Spread icing on walls and roof of the cardboard house, one section at a time. Press large cookie pieces for walls and roof into place. Spread icing on roof and top with overlapping rows of half-round cookies. Use the icing to add icicles to roof and to glue candy decorations to house. Spread icing on base of house and decorate with candy.

**MAKES 1 HOUSE
CARDBOARD HOUSE FRAME
(SEE PRECEDING COOKIE
AND CANDY HOUSE)**

INGREDIENTS

1 cup honey
1 cup molasses
5 cups sugar
¾ cup butter or margarine
1 cup orange juice
3 eggs
3 egg yolks
1 bag (5 pounds) all-purpose
   flour, unsifted
¼ cup (that's right)
   baking powder

1 tablespoon each ground
   ginger, cinnamon,
   allspice and nutmeg
1 teaspoon salt
1 recipe Royal Icing (see
   Cookie and Candy House)
Nonpareils, gumdrops,
   peppermints, lollipops,
   silver dragees, candy canes,
   M & M's, chocolate kisses

*POPCORN BALLS

1 Place popcorn in a shallow pan in a preheated 225°F oven to warm through.

2 Combine brown sugar, sugar, honey and water in a 2-quart saucepan and bring to boil. Boil until a candy thermometer registers 242°F. Stir in butter.

3 Pour popcorn into a buttered 2-quart bowl. Pour syrup over

MAKES 12

INGREDIENTS
2 quarts popped popcorn
⅔ cup firmly packed
    light brown sugar
⅔ cup sugar
⅓ cup honey
6 tablespoons water
1 tablespoon butter
    Cinnamon red hots
    Plastic wrap
    Red and green ribbon

popcorn and stir with a buttered spoon until all popcorn is coated. With buttered hands, shape the popcorn into 12 balls. Press cinnamon red hots onto one side of ball to form eyes, nose and mouth.

4 Wrap popcorn ball with a large square of plastic wrap, pulling excess to bottom. Tie plastic wrap with red or green ribbon.

BREAD SCULPTURE DOUGH (NOT EDIBLE)

1 In a large bowl, combine ingredients and knead until smooth and claylike. This dough can be shaped into fruits, vegetables, animals, flowers or any other figures. It can be rolled to ¼-inch thickness and cut with a knife or cookie cutter into desired shapes, or formed into circles and used as napkin rings. You can also press designs into the surface, using a

MAKES 4 POUNDS

INGREDIENTS
4 cups unsifted
    all-purpose flour
2 cups salt
2 cups cold water

toothpick, a beer can opener, the tip of a spoon, the tines of a fork etc.

2 Place finished shapes on cookie sheets; bake in preheated 200°F oven until firm to the touch, overnight or at least 8 hours. Paint with acrylic colors, let dry; spray with clear lacquer.

CEREAL WREATH

1 Combine marshmallows and butter in the top part of a double boiler set over simmering water and stir until melted. Remove from heat and stir in vanilla and food coloring.

2 Pour cornflakes into a buttered 2-quart bowl. Add syrup and stir with a buttered spoon until cornflakes are well coated.

MAKES ONE 8-INCH WREATH

INGREDIENTS
36 marshmallows
½ cup butter
2 teaspoons vanilla
2 teaspoons green
  food coloring
4 cups cornflakes
15 candied cherries
  Red ribbon bow

3 Drop mixture by heaping spoonfuls onto buttered foil, shaping a ring 8 inches in diameter. Arrange 5 clusters of 3 cherries each on top of ring. Add red ribbon bow and let stand until set. Remove from foil and place on serving platter with a fat red candle in the center.

SPARKLING MARSHMALLOWS

1 In a small bowl, mix dry lime gelatin with enough green coloring to make a rich green. In another small bowl, do the same with strawberry gelatin and red coloring.

MAKES 36

INGREDIENTS
1 package (3 ounces)
  lime gelatin
  Green food coloring
1 package (3 ounces)
  strawberry gelatin
  Red food coloring
36 marshmallows
1 egg white,
  beaten until foamy

2 Brush marshmallows lightly on all sides with egg white. Roll 18 in red sugar mixture and 18 in green sugar mixture. Place on waxed paper and let stand several hours or until dry.

Opposite: Christmas Cutout Cookies, page 53

SANTA'S PILLOWS

MAKES 4 CUPS

INGREDIENTS

1 package (6 ounces) semi-sweet chocolate chips
2 tablespoons vegetable shortening
½ cup smooth peanut butter
3 cups spoon-size Shredded Wheat
½ cup finely chopped peanuts

1 In the top part of a double boiler set over simmering water, combine chocolate and shortening and stir until melted. Remove from heat but keep chocolate mixture over hot water. Stir in peanut butter.

2 Using a fork, dip Shredded Wheat biscuits one at a time into chocolate, covering them completely. Roll in chopped peanuts. Let stand at room temperature until firm.

SNOWBALLS

MAKES 36

INGREDIENTS

1 cup nonfat dry milk powder
1 cup crunchy peanut butter
1 cup honey
1 teaspoon vanilla
Grated rind of 1 orange
8 ounces white chocolate or coating chocolate
¼ cup vegetable shortening
Flaked coconut

1 With your hands, mix the milk powder, peanut butter, honey, vanilla and orange rind in a 1-quart bowl until mixture becomes creamy and shapable. Cut into 36 equal pieces and roll each piece into a ball.

2 In the top part of a double boiler set over simmering water, melt chocolate with shortening until smooth. Dip balls into chocolate to coat and remove with a fork, draining off excess.

3 Roll balls in coconut and let stand at room temperature until firm.

GIFTS FROM THE KITCHEN

From Simple to Sophisticated

*I*t is always appropriate to bring along a "house specialty" when visiting, or to offer it as a parting gift for friends to take home. Though there are mail-order catalogs featuring specialty foods for every taste and budget, nothing quite competes with a homemade gift; because they bespeak the time and effort you have put into them, they are truly full of love. These treats can be for simple or sophisticated palates, and they needn't be complicated to prepare. Herbed vinegars and special mustards, for instance, take hardly any time at all, but they make for a very elegant presentation and can be enjoyed for a long time to come. Pâtés and pasta sauces require more time and more expensive ingredients, but because they are the kinds of special dishes that we rarely make for ourselves, they are much appreciated. Don't forget to refer to the bread, pie and sweetmeat sections of the book for more gift ideas.

All the starred (*) recipes are suitable for shipping. When shipping, use a box large enough to surround your gifts with popped popcorn or sealed bags of air-puffed snacks; they are great shock absorbers and edible as well.

Bubble paper and styrofoam pieces can be saved from other packages during the year and used for Christmas packing.

PÂTÉ MAISON

**MAKES ONE 9- X 5- X 3-INCH LOAF
OR 2-QUART TERRINE**

INGREDIENTS
1½ pounds ground veal
1½ pounds ground pork
2 eggs
2 teaspoons salt
1 teaspoon white pepper
1 tablespoon each
   chopped fresh rosemary
   and marjoram
   (or 1 teaspoon each dried)
2 cloves garlic, minced
6 green onions, chopped
½ cup dry sherry
8 ounces Virginia ham, cut
   into ½-inch cubes
½ cup shelled
   natural pistachios
1 pound sliced bacon

1 In a large bowl, combine veal, pork, eggs, salt, pepper, herbs, garlic, onions and sherry and mix just until blended. Mix in ham cubes and pistachios.

2 Use bacon to line the bottom and sides of an ungreased 9- x 5- x 3-inch loaf pan or 2-quart terrine, allowing bacon to hang over sides of terrine. Pack meat mixture tightly into pan and cover with bacon slices hanging over sides of terrine. Place in a shallow pan containing 1 inch of water.

3 Bake in a preheated 350°F oven for 1½ hours. Cool, then refrigerate.

4 To present as a gift, clean the edges of the pan and overwrap with plastic. Add a loaf of thinly sliced Belgian Dark Bread (see Index), a jar of cornichons and a crock of Dijon or coarse-grain mustard. Pâté will keep, refrigerated, for 2 weeks.

Opposite: Assorted Gifts from the Kitchen

SHRIMP PÂTÉ

1 Combine shrimp, capers, onions, butter, cream and Pernod in a food processor and puree until smooth. Season to taste with salt and pepper.

2 Pack mixture into a decorative crock and sprinkle with

MAKES ABOUT 1 QUART

INGREDIENTS
2 pounds shrimp, cooked, shelled and deveined
3 tablespoons drained capers
2 green onions, chopped
½ cup soft butter
½ cup heavy cream
2 teaspoons Pernod
Salt and pepper
Chopped parsley

chopped parsley. Cover and chill. If desired, top with a few cooked shelled and deveined shrimp.

3 To present as a gift, pack with a handcrafted wooden spreader and a box of special crackers.

MUSHROOMS AND CAULIFLOWER À LA GRECQUE

1 Combine cauliflower and mushrooms in a large bowl and cover with boiling water. Let stand 2 minutes, then drain and cool.

2 Divide cauliflower and mushrooms among canning jars. Add 4 peppercorns, 1 bay leaf, 1 dill sprig and ½ teaspoon each oregano and marjoram to each jar.

MAKES 6 TO 8 PINTS

INGREDIENTS
1 head cauliflower, broken into bite-size florets
1 pound small whole mushrooms, trimmed
Black peppercorns
Bay leaves
Sprigs of fresh dill
Crumbled dried oregano and marjoram
1½ cups olive oil
1½ cups mild red wine vinegar or white wine vinegar
1 tablespoon salt

3 In a nonaluminum saucepan, combine oil, vinegar and salt and bring to boil. Pour into jars, covering contents completely. Seal and cool, then refrigerate.

4 To present as a gift, use jars with decorative lids and add a pretty label. Tie with ribbons and add a pickle fork for spearing.

Opposite: Shrimp Pâté, page 67

SAUSAGE AND MEAT
BOLOGNESE SAUCE FOR PASTA

1 Combine the first 7 ingredients in a food processor and chop finely. Transfer to a 3-quart saucepan and simmer for 5 minutes, stirring.

2 In a skillet, sauté beef and sausages until brown and crumbly. Drain excess fat. Add meat to saucepan with remaining ingredients, cover tightly and simmer 1 hour, stirring occasionally. Adjust seasoning with salt and pepper.

MAKES 2 QUARTS

INGREDIENTS

3 slices bacon
1 ounce sliced prosciutto
2 cloves garlic
1 onion, quartered
2 carrots, cut into
*   1-inch chunks*
2 stalks celery, cut into
*   1-inch chunks*
8 ounces mushrooms,
*   trimmed and halved*
1 pound lean ground round
4 sweet Italian sausages,
*   removed from casing*
1 can (2 pounds, 3 ounces)
*   Italian plum tomatoes,*
*   undrained*
½ cup marsala
1 can (6 ounces) tomato paste
½ cup water
1 tablespoon each chopped
*   fresh oregano and basil*
*   (or 1 teaspoon each dried)*
Salt and pepper

3 Pack sauce into decorative jars and add pretty labels. To present as a gift, tie with ribbon and add bunches of special pasta made with spinach, carrot or herbs. Sauce will keep in refrigerator for 2 weeks or in freezer for 2 months.

ALL-PURPOSE CHEESE SAUCE
FOR PASTA, VEGETABLES, CHICKEN OR FISH

1 In a glass or enamel medium saucepan, melt butter. Stir in flour; gradually stir in milk and cream. Stir over medium heat until mixture bubbles. Add cheese, a handful at a time, stirring after each addition until cheese is melted. Stir in brandy, nutmeg, mustard, and salt and pepper to taste.

MAKES 1 QUART

INGREDIENTS
¼ cup butter
¼ cup all-purpose flour
2½ cups milk
½ cup heavy cream
1 cup (4 ounces) shredded Gruyère cheese
1 cup (4 ounces) shredded sharp cheddar cheese
2 tablespoons brandy
Pinch of ground nutmeg
1 teaspoon dry mustard
Salt and pepper

2 Pour hot sauce into decorative jars with pretty lids. Cool and refrigerate.

3 To present as a gift, add decorative labels and pack jar into a new contemporary-style enamel or glass saucepan along with a wooden spoon. Sauce will keep in refrigerator for 1 week.

HERB AND GARLIC BUTTER

1 In a small bowl, mix all ingredients until well blended. Pack into small decorative crocks with lids and refrigerate.

MAKES 2 CUPS

INGREDIENTS
1 pound salted butter, at room temperature
2 cloves garlic, minced
1 tablespoon each chopped fresh thyme, chervil, marjoram and summer savory (or 1 teaspoon each dried)

2 To present as a gift, tie with ribbons and add written suggestions for use—on garlic bread, for broiling fish or chicken, for sautéing beef or veal scaloppini, or for tossing with hot vegetables, pasta or rice.

*HERB AND SPICE BLENDS

MAKES ⅓ CUP OF EACH BLEND

To present as gifts, pack mixes into small jars with lids and labels. Tie jars onto a cookbook filled with herb and spice recipes. Herbs will keep for 6 months, tightly closed, in a cool, dry place.

FOR BEEF

Mix 1 tablespoon coarsely ground black pepper, 1 tablespoon red pepper flakes, 2½ tablespoons garlic powder and 1 tablespoon dried minced onions.

FOR FISH

Mix 2 tablespoons dried dillweed, 2 tablespoons crumbled bay leaves and 2 tablespoons freeze-dried chives.

FOR FRUIT PIES, SPICE CAKES AND COOKIES

Mix 2 tablespoons ground cinnamon, 1 tablespoon ground nutmeg, 1 tablespoon ground mace, 1 tablespoon ground allspice, 2 teaspoons ground cloves and 2 teaspoons ground cardamom.

FOR VEGETABLES

Mix 2 tablespoons dried thyme, 2 tablespoons dried oregano and 2 tablespoons dried basil.

FOR CHICKEN

Mix 2 tablespoons curry powder, 2 tablespoons paprika and 2 tablespoons dried lemon rind.

FOR TOMATO SAUCE

Mix 2 tablespoons crumbled basil, 2 tablespoons dried minced onions, 1 tablespoon red pepper flakes and 1 tablespoon crumbled dried oregano.

FOR LAMB

Mix 1½ tablespoons dried marjoram, 1 tablespoon crumbled dried rosemary, 1 tablespoon white pepper and 2 tablespoons garlic powder.

Opposite: Shrimp Pâté, page 67; Pâté Maison, page 64

MUSTARD BLENDS

**MAKES ABOUT 1½ CUPS
OF EACH BLEND**

Pack mustard blends into small jars or crocks and refrigerate. To present as a gift, wrap and tie with ribbons and add a wooden mustard spoon. Will keep, refrigerated, for 2 months.

FOR BEEF OR FRANKFURTERS

Mix 1 cup Dijon mustard with ½ cup well-drained pickle relish, 1 tablespoon prepared white horseradish and 2 tablespoons chopped green peppercorns.

FOR FISH

Mix ½ cup coarse-grain mustard with juice of 1 lemon and 1 cup mayonnaise.

FOR SALAD DRESSING

Combine 1 cup olive oil, ⅓ cup red wine vinegar, 3 tablespoons Dijon mustard, 1 teaspoon salt, 1 tablespoon honey and 2 tablespoons minced onion, and beat until thick.

FOR LAMB, VEAL OR CHICKEN

Mix 1 cup coarse-grain mustard with 2 tablespoons capers, 2 tablespoons lemon juice and 2 tablespoons white wine.

FLAVORED VINEGARS

MAKES ABOUT 1 QUART EACH

To present as a gift, pack into old-fashioned pressed glass bottles or simple clear decanters. Tie with ribbons and a small scroll of recipes for using the vinegar.

RASPBERRY, LEMON AND ORANGE VINEGAR

Mix 3 cups white wine vinegar and ½ cup frozen unsweetened raspberries. Pour into a 1-quart bottle. Cut the rinds of 1 lemon and 1 orange into long strips and add to bottle. Close tightly and let stand at room temperature at least 2 weeks.

ORANGE, BASIL AND DILL VINEGAR

Pour 3 cups red wine vinegar into a 1-quart bottle. Add the rind of 1 orange cut into long strips, 6 sprigs fresh dill and 1 sprig fresh basil or 2 teaspoons dried. Close tightly and let stand at room temperature at least 2 weeks.

Opposite: Assorted Gifts from the Kitchen

CRANBERRY ORANGE BREAD
WITH COINTREAU BUTTER

1 For bread, mix flour, sugar, baking powder, salt, baking soda and orange rind in a large bowl. Add orange juice, melted shortening and eggs and stir until all particles are just moistened. Fold in pecans and cranberries.

2 Spoon dough into 8 greased and floured 2½- x 4- x 1½-inch small loaf pans.

3 Bake in a preheated 350°F oven for 30 to 35 minutes or until golden brown and firm to the touch. Cool in pans for 5 minutes, then turn out onto racks to cool.

MAKES EIGHT 2 ½- X 4- X 1 ½-INCH LOAVES AND 2 CUPS BUTTER

INGREDIENTS

BREAD
3 cups sifted all-purpose flour
1½ cups sugar
2 teaspoons baking powder
½ teaspoon salt
1 teaspoon baking soda
2 tablespoons grated orange rind
1 cup orange juice
3 tablespoons melted vegetable shortening
2 eggs, well beaten
1½ cups coarsely chopped pecans
1½ cups halved fresh cranberries

COINTREAU BUTTER
1 pound unsalted butter, at room temperature
Grated rind of 2 oranges
⅓ cup Cointreau or other orange liqueur

4 For Cointreau butter, mix butter, orange rind and liqueur in a small bowl until well blended. Pack into a crock and refrigerate.

5 To present as a gift, line the loaves up on a long cutting board. Add a serrated bread knife and tie a spreader onto the crock of butter. Overwrap and tie with ribbons.

*RED AND GREEN PEPPER RELISH

MAKES ABOUT 6 PINTS

INGREDIENTS

2 quarts thinly sliced
  unpeeled cucumber
  (about 4 to 6 cucumbers
  depending on size)
3 yellow onions, thinly sliced
2 green bell peppers, seeded
  and cut into slivers
2 red bell peppers, seeded
  and cut into slivers
¼ cup coarse salt
3 cups cider vinegar
3 cups sugar
1 tablespoon mustard seed
1 teaspoon celery seed
½ teaspoon each ground
  allspice and cloves

1 In a large glass bowl, combine cucumber, onions, peppers and salt. Cover and refrigerate for 12 hours.

2 Drain vegetables. In a large nonaluminum kettle, combine remaining ingredients and bring to boil. Add vegetables and bring to boil again.

3 Pack mixture into sterilized jars, adding enough hot liquid to cover vegetables completely. Seal and cool.

4 To present as a gift, add pretty labels and a small bowl and spoon for serving.

*CRANBERRY RASPBERRY SAUCE

MAKES ABOUT 1 QUART

INGREDIENTS
4 cups (1 pound) cranberries
2 cups water
2 cups sugar
*1 package (10 ounces) frozen
raspberries in syrup*

1 In a 2-quart nonaluminum saucepan, combine cranberries and water and bring to boil. Boil for 5 minutes. Add sugar and raspberries and boil for another 5 minutes.

2 Press mixture through a food mill or sieve to remove seeds. Pour while hot into small soufflé dishes or pot de crème dishes and chill until firm.

3 To present as a gift, cover dishes with plastic wrap and place on a tray. Overwrap with plastic and tie with ribbons.

RUM DRIED FRUIT COMPOTE

MAKES ABOUT 6 PINTS

INGREDIENTS
*2 pounds mixed dried fruits,
pitted as necessary*
*1 pound dried figs,
stemmed and halved*
*3 lemons, cut into paper-thin
slices and seeded*
3 cups (about) honey
2 cups (about) dark rum

1 Divide dried fruits among 6 pint-size jars, filling them slightly more than half full. Add ½ sliced lemon to each jar.

2 Mix honey and rum. Fill jars to within 1 inch of the top, adding more honey and rum if necessary. Cover tightly and store at room temperature for 1 month before using.

3 To present as a gift, pack into decorative jars with lids and pretty labels. Give a jar with a sponge cake, angel food cake or container of homemade vanilla ice cream; the fruit and its syrup makes a delicious topping.

Opposite: Assorted Gifts from the Kitchen

*APPLE PECAN CHUTNEY

1 Chop the apples, lemons, onion, garlic, dates and pecans in a food processor. Transfer to a large nonaluminum kettle and add remaining ingredients. Simmer, stirring occasionally, for 20 to 25 minutes or until thick and jamlike.

MAKES ABOUT 4 PINTS

INGREDIENTS
2 pounds greening apples,
  peeled and cored
2 unpeeled lemons, seeded
1 small onion
1 clove garlic
1 pound pitted dates
1 cup pecans
1 pound raisins
1 pound light brown sugar
2 teaspoons ground ginger
½ teaspoon salt
1 teaspoon red pepper flakes
1 cup tarragon vinegar
2 cups cider vinegar

2 Pour into sterilized jars while hot. Seal and cool.

3 To present as a gift, add decorative labels and tie on your favorite recipe for lamb curry.

*PINEAPPLE CARROT PRESERVES

1 In a 2-quart saucepan, combine all ingredients and simmer, stirring occasionally, until thick, about 20 to 25 minutes.

2 Spoon while hot into sterilized jars. Seal and cool.

MAKES ABOUT 4 PINTS

INGREDIENTS
4 cups undrained
  crushed pineapple
Rind of 1 orange, slivered
Rind of 1 lemon, slivered
3 carrots, coarsely shredded
3 cups sugar

3 To present as a gift, add pretty labels and a dish and silver spoon for serving.

BRANDIED PEARS

MAKES ABOUT 4 PINTS

INGREDIENTS
4 pounds Seckel pears
8 cups sugar
4 cups water
2 cups brandy
Whole star anise (optional)

1 Peel pears and leave them whole; leave stems attached. With the tip of a knife, remove the blossom end of each pear.

2 In a kettle, combine sugar and water and bring to boil. Boil 5 minutes, then add pears. Simmer for 5 to 6 minutes or until pears are tender but still firm.

3 Remove pears with a slotted spoon and transfer to sterilized wide-mouth jars. Boil liquid for another 5 minutes or until reduced to a syrup consistency. Remove from heat and stir in brandy.

4 Pour hot syrup into jars, covering pears completely. If desired, place 1 whole star anise into each jar for added flavor. Seal and cool.

5 To present as a gift, use imported French canning jars with wire closures. Tie with ribbons and greens.

CHOCOLATE-DIPPED DRIED FRUITS AND RAISIN NUT CLUSTERS

1 In the top part of a double boiler set over simmering water, combine chocolate and shortening and stir until melted; keep mixture over hot water, off heat, while dipping.

2 Dip dried fruits into the chocolate one by one, covering them only halfway. Arrange on foil-lined cookie sheets and let stand in a cool place until firm.

MAKES 24 DATES, 24 FIGS, 24 APRICOTS, 24 RAISIN NUT CLUSTERS

INGREDIENTS

1½ pounds semisweet chocolate, coarsely chopped
¼ cup vegetable shortening
24 each pitted dates, black mission figs and dried apricots
2 cups unsalted peanuts
1 cup raisins

3 Stir peanuts and raisins into the remaining chocolate; drop by heaping teaspoons onto foil-lined cookie sheet. Let stand in a cool place until firm. Place fruits and clusters in small paper or foil crinkle cups.

4 To present as a gift, pack in small baskets and tie with ribbons, or present in a covered candy dish.

Opposite: Chocolate-Dipped Dried Fruits and Raisin Nut Clusters, page 81; Cranberry Orange Bread, page 74

*COGNAC BALLS

1 In a large bowl, combine first 6 ingredients and mix with fingers until well blended. Add more cognac, if necessary, until mixture holds together. Roll into 1-inch balls. Leave plain or roll balls in confectioners' sugar.

MAKES ABOUT 1 POUND

INGREDIENTS
6 tablespoons unsweetened
  cocoa powder
3 cups sifted
  confectioners' sugar
About ¾ cup cognac
6 tablespoons light corn syrup
8 cups finely crushed
  vanilla wafers
3 cups finely chopped pecans
Additional confectioners'
  sugar

2 To present as a gift, pack the balls into a brandy snifter; accompany with liqueur glasses and a small bottle of cognac.

*SPICED CAFÉ AU LAIT MIX

1 Mix all ingredients until well blended and place in an airtight container.

2 For 1 serving, place ¼ cup of the café au lait mix into a mug and add ⅔ cup boiling water. Stir to blend. Top with whipped cream if desired.

MAKES ABOUT 2 CUPS

INGREDIENTS
2 cups nonfat dry milk
  powder
½ cup instant coffee powder
½ cup confectioners' sugar
½ teaspoon each ground cinnamon, cloves and allspice

3 To present as a gift, spoon ¼-cup portions onto squares of foil. Seal foil and place packets in a decorative box. Tie with a coffee mug and the recipe.

COFFEE LIQUEUR

MAKES ABOUT 2 PINTS

INGREDIENTS
2 cups water
3 cups sugar
½ cup instant espresso
3½ cups vodka
1 tablespoon vanilla

1 In a 1-quart saucepan, combine water and sugar and bring to boil. Lower heat and simmer for 10 minutes. Remove from heat and stir in instant coffee. Cool.

2 Mix coffee syrup with vodka and vanilla. Pour into small bottles, cover and chill.

3 To present as a gift, pour into a small crystal decanter and package with liqueur glasses.

CRANBERRY CORDIAL

MAKES ABOUT 3 CUPS

INGREDIENTS
4 cups cranberries, chopped in a food processor
3 cups sugar
2 cups (1 pint) gin or vodka

1 Mix all ingredients in a 2-quart jar. Cover and store in a cool place for 3 weeks, shaking the jar gently every day to blend ingredients.

2 Strain cordial through several thicknesses of dampened cheesecloth and pour into a decanter.

3 To present as a gift, wrap decanter with ribbons and sprigs of holly with red berries.

Party Snacks
and Hors d'oeuvres

*C*hristmas is the season of cocktail parties
and open houses—where guests drop in between
certain hours, stay a while to catch up on the year's news, and
perhaps go on to other parties. Everyone expects wonderful, festive food but in
small samples, because they will be eating a lot.

Holiday-season parties tend also to be more food-oriented than parties at other
times of the year. People look forward to Christmas as a time for indulging in
specialties they won't see again for a year. And because the holidays often bring large
groups of people together, mixing relatives with business associates and close friends
with casual acquaintances, it's nice to serve food that sparks the conversation. Served
before dinner, these snacks tease the appetite but do not overwhelm it. For a party,
they are tantalizing little bites that are perfect with drinks (please make sure you
offer guests enough food when you are serving liquor). And whether you are
planning a casual gathering of close friends or a formal reception, they offer
variety and ease of preparation.

HOW TO ARRANGE A CHEESE PLATTER FOR CHRISTMAS
Choose cheeses that vary in flavor, texture, shape and color. Let the cheese
warm to room temperature for 1 hour before serving for the best
flavor. Cut bell-shaped pieces of paper and write the name and
general description of each cheese on them. Spear papers
on toothpicks and insert into cheeses. Serve hard

cheeses with a cheese plane or knife, soft cheeses with a spreader or cheese scoop. Cut three pieces of cardboard into large Christmas tree shapes and cover with foil. On one, place the assortment of cheeses. On the second, place an assortment of unsalted crackers or thinly sliced French bread. For the calorie conscious, add thinly sliced raw vegetables such as carrots, zucchini, mushroom caps or endive leaves. On the third, place small bunches of grapes and wedges of unpeeled apple or pear.

QUICK AND EASY APPETIZER SUGGESTIONS

CAVIAR POTATOES
Cook unpeeled tiny new potatoes until tender. Cut in half and chill. Serve topped with caviar and sour cream.

ITALIAN MELON
Wrap pieces of melon with thinly sliced prosciutto. Serve with fresh lemon or lime juice for dipping. Pieces of peeled pear, avocado, or banana can be substituted for melon.

GRAPE GRILLS
Wrap seedless red or green grapes in small pieces of bacon and broil until crisp on all sides. Spear on toothpicks.

DATE NUT DIPS
Make sandwiches of date nut bread and cream cheese. Cut into small squares or triangles. Spear on toothpicks and dip into purchased Chinese sweet-and-sour sauce.

ORIENTAL BROILS

Dip cooked, shelled and deveined shrimp into soy sauce. Top with a pineapple chunk and a sliver of green onion. Wrap in bacon and broil until crisp on all sides. Spear on toothpicks.

SOUFFLÉD SANDWICHES

Top party rye or pumpernickel bread slices with thin slices of chicken, turkey, duck or ham. Mix 1 cup grated sharp cheddar with ½ cup mayonnaise and spread a layer ½ inch thick on top, covering meat. Broil until topping is puffed and brown.

BEEF TOASTS

Cut thin slices of French bread and toast on one side. Spread untoasted side with a ½-inch-thick layer of good-quality ground round. Sprinkle with salt and pepper and broil lightly. Serve spread with steak sauce.

MEXICAN PORK

Bake unseasoned 1-inch cubes of pork in a preheated 300°F oven for 1 hour or until crisp and brown. Drain and serve hot, speared on toothpicks. Dip into homemade or purchased guacamole.

WAFFLED SANDWICHES

Make a ham and cheese sandwich using white bread. Brush outside of sandwich with melted butter. Place sandwich into the center of a hot waffle iron. Close lid and grill about 5 to 6 minutes, until crusty and brown. Cut into quarters to serve.

STUFFED OLIVE DUNKS

Stuff a large, pitted black olive with julienne strips of green onion or carrot. Spear on toothpicks and dip into a creamy Italian salad dressing.

Opposite: Assorted Holiday Tidbits

CHEESE NUT SNACKS
Shape grated sharp cheddar cheese into ¾-inch balls. Sandwich each between 2 pecan halves.

STUFFED TOMATOES
Hollow out cherry tomatoes and stuff with deviled ham, blue cheese, Camembert, a rolled anchovy, a tiny stuffed olive, a piece of pâté, a bit of smoked salmon, or egg or tuna salad.
Small raw mushroom caps can be substituted for tomatoes.

LYCHEES CHINOISE
Stuff well-drained canned lychees with whipped cream cheese and a small piece of crystallized ginger.

ONION DAINTIES
Cut 3-inch rounds of thinly sliced firm white bread. Spread one side of each round with mayonnaise. Top half of the rounds with very thin slices of red onion. Top with remaining rounds, mayonnaise side down. Spread sides of sandwich with mayonnaise and roll sides in minced parsley.

SEAFOOD ORGY
Arrange cooked, shelled and deveined shrimp, crabmeat chunks, lobster chunks, scallops and pieces of cooked fresh salmon on a large platter. Surround with bowls of tartar sauce, Russian dressing, cocktail sauce and herb dressing for dipping.

CRUNCH CHUNKS
Dip bite-size pieces of turkey, ham or chicken into mayonnaise thinned slightly with pineapple juice. Roll in chopped peanuts.

Opposite: Cheese Nut Snacks, page 89
Stuffed Tomatoes, page 89; Italian Melon, page 85

Gorgonzola Crisps
Spread mashed gorgonzola on thin slices of crisp apple or pear. Sprinkle with toasted pine nuts.

Brandied Cheese
Marinate 1-inch cubes of sharp cheddar cheese in brandy to cover for several hours. Serve cubes on picks.

Bite-Size Steak Tartare
Mix ground sirloin with minced onion, salt and pepper to taste. Shape into small balls. Chill until ready to serve. Serve on toothpicks with pickled onions and cornichons. and cornichons.

Mozzarella Melts
Top oblong pieces of toast with skinless and boneless sardines. Top with tomato puree and a thin slice of mozzarella cheese. Broil until cheese melts.

Opposite: Seafood Orgy, page 89

CRUDITÉS WITH CURRY HERB DIP

SERVES 10 TO 12

1 In a bowl, mix yogurt, sour cream, curry, parsley, dill, onions, eggs and salt to taste. Chill.

INGREDIENTS

1 cup plain yogurt
1 cup sour cream
1 to 2 teaspoons curry powder
¼ cup minced parsley
2 tablespoons chopped fresh dill
2 tablespoons chopped green onions
2 hard-cooked eggs, sieved
Salt
Bite-size pieces of raw vegetables—zucchini, carrots, bell peppers of various colors, jicama, snow peas, mushrooms, broccoli florets, cauliflower florets, celery pieces, tomato wedges.

2 Shortly before serving time, arrange the vegetables in a circle on a round platter to resemble a Della Robbia wreath. Place dip in center. Chill until ready to serve.

Opposite: Bite-Size Steak Tartare, page 90; Caviar Potatoes, page 85; Stuffed Olive Dunks, page 86

PICKLED SHRIMP AND OLIVES WITH CHRISTMAS CHEESE BALLS

SERVES 8 TO 10

INGREDIENTS

2 pounds medium shrimp,
cooked, shelled and deveined
2 cups black olives
1 red onion, thinly sliced
1 cup prepared Italian oil and
vinegar dressing
1 tablespoon Dijon mustard
1 bay leaf
1 pound sharp cheddar cheese
½ cup chopped stuffed green olives
1 can (4 ounces) sweet green
chilies, drained and chopped
Chopped parsley
2 packages (8 ounces each)
soft cream cheese
1 cup crushed pineapple
1 teaspoon curry powder
2 teaspoons grated fresh ginger
Chopped salted cashews
8 ounces Roquefort cheese
½ cup soft butter
2 cups (8 ounces) grated
Gruyère cheese
1 tablespoon brandy
¼ cup minced parsley
2 tablespoons minced green
onion
Paprika

1 In a large bowl, combine shrimp, drained, pitted black olives and onion rings. In a small bowl, mix dressing, mustard and bay leaf. Pour over shrimp mixture. Cover and refrigerate for several hours.

2 In a bowl, mix grated cheddar, green olives and chilies. Shape into a ball and roll in chopped parsley.

3 Mix cream cheese, drained pineapple, curry and ginger; shape into a ball and roll in cashews.

4 Mix Roquefort, butter, Gruyère, brandy, parsley and onion; shape into a ball and roll in paprika. Chill all three cheese balls.

5 When ready to serve, drain shrimp, olives and onions. Place shrimp, olives and onions on platter. Serve with picks. Garnish with chopped parsley.

6 Arrange cheese balls on a board with spreaders. Serve with thinly sliced party rye or pumpernickel or crackers.

7 If desired, shrimp and olives can be speared on toothpicks and arranged in diagonal rows on a 10-inch styrofoam cone. Place onion rings on top of cone. Garnish with parsley sprigs.

PASTA SHELLS STUFFED WITH CRABMEAT SALAD

1 In a large saucepan, cook pasta shells in boiling salted water until tender but still firm. Drain and place in cold water.

2 In a bowl, mix crabmeat, nuts, celery, carrot, lemon juice, curry, mayonnaise and tarragon. Drain pasta shells and dry on paper towels. Spoon crabmeat mixture into shells.

SERVES 6

INGREDIENTS

24 *large pasta shells*
3 *cups flaked crabmeat*
½ *cup coarsely chopped macadamia nuts*
⅓ *cup minced celery*
¼ *cup shredded carrot*
2 *tablespoons fresh lemon juice*
Pinch of curry powder
½ *cup mayonnaise*
¼ *teaspoon crumbled dried tarragon*
Minced red and green bell pepper

3 Top half of the shells with red pepper and the other half with green pepper. Place 4 shells, alternating red and green pepper, on each serving plate. Chill until ready to serve.

Page following: Assorted Holiday Tidbits

SALMON MOUSSE

MAKES ONE 1½-QUART MOLD

INGREDIENTS

2 cups cooked fresh or canned
   flaked salmon
¼ cup minced celery
¼ cup minced onion
   Juice of 1 lemon
1 dill pickle, minced
2 cups chicken broth
2 cups (1 pint) plain yogurt
3 envelopes unflavored gelatin
   Salt
   Finely chopped fresh dill
   Finely shredded iceberg
      lettuce
1 cup mayonnaise
½ cup heavy cream, whipped
   Thinly sliced seedless
      cucumber (optional)

1 In a blender, combine salmon, celery, onion, lemon juice, pickle and 1 cup of the chicken broth and process until pureed. Pour into a bowl and stir in yogurt.

2 In a small saucepan, sprinkle gelatin over remaining chicken broth and let stand until softened, about 5 minutes. Stir over low heat until gelatin is dissolved and broth is hot. Stir into salmon mixture. Season to taste with salt.

3 Chill until mixture has thickened to the consistency of unbeaten egg whites. Stir to blend well, then pour into a lightly oiled 1½-quart ring mold (or use a 1½ quart decorative bowl or dish of the same capacity). Chill until firm.

4 To unmold, dip ring mold into lukewarm water for a few seconds. Tap to loosen and invert onto a serving platter. Sprinkle top with chopped dill and surround with shredded lettuce.

5 Fold mayonnaise and heavy cream together. Pour into a bowl and place in center of ring mold. Chill until ready to serve.

6 To serve in bowl, mousse does not have to be unmolded. Serve with a spreader. Spread mousse on thin seedless cucumber slices.

SPICY DEVILED EGGS

1 Cut off the pointed ends of the eggs 1 inch from the top. Cut a thin slice from the rounded end of each egg to allow it to stand upright. With the tip of a demitasse spoon, scoop yolks from eggs carefully so whites stay whole.

2 Press yolks through a sieve into a bowl. Stir in mustard, chili

SERVES 12

INGREDIENTS
12 jumbo eggs, hard-cooked and shelled
2 tablespoons Dijon mustard
2 tablespoons chili sauce
¼ cup mayonnaise
1 jar (2 ounces) salmon caviar
Italian parsley sprigs
Leaf lettuce or radicchio leaves (optional)

sauce and mayonnaise. Restuff egg whites with mixture.

3 Spoon salmon caviar on top of egg yolk mixture. Press a small parsley sprig into the caviar. Serve as is or arrange eggs on a bed of lettuce and chill until ready to serve.

ENDIVE STUFFED WITH GOAT CHEESE AND GRAPES

1 In a bowl, mash cheese until creamy. Stir in capers, oil and bacon. Spoon mixture into endive leaves and top with halved red grapes. Chill until ready to serve.

SERVES 8

INGREDIENTS
24 Belgian endive leaves, all one size
12 ounces goat cheese
¼ cup capers
2 tablespoons green olive oil
8 slices crisp-cooked bacon, crumbled
Seedless red grapes, halved
Carrot curls

2 Place stuffed leaves in a circle on a large round platter to resemble a poinsettia. Pile carrot curls in the center of the platter.

THREE-CAVIAR MOSAIC

1 On a 10-inch square platter, spoon the black caviar in a diagonal line to resemble the trunk of a Christmas tree. Spoon the red caviar on one side in a triangle to resemble tree branches. Repeat on the other side using the golden caviar.

2 Sprinkle onion evenly over red and golden caviar. Surround tree with parsley. Serve with toast slices.

SERVES 10 TO 12

INGREDIENTS

1 jar (2 ounces) black
    lumpfish caviar
1 jar (2 ounces) red lumpfish
    caviar
1 jar (2 ounces) golden caviar
1/3 cup minced green onion
    Chopped Parsley
    Stemmed cherry tomatoes
    (optional)
    Raw mushroom caps
    (optional)
    Small zucchini slices
    (optional)
    Purchased 1½-inch tartlet
    shells (optional)

3 If desired place the platter on a larger round platter. Fill spaces on round platter with cherry tomatoes, mushroom caps, slices of zucchini and tartlet shells. Add small serving spoons. Spoon caviar on mushrooms, zucchini slices or tartlet shells.

CREAM CHEESE AND CHUTNEY SNACKS

1 Mix cream cheese and pecans. Mound cheese on a serving platter and form with a knife or spatula into a small bell shape.

2 Spoon pureed chutney around cheese. Decorate with

SERVES 10 TO 12

INGREDIENTS

2 packages (8 ounces each)
    soft cream cheese
½ cup finely chopped pecans
1 cup mango chutney, pureed
    in a blender
    Red bell pepper strips
    Thin apple slices or thin slices
    of date nut bread

strips of red pepper. Chill until ready to serve.

3 Surround with apple or date nut bread slices. Serve with spreaders.

SMOKED MOZZARELLA WITH TAPENADE

1 Arrange overlapping slices of cheese on a long, narrow rimmed serving platter.

SERVES 8

INGREDIENTS
1 pound smoked mozzarella, cut into ¼-inch-thick slices
½ cup olive oil
1 clove garlic, minced
2 tablespoons minced parsley
1 teaspoon crumbled dried thyme
6 pitted black olives
4 rolled anchovy fillets
2 tablespoons fresh lemon juice
½ cup canned tuna
Red and green pickled cherry peppers

2 Combine remaining ingredients except peppers in a blender and puree. Pour mixture evenly over cheese. Chill until ready to serve. Garnish with cherry peppers.

EASY BRIE CHEESE FONDUE

1 With a lightly oiled knife, thinly slice the top rind from each wheel of Brie. Place cheese cut side up on a heatproof platter. Place under broiler and broil until cheese melts.

SERVES 6

INGREDIENTS
2 wheels (8 ounces each) Brie cheese
2-inch squares of thinly sliced firm rye or pumpernickel bread

2 Remove from heat and use bread squares to scoop melted cheese; rind can also be eaten if desired. If cheese firms during serving, place under broiler again for a few minutes to soften.

PINE CONE BLUE CHEESE

SERVES 10 TO 12

INGREDIENTS

8 ounces soft blue cheese
2 packages (8 ounces each)
   soft cream cheese
½ cup soft butter
8 ounces goat cheese
   (Montrachet or Bucheron)
1 teaspoon ground caraway
   seeds
2 tablespoons chopped capers
1 tablespoon anchovy paste
1 tablespoon Dijon mustard
2 tablespoons minced green
   onion
1 pound whole almonds
¼ cup butter
   Pine sprigs
   Sesame seed crackers

1 In a bowl, mix blue cheese, cream cheese, softened butter, goat cheese, caraway, capers, anchovy paste, mustard and onion until well blended. Pile cheese in a mound on a board and shape with a knife or spatula into a small football shape. Chill.

2 To blanch almonds, drop them into a large pot of boiling water and boil for 30 seconds. Cool almonds in water, then drain and slip off skins. While almonds are still wet, split them in half with the tip of a knife.

3 In a large skillet, melt butter and sauté almonds, stirring constantly, until golden brown. Cool on paper towels.

4 Press almond halves, rounded side up, into the cheese mound in overlapping rows to resemble the brown scales of a pine cone. Garnish with pine sprigs. Add a spreader and surround with sesame crackers.

Opposite: Endive Stuffed with Goat Cheese and Grapes, page 99;
Pine Cone Blue Cheese, page 102

SMOKED SALMON AND STURGEON WITH HORSERADISH CREAM

SERVES 6 TO 8

INGREDIENTS

8 ounces each thinly sliced smoked salmon and sturgeon
1 cup (½ pint) heavy cream, whipped
3 tablespoons prepared white horseradish
2 tablespoons minced green onions

1 Chill smoked fish. In a bowl, mix whipped cream with horseradish and onions. Spread some of the cream on each slice of smoked fish and roll up.

2 Alternate rolls side by side on a long platter or board to resemble a giant candy cane. Chill until ready to serve. Serve with toothpicks for spearing.

CARPACCIO

SERVES 6 TO 8

INGREDIENTS

1 pound lean beef fillet or sirloin
½ cup green olive oil
½ cup fresh lemon juice
2 tablespoons Dijon mustard
2 tablespoons minced onion
2 tablespoons drained capers
Salt
Fresh rosemary sprigs
Red cord

1 Freeze beef until it is almost hard. With a very sharp, heavy knife, cut the frozen beef into paper-thin slices; overlap slices on serving platter. Chill.

2 In a bowl, beat oil, lemon juice, mustard, onion and capers until thick, adding salt to taste. Let stand at room temperature for 1 hour, then beat again. Pour mixture evenly over beef.

3 Garnish each serving with a sprig of fresh rosemary tied into a small wreath with red cord.

POLPETTE
(ITALIAN MEATBALLS)

1 In a bowl, mix meats, garlic, salt, cheese, crumbs, eggs, wine, oregano and basil. Shape mixture into 1-inch balls. Roll balls in flour.

2 In a large skillet, heat ⅛ inch of olive oil and sauté meatballs until brown on all sides. Drain on paper towels. Keep warm over low heat.

SERVES 8 TO 10

INGREDIENTS
1 pound ground chuck
1 pound ground veal
2 cloves garlic, crushed
2 teaspoons salt
½ cup grated Parmesan cheese
½ cup dry breadcrumbs
2 eggs
2 tablespoons dry red wine
1 teaspoon each crumbled
   dried oregano and basil
All-purpose flour
Olive oil
Purchased pesto sauce and
   marinara sauce
Large round loaf of Italian
   bread

3 Heat sauces separately in two saucepans and pour into candle warmer dishes.

4 Slice top from bread and scoop out inside, leaving a shell about 1 inch thick. Place meatballs into bread. Spear meatballs on picks and dip into desired sauce.

LIVER PÂTÉ WREATH

SERVES 10 TO 12

INGREDIENTS
2 pounds chicken livers
2 small onions, minced
1 clove garlic, minced
½ cup rendered chicken fat or butter
4 hard-cooked eggs, sieved
¼ cup Calvados or apple brandy
Salt and pepper
2 large green bell peppers
Toasted party rye slices
Pickled Cranberries (see following page), optional

1 Trim chicken livers and cut into halves. Mix livers with onions and garlic.

2 In a large skillet, heat fat and sauté livers over medium heat for 10 minutes or until brown outside but still slightly pink inside. Pour the entire contents of the skillet into a food processor and chop. Scrape into a bowl and stir in eggs, Calvados and salt and pepper to taste.

3 Spoon liver into a small ring shape to resemble a wreath in the center of a large round platter. With a sharp knife, cut oval pieces from the green peppers to resemble leaves. Press them in a circle into the top of the liver pâté ring. Chill until ready to serve.

4 Surround with rye slices and add a spreader. If desired, garnish and serve with Pickled Cranberries.

Opposite: Cream Cheese and Chutney Snacks, page 100; Liver Pâté Wreath, page 106

SESAME CHICKEN WINGS

1 Wash chicken and pat dry. Place in a bowl. Combine all remaining ingredients except sesame seeds in a blender and puree. Pour over chicken and stir to coat all pieces. Refrigerate for at least 2 hours.

SERVES 6 TO 8

INGREDIENTS

36 chicken drumettes (bottom part of chicken wing)
2 cloves garlic
1-inch piece fresh ginger, peeled
1 onion, quartered
1 teaspoon red pepper flakes
2 teaspoons salt
2 teaspoons ground coriander
3 tablespoons soy sauce
3 tablespoons fresh lemon juice
2 tablespoons sesame oil
2 tablespoons sugar
About 1/2 cup sesame seeds

2 Remove from marinade and sprinkle with seeds. Place under broiler and broil for 5 to 6 minutes on each side. Serve hot.

PICKLED CRANBERRIES

1 In a 2-quart nonaluminum saucepan, combine sugar, water, vinegar and pickling spice and bring to boil; boil for 5 minutes. Add cranberries and return to boil; boil for 2 minutes.

MAKES ABOUT 3 CUPS

INGREDIENTS

1 cup sugar
1 cup water
1/2 cup red wine vinegar
1 tablespoon whole pickling spice
4 cups (1 pound) cranberries

2 Cool, then chill cranberries in syrup.

SESAME CHICKEN WINGS

1 Wash chicken and pat dry. Place in a bowl. Combine all remaining ingredients except sesame seeds in a blender and puree. Pour over chicken and stir to coat all pieces. Refrigerate for at least 2 hours.

SERVES 6 TO 8

INGREDIENTS
36 chicken drumettes (bottom part of chicken wing)
2 cloves garlic
1-inch piece fresh ginger, peeled
1 onion, quartered
1 teaspoon red pepper flakes
2 teaspoons salt
2 teaspoons ground coriander
3 tablespoons soy sauce
3 tablespoons fresh lemon juice
2 tablespoons sesame oil
2 tablespoons sugar
About ½ cup sesame seeds

2 Remove from marinade and sprinkle with seeds. Place under broiler and broil for 5 to 6 minutes on each side. Serve hot.

PICKLED CRANBERRIES

1 In a 2-quart nonaluminum saucepan, combine sugar, water, vinegar and pickling spice and bring to boil; boil for 5 minutes. Add cranberries and return to boil; boil for 2 minutes.

MAKES ABOUT 3 CUPS

INGREDIENTS
1 cup sugar
1 cup water
½ cup red wine vinegar
1 tablespoon whole pickling spice
4 cups (1 pound) cranberries

2 Cool, then chill cranberries in syrup.

CREAMED SWEETBREADS AND OYSTERS IN TOAST CUPS

1 Brush both sides of the bread slices with ⅓ cup melted butter. Place bread in muffin pans, pushing down in the center to shape a cup. Bake in a preheated 400°F oven for 12 to 15 minutes or until golden brown. Remove from pans and set aside.

2 In a medium saucepan, cover sweetbreads with water. Bring to boil, lower heat and simmer for 20 minutes. Drain and cool. Remove membranes and tubules. Dice sweetbreads and mix with oysters and mushrooms.

MAKES 8 APPETIZER SERVINGS

INGREDIENTS
8 slices white bread, crusts trimmed
⅓ cup melted butter
1 pair sweetbreads
1 cup shucked oysters
1 cup sliced mushrooms
¼ cup butter
¼ cup all-purpose flour
1½ cups milk
½ cup dry sherry
Salt and pepper
Green bell pepper and pome-granate seeds (optional garnish)

3 In a medium saucepan, melt ¼ cup butter. Add sweetbread mixture and sauté for 5 minutes. Stir in flour, then gradually stir in milk and sherry and simmer for 5 minutes. Season to taste with salt and pepper.

4 Place toast cups on serving plates and fill with sweetbread mixture. If desired, garnish with pieces of green pepper cut with a sharp knife into holly leaf shapes; sprinkle with a few pomegranate seeds.

*Page following: Minestone, page 112;
Chestnut, Herb and Sausage Soup, page 124*

THE STEAMING TUREEN

Soups Both Hearty and Delicate

*M*any good things come to the table in big
bowls—salad, fruit, punch, popcorn and, best of all,
soup. Served at the beginning of a dinner it can be light, elegant—
a kind of supple warm-up to the meal. But soup can also be a complete
lunch or supper in itself. Whether rich minestrone or delicate chicken broth, soup
is one of the true comfort foods. It is easy to prepare and easy to eat—a good
combination for any cook.

Making soup is also one of the most nutritious ways we have of preparing food. The
precious vitamins and minerals in vegetables are often thrown out with the water
we cook them in. Since the cooking liquids of vegetables and meats are generally used
in soups, the comfort soup provides is in more than just its savor. Although it's a
wonderful and economical crowd-pleaser, soup can be tricky to serve to a large
group, as soup bowls are shallow and difficult to maneuver. Try using mugs, or even
serve from a punchbowl in punch cups.

MINESTRONE

SERVES 6 TO 8

INGREDIENTS

⅓ cup olive oil
1 large onion, chopped
2 leeks, trimmed, sliced,
    washed and drained
2½ quarts chicken broth
1½ teaspoons each chopped fresh
    marjoram and rosemary
    or ½ teaspoon each dried
3 tomatoes, peeled, seeded
    and chopped
2 boiling potatoes, peeled
    and diced
2 carrots, diced
2 zucchini, diced
1 cup sliced celery
1 cup 1-inch pieces green
    beans
½ cup ditalini pasta
1 pound escarole, trimmed
    and coarsely chopped
2 cups well-drained cooked or
    canned cannellini beans
Salt and pepper
Grated Parmesan cheese

*I*n a kettle, heat oil and sauté onion and leeks for 5 minutes or until golden brown. Add broth, herbs, vegetables and pasta. Bring to boil, lower heat and simmer, covered, for 15 minutes or until vegetables and pasta are tender.

Stir in escarole and cannellini beans and simmer for 5 minutes. Season to taste with salt and pepper. Serve minestrone in large bowls, sprinkled with cheese. This is a thick, hearty soup.

BLACK BEAN SOUP

1 In a kettle, combine ham bone and water. Cover and simmer for 2 hours, skimming fat from time to time. Cool, then remove bone.

2 In a 3-quart saucepan, melt butter and sauté onions and celery over medium heat for 10 minutes. Add beans and ham broth and simmer 20 minutes.

MAKES 8 SERVINGS

INGREDIENTS

*1 ham bone (saved from
  holiday ham), cracked*
8 cups water
¼ cup butter
2 onions, chopped
2 cups sliced celery
*2 cans (1 pound each) black
  beans, drained*
½ cup dry sherry
Salt and pepper
Peeled lemon slices
Finely chopped smoked ham

3 Puree soup in batches in blender. Return to saucepan, stir in sherry and simmer for 10 minutes. Season to taste with salt and pepper. Top each serving with a lemon slice and chopped ham.

CREAM OF CELERY AND LEEK SOUP

1 In a 3-quart saucepan, melt butter and sauté celery and leeks over low heat for 10 minutes, or until wilted but not brown. Sprinkle with flour.

2 Gradually stir in broth and herbs. Cover and simmer for 20 minutes or until vegetables are tender.

MAKES 8 SERVINGS

INGREDIENTS

⅓ cup butter
*2 cups chopped celery
  with leaves*
*2 cups sliced leeks, green and
  white parts*
⅓ cup all-purpose flour
6 cups chicken broth
*½ teaspoon each dried chervil
  and summer savory*
1 cup (½ pint) heavy cream
Salt and white pepper
*Finely chopped celery leaves
  (garnish)*

3 Puree soup in batches in blender. Return to saucepan and stir in cream. Season to taste with salt and pepper. Serve topped with finely chopped celery leaves.

ONION SOUP WITH CHEESE CUSTARD

MAKES 6 SERVINGS

INGREDIENTS

CUSTARD

3 eggs
1 cup milk
⅓ cup grated Parmesan cheese

SOUP

3 large Spanish onions, thinly sliced
¼ cup butter
1½ quarts beef broth
½ cup marsala
Pinch of ground mace
Salt and pepper
Salted whipped cream or sour cream

1 For custard, beat eggs with milk and cheese in a small bowl until well blended. Pour mixture into a greased 9- x 5- x 3-inch loaf pan. Bake in a preheated 325°F oven for 30 to 35 minutes or until a knife inserted in center comes out clean. Cool, then chill. (This custard will only be about 1 inch thick.)

2 For soup, sauté onions in butter in a 2-quart saucepan over low heat for 20 minutes or until they are very soft but not brown. Add broth, wine and mace, cover and simmer for 30 minutes. Season to taste with salt and pepper.

3 Cut custard into ¾-inch squares and divide among serving bowls. Top with soup.

QUICK MUSHROOM AND SEAFOOD SOUP

1 In a 2-quart saucepan, melt butter and sauté garlic for 2 minutes. Add flounder, wine and chicken broth. Cover and simmer for 5 minutes or until flounder is cooked.

MAKES 6 SERVINGS

INGREDIENTS

¼ cup butter
1 clove garlic, minced
1 pound flounder fillets, cut into 1-inch cubes
1 cup dry white wine
1 cup chicken broth
1 cup chopped cooked, shelled and deveined shrimp
1 cup cooked lobster or King crab
1 can (10¾ ounces) condensed golden mushroom soup, undiluted
6 tablespoons dry sherry

2 Stir in shrimp, crabmeat and condensed soup; reheat only until soup starts to bubble. Top each serving with 1 tablespoon sherry.

PUMPKIN OR SQUASH SOUP

1 In a large kettle, combine squash and 2 quarts chicken broth. Cover and simmer until squash is very tender, about 40 to 45 minutes.

2 Puree mixture in a blender in several batches. Return to kettle. Stir in cream and salt and pepper to taste. If soup is too thick, thin it with additional chicken broth.

MAKES 8 SERVINGS

INGREDIENTS
2 quarts diced peeled and seeded pumpkin, or butternut or acorn squash
2 quarts (or more) chicken broth
2 cups (1 pint) heavy cream
Salt and pepper
Freshly grated nutmeg
Whipped cream (optional)

3 Serve in bowls topped with a dusting of nutmeg or a dollop of whipped cream.

WILD MUSHROOM BROTH

1 In a bowl, mix mushrooms and water and let stand at room temperature for 30 minutes.

2 Transfer mushrooms to a 3-quart saucepan. Strain liquid through several thicknesses of dampened cheesecloth or a paper coffee filter and add to saucepan

MAKES 8 SERVINGS

INGREDIENTS
⅔ cup dried porcini mushrooms
1 cup warm water
2 cloves garlic, minced
2 tomatoes, quartered
8 cups chicken broth
1 cup (½ pint) heavy cream
Salt
Grated Parmesan cheese
Chopped parsley

with garlic, tomatoes and chicken broth. Cover and simmer for 1 hour.

3 Strain soup through a sieve, pressing out all liquid. Return to saucepan and stir in cream and salt to taste. Top each serving with cheese and parsley.

Opposite: Pumpkin Soup, page 116;
Cream of Celery and Leek Soup, page 113

RED AND GREEN SOUP

MAKES 8 SERVINGS

INGREDIENTS

RED SOUP
¼ cup butter
1 small onion, minced
¼ cup all-purpose flour
3 cups half-and-half
3 cups crushed tomatoes,
    pureed in blender
½ teaspoon crumbled dried
    basil
½ teaspoon garlic powder
    Salt

GREEN SOUP
2 packages (10 ounces each)
    frozen peas
6 cups chicken broth
¼ cup soft butter mixed with
    ¼ cup all-purpose flour
    Salt
    Thinly sliced white bread

1 For red soup, melt butter in a 2-quart saucepan over medium heat and sauté onion for 10 minutes. Sprinkle with flour. Gradually stir in half-and-half. Stir over medium heat until mixture bubbles and thickens. Stir in tomatoes, basil, garlic and salt to taste. Keep warm.

2 For green soup, combine peas and broth in a 2-quart saucepan, and simmer, covered, for 15 minutes. Puree in blender, then return to saucepan. Add butter/flour mixture and stir over medium heat until soup bubbles and thickens. Season to taste with salt.

3 Using 2 ladles, placed at either side of the bowl, pour in soup simultaneously so colors remain separate. Garnish with minced parsley.

4 For another garnish, use a cookie cutter, and cut Christmas trees from bread slices and toast. Place on soup and serve.

CRAB AND SCALLOP SOUP

MAKES 6 SERVINGS

INGREDIENTS
½ cup uncooked wild rice
3 cups water
½ teaspoon salt
6 cups chicken broth
1 cup chopped cooked King
    crab or snow crab
8 ounces bay scallops
6 tablespoons dry white wine

1 In a covered 1-quart saucepan, cook rice in boiling water with salt for 35 to 40 minutes or until tender.

2 Drain rice and transfer to a 2-quart saucepan. Add broth, crabmeat and scallops and simmer uncovered for 5 minutes. Season with salt to taste. Add 1 tablespoon white wine to each serving.

SWEDISH FRUIT SOUP

MAKES 6 SERVINGS

INGREDIENTS
3 tablespoons quick-cooking
    tapioca
3 cups unsweetened pineapple
    juice
2 tablepoons honey
1 package (10 ounces) frozen
    raspberries, thawed
2 navel oranges, sectioned
    Peeled, shredded tart apple

1 In a 2-quart nonaluminum saucepan, combine tapioca and pineapple juice. Bring to boil, remove from heat and let stand until lukewarm.

2 Stir in honey, raspberries with their syrup, and orange sections. Chill. Serve very cold in small bowls, topped with shredded apple.

OYSTER STEW

MAKES 8 SERVINGS

INGREDIENTS

1/4 cup butter
1 small onion, minced
1/2 cup minced celery with
  leaves
3 cups shucked oysters and
  their liquor
2 cups milk
1 cup (1/2 pint) heavy cream
1/2 teaspoon paprika
3 tablespoons minced parsley
3 egg yolks
  Salt and pepper
  Sliced firm white bread

1 In a 2-quart saucepan, melt butter over medium heat and sauté onion and celery for 5 minutes. Add oysters, milk, cream and paprika and simmer for 5 minutes. Stir in parsley.

2 Beat egg yolks in a small bowl and beat in 1/2 cup of the hot soup. Return mixture to soup, stirring constantly. Reheat but do not boil or egg will curdle. Season to taste with salt and pepper. Serve sprinkled with paprika.

3 If desired, cut bell shapes from bread slices; toast until golden. Place on bowls of soup and serve.

TURKEY GIBLET SOUP

MAKES 8 SERVINGS

INGREDIENTS

1 turkey carcass, cracked
Turkey giblets, neck and liver
2 onions, sliced
4 whole cloves
1 bay leaf
6 peppercorns
2 quarts water
1 quart chicken broth
1 large package (2 pounds) soup greens, cleaned and diced
½ cup ditalini pasta
1 teaspoon crumbled dried thyme
Salt and pepper
Italian bread

1 In a large kettle, combine turkey carcass, giblets, neck, liver, onions, cloves, bay leaf, peppercorns, water and chicken broth. Cover and simmer for 2 hours, skimming foam from time to time.

2 Strain broth into a 4-quart saucepan. Chop giblets, neck meat and liver and add to broth. Add soup greens, pasta and thyme and simmer, uncovered, for 20 to 25 minutes or until vegetables are tender. Season to taste with salt and pepper. Serve with toasted, thinly sliced Italian bread.

Opposite: Crab and Scallop Soup, page 120; Oyster Stew, page 121

CHESTNUT, HERB AND SAUSAGE SOUP

MAKES 8 SERVINGS

INGREDIENTS

1 pound chestnuts
1 cup chopped carrots
1 cup chopped celery
1 cup chopped onion
8 ounces bulk sausage,
*   crumbled*
5 cups (or more) chicken
*   broth*
½ teaspoon each dried thyme
*   and rosemary*
3 egg yolks
1 cup (½ pint) heavy cream
*   Salt and pepper*
*   Fresh herb sprigs (optional*
*   garnish)*

1 Slash one side of the chestnuts and strip off the shell. Place in a saucepan and cover with water. Cover and simmer for 40 to 45 minutes or until easily pierced. Cool chestnuts in water. Remove them one at a time and strip off the thin brown skin. Place peeled chestnuts in a food processor and puree.

2 In a 3-quart saucepan, combine carrots, celery, onion and sausage. Sauté for about 15 minutes, or until sausage is brown and crumbly. Drain excess fat.

3 Add chestnut puree, 5 cups chicken broth and herbs. Cover and simmer for 20 minutes.

4 Beat egg yolks with cream in a small bowl. Gradually stir this mixture into the hot soup; reheat but do not boil. Season to taste with salt and pepper. If soup is too thick, thin it with additional chicken broth. Serve topped with a small herb sprig, if available.

CHRISTMAS DINNER

Dramatic Dishes
Minimal Effort–Happy New Year
Buffet and Dinner

Our image of Christmas dinner is usually of crystal and candlelight, a steaming turkey or roast, mounds of fragrant winter vegetables, and familiar faces ranged around the table all shining with anticipation. This Norman Rockwell portrait of the holiday is something we devote ourselves to achieving year after year because it satisfies something deep in us, something about nostalgia and continuance, love and remembering. But what it takes to create this scene at the dining table can be quite a project. These days, it seems, everyone has to travel home for Christmas. Bed rolls, inflatable mattresses, old cribs and daybeds are aired and set up in any empty corner or room. While presents are being unwrapped, everyone is busy talking and catching up with family news. Dinner is hustled together in the kitchen with lots of extra help–sometimes too much of it! By late afternoon, all is ready. The big table, pieced together from several smaller ones, is surrounded by hungry people. The center of everyone's attention is always the main dish and its presentation.

The recipes in this chapter are designed for a maximum of drama, flavor and nostalgia–and a minimum of work. They involve straightforward preparation, a set cooking time without too much supervision, and easy final presentation. After all, you want to be able to spend the day with your family and company, and to enjoy the process of preparing this special meal in the spirit of the season.

STANDING RIB ROAST WITH HORSERADISH SAUCE AND YORKSHIRE PUDDING

1 Sprinkle roast with pepper, herbs, onions and garlic. Place fat side up on a rack set into a roasting pan. Roast in a preheated 350°F oven for 2 hours or until a meat thermometer inserted in the thickest part registers 150°F for medium rare. Pour off fatty part of the drippings from roasting pan and use for pudding and sauce. Keep roast warm.

2 For pudding: turn oven to 425°F. In a bowl, mix flour and salt. Add eggs and milk, beat with electric mixer until well blended. Pour drippings into a 9- x 13- x 2-inch pan; tilt pan to cover bottom evenly. Pour batter into pan. Bake for 10 minutes, then lower temperature to 325°F for 30 minutes. Bake until puffed and brown. Cut into squares to serve. For individual servings, divide batter between 8 greased custard cups or popover pan. Bake the same length of time.

MAKES 8 SERVINGS

INGREDIENTS
10-pound standing beef
   rib roast
2 teaspoons cracked pepper
2 teaspoons crumbled
   dried marjoram
2 teaspoons crumbled
   dried thyme
2 onions, finely chopped
2 cloves garlic, minced

PUDDING
2 cups unsifted
   all-purpose flour
1 teaspoon salt
4 eggs
2 cups milk
½ cup beef drippings
   or melted butter

SAUCE
½ cup beef drippings or butter
½ cup all-purpose flour
2 cups beef broth
2 cups half-and-half
½ cup prepared white
   horseradish
Salt and pepper
Red onion flowers
   (see below)

3 While pudding is baking, prepare sauce. In a 1½-quart saucepan, heat drippings and stir in flour. Stir over low heat for 10 minutes. Gradually add beef broth and half-and-half. Stir over medium heat until sauce bubbles and thickens. Stir in horseradish and salt and pepper to taste.

4 Place roast on platter and garnish with sautéed onions and cherry tomatoes. Can also be garnished with long-needled pine boughs and red onion flowers. To prepare onion flowers, peel small red onions. Starting at the pointed end, cut onions into quarters, cutting to within ½ inch of the bottom. Cut each quarter into ⅛-inch-wide strips to within ½ inch of the bottom. Place in cold water and onions will open to resemble chrysanthemums. Serve pudding separately and pass sauce.

Opposite: Standing Rib Roast, page 127

DIJON SHELL OF BEEF

1 Place beef bone side down on roasting pan. Score fat into diamonds. In a bowl, mix remaining ingredients and spread over fat on roast. Roast in a preheated 325°F oven for about 1½ hours or until meat thermometer inserted in thickest part registers 140°F for rare and 160°F for medium rare.

SERVES 10 TO 12

INGREDIENTS
1 whole shell of beef, fat
   trimmed, about 10 pounds
2 cloves garlic, crushed
1 teaspoon white pepper
2 teaspoons fines herbes
½ cup Dijon mustard

2 Serve with Scalloped White and Sweet Potatoes, Fresh Spinach Croustade and Cranberry Wine Mold, with Cheese-Crusted Deep-Dish Apple Cranberry Pie and Maple Walnut Ice Cream for dessert (see Index for recipes).

SPICY BEEF FILETS

1 Rub filets with garlic and sprinkle with salt and pepper. In a large skillet, melt butter and brown filets over medium heat for 5 minutes on each side; they will be medium rare. Remove filets and keep warm.

2 Sprinkle flour into pan drippings, then gradually stir in broth and wine. Cook, scraping

MAKES 6 SERVINGS
INGREDIENTS
6 filets mignons,
   each 1½ inches thick
2 cloves garlic, mashed
   Salt and pepper
¼ cup butter
2 tablespoons all-purpose flour
1 cup beef broth
1 cup dry red wine
2 tablespoons Dijon mustard
1 teaspoon Worcestershire sauce
6 thin slices rye toast
2 red bell peppers, thinly sliced
   into rings

up all brown particles, until sauce bubbles and thickens slightly. Stir in mustard and Worcestershire sauce and simmer for 5 minutes. Season to taste with salt, if necessary.

3 Place filets on serving plates and top with sauce. Cut pepper rings in half; surround filets with a wreath of halved pepper rings.

Opposite: Standing Rib Roast, page 127

129

ROAST VEAL SHOULDER WITH EGGPLANT AND PEPPERS

1 Brush veal with ¼ cup olive oil and sprinkle with oregano, 1 teaspoon thyme and sage. Place on a rack set into a roasting pan. Roast in a preheated 350°F oven for 2 to 2½ hours or until a meat thermometer inserted in thickest part registers 170°F.

2 While veal is roasting, place eggplant in a bowl and sprinkle with salt. Let stand at room temperature for 1 hour. Drain.

MAKES 6 TO 8 SERVINGS

INGREDIENTS

5-pound boneless
   veal shoulder
¼ cup olive oil
1 teaspoon crumbled
   dried oregano
1 teaspoon crumbled
   dried thyme
1 teaspoon crumbled
   dried sage
   Salt and pepper
1 unpeeled eggplant,
   cut into 1-inch cubes
¼ cup olive oil
1 red onion, thinly sliced
1 red and 1 green bell pepper,
   cut into strips
1 can (1 pound) tomatoes
1 teaspoon crumbled
   dried basil
1 teaspoon crumbled
   dried thyme

3 In a 2-quart saucepan, heat ¼ cup olive oil and sauté onion and peppers over medium heat for 5 minutes. Add eggplant and sauté for another 5 minutes. Add tomatoes, basil and 1 teaspoon thyme. Cover and simmer gently for 25 to 30 minutes or until eggplant is tender. Season to taste with salt and pepper.

4 Slice veal and serve with eggplant mixture.

5 Serve veal with Turkey Manicotti, Stuffed Baby Artichokes (see Index for recipes).

BRAISED VEAL CHOPS WITH SAGE AND PROSCIUTTO

1 With a sharp knife, slash chops horizontally to form a pocket. Push a slice of prosciutto into each chop. Press cut edges together. Sprinkle with salt, pepper and sage. Coat with flour, shaking off excess.

2 Divide butter between 2 large skillets. Melt butter over medium-high heat and brown 3 chops on both sides in each skillet. Divide wine between skillets, cover and simmer for 20 to 25 minutes or until veal is tender.

MAKES 6 SERVINGS

INGREDIENTS

6 *veal loin chops, 1 inch thick*
6 *thin slices prosciutto*
 Salt and pepper
2 *teaspoons crumbled*
  dried sage
 All-purpose flour
¼ *cup butter*
1 *cup marsala*
6 *lemon wedges*
6 *slices prosciutto*

3 Place chops on serving plates. Boil pan juices for 2 minutes to loosen all particles; spoon over veal.

4 Cut the lemon wedges in half crosswise, cutting not quite all the way through. Loosely roll up each of the 6 remaining prosciutto slices and pinch one side; the other side will resemble a rose. Place pinched side into slit in lemon wedges and use as a garnish.

Opposite: Roast Veal Shoulder with Eggplant and Peppers, page 131

HOT VEAL GALANTINE

SERVES 6

INGREDIENTS

1 boned breast of veal, about
   3 to 4 pounds
   Salt and pepper
8 slices prosciutto
1 pound bulk sausage
1 onion, chopped
2 carrots, diced and cooked
½ cup chopped parsley
2 cups dry herb stuffing
2 eggs, well beaten
¼ cup butter
3 onions, sliced
3 carrots, sliced
2 white turnips, peeled and
   diced
2 cups sliced celery
1 bay leaf
1½ teaspoons chopped fresh
   thyme or ½ teaspoon dried
2 cups dry white wine

*P*ound veal to ½ inch thickness. Sprinkle lightly with salt and pepper. Cover with prosciutto slices. In a bowl, mix sausage, onion, carrots, parsley, stuffing and eggs until well blended. Spread evenly over veal. Roll up veal like a jelly roll and tie with string. Heat butter in a Dutch oven and sauté vegetables with herbs until tender. Add wine. Cover tightly and simmer for 2 to 2½ hours or until veal is tender. Place on serving platter and remove string. Spoon vegetables and pan juices around veal. Cut into thick slices and serve with vegetables and juices.

Opposite: Hot Veal Galantine, page 135

VEAL CHOPS WITH SUN-DRIED TOMATOES, CAPERS AND CREAM SAUCE

1 Sprinkle chops with salt and pepper. Cut a slash into side of each chop, forming a pocket. In a bowl, mix tomatoes, spinach and celery. Use mixture to stuff chops; fasten openings with toothpicks. Divide butter and oil between two large skillets and heat. Brown chops over medium heat for 5 minutes on each side. Combine all chops in one skillet, cover and simmer for 15 minutes.

SERVES 6

INGREDIENTS

6 *loin veal chops, each 1 inch thick*
  Salt and pepper
4 *ounces sun-dried tomatoes, chopped*
1 *package (10 ounces) frozen chopped spinach, cooked and squeezed dry*
½ *cup minced celery*
2 *tablespoons butter*
2 *tablespoons olive oil*
4 *shallots, minced*
1 *small tart green apple, peeled, cored and finely diced*
½ *cup apple brandy*
  Juice of ½ lemon
1 *cup (½ pint) heavy cream*
2 *teaspoons Dijon mustard*
3 *tablespoons drained capers*
3 *tablespoons chopped parsley*

2 Meanwhile, add shallots and apple to empty skillet and sauté over medium heat for 5 minutes or until golden. Add brandy and lemon juice and simmer uncovered for 5 minutes. Stir in cream and simmer for 10 minutes or until slightly thickened. Stir in mustard, capers and parsley and simmer 1 minute. Place chops on serving platter and remove toothpicks. Stir pan juices from chops into sauce. Season to taste with salt. Spoon sauce evenly over chops.

CROWN ROAST OF PORK
WITH APPLE, APRICOT AND RICE STUFFING

1 Have butcher crack bottom bones on loins and shape them into a crown roast. After trimming, have the butcher grind the trimmings.

2 Rub roast with garlic, caraway and salt. In a 3-quart saucepan, melt butter and sauté onion, peppers and celery over medium heat for 5 minutes or until wilted. Add ground pork trimmings and sauté for another 5 minutes. Add rice and chicken broth, cover and simmer for 20 minutes or until rice is tender and liquid is absorbed. Stir in parsley, apple, fines herbes and apricots.

MAKES 10 TO 12 SERVINGS

INGREDIENTS
2 center-cut pork loins, chine
  bone removed
2 cloves garlic, mashed
1 teaspoon ground
  caraway seeds
2 teaspoons salt
½ cup butter
1 red onion, chopped
2 green bell peppers, chopped
1 cup chopped celery
3 cups uncooked Arborio
  or long-grain rice
6 cups chicken broth
½ cup chopped parsley
2 cups diced peeled apple
2 teaspoons crumbled
  dried fines herbes or
  Herbes de Provence
½ cup finely chopped
  dried apricots
Candied kumquats
Chicory leaves
Crabapples

3 Place crown roast on a foil-lined pan. Pack rice mixture into center of roast. Cover stuffing with a piece of oiled foil. Roast in a preheated 350°F oven for 2 hours.

4 Place roast on a serving platter, and remove foil. Garnish with candied kumquats and clusters of crabapples. Add sprigs of chicory.

MARINATED RACK OF LAMB

SERVES 6

INGREDIENTS
3 racks of lamb
1⅓ cups French olive oil
⅔ cups white wine vinegar
2 teaspoons salt
½ teaspoon white pepper
4 cloves garlic, mashed
2 tablespoons chopped fresh
     rosemary or 2 teaspoons
     dried

1 Trim excess fat from lamb racks and place fat side down in a glass or earthenware dish. Beat remaining ingredients in a bowl until thick and pour evenly over lamb. Refrigerate overnight.

2 Turn lamb and let stand at room temperature for 2 hours. Drain and place in roasting pan. Roast in a preheated 350°F oven for 1 hour or until a meat thermometer inserted into thickest part registers 160°F.

3 Place 2 racks on a serving platter with bones crossed. Slice remaining rack and arrange around whole racks. Garnish with pine sprigs and bunches of fresh thyme, or with pineapple slices and red bell pepper rings. Serve with cooked wild rice and Asparagus with Mint and Snow Peas (see Index).

CRUSTED DOUBLE LAMB CHOPS

1 Trim excess fat from chops. In a small bowl, mix all remaining ingredients except jelly. Roll chops in mixture, pressing firmly to make crumbs adhere.

MAKES 6 SERVINGS

INGREDIENTS

6 double-rib loin lamb chops
1 clove garlic, mashed
1 teaspoon salt
½ teaspoon pepper
1 cup dry breadcrumbs
⅓ cup olive oil
1 teaspoon crumbled
   dried mint leaves
1 teaspoon crumbled
   dried rosemary
Mint jelly (optional garnish)

2 Arrange chops side by side on an oiled baking sheet. Roast in a preheated 400°F oven for 15 minutes; chops will be pink inside. If desired, garnish with a few cubes of mint jelly.

LEG OF LAMB WITH BOMBAY SAUCE

1 Make small slashes all over the fatty side of the leg of lamb. Insert a sliver of garlic into each slash. Rub lamb with rosemary, salt and pepper. Place in a roasting pan and roast in a preheated 350°F oven for 2 hours; lamb will be pink.

MAKES 10 TO 12 SERVINGS

INGREDIENTS

1 leg of lamb, about 8 pounds
3 cloves garlic, cut into slivers
2 teaspoons crumbled
dried rosemary
Salt and pepper
½ cup butter
2 large onions, chopped
2 green apples, peeled,
cored and diced
Rind of 1 orange,
cut into slivers
2 teaspoons curry powder
½ cup all-purpose flour
3 cups chicken broth
1 cup (½ pint) heavy cream
½ cup finely chopped
mango chutney
Pine sprigs and pine cones

2 While lamb is roasting, melt butter in a 2-quart saucepan over medium-high heat. Sauté onions, apples, orange rind and curry for 5 minutes. Sprinkle with flour; gradually stir in chicken broth and cream. Stir over medium heat until sauce bubbles and thickens. Stir in chutney and season to taste with salt and pepper. Serve with Twice-Baked Idaho Potatoes and Corn Custard with Scalloped Tomatoes (see Index for recipes).

SPICED GLAZED HAM WITH MINTED PEARS AND ROSY SPICED APPLES

1 Trim skin from ham shank and score fat into diamonds. Insert a whole clove into the center of each diamond.

2 In a bowl, mix all remaining ingredients. Place ham, fatty side up, on a rack set into a shallow roasting pan. Roast in a preheated 350°F oven for 1 hour. Spoon apricot mixture evenly over ham. Roast another hour.

MAKES 12 TO 14 SERVINGS

INGREDIENTS
*1 precooked smoked whole
ham, 10 to 12 pounds
Whole cloves
¼ cup Dijon mustard
2 tablespoons brandy
1 cup orange liqueur
2 cups apricot preserves
Minted Pears and Rosy
Spiced Apples
(see following recipes)*

3 Remove ham from oven and place on serving platter; keep warm. Pour off excess fat from roasting pan. Add 1½ cups water to pan; place on top of range and boil, scraping up all particles. Pour into sauceboat. Serve ham garnished with Minted Pears, Rosy Spiced Apples and parsley. Serve with Baked Succotash, red and green seedless grapes and slices of English Fruit Cake for dessert. Can also be served with Spiced Cranberries, julienne of carrots, zucchini and green beans, Fruited Slaw, and Rum-Baked Acorn Squash (see Index for recipes).

Opposite: Leg of Lamb with Bombay Sauce, page 143

MINTED PEARS

1 Peel pears, leaving them whole with stems attached. With tip of a knife, remove the blossom ends.

MAKES 12

INGREDIENTS
12 small firm Bosc pears
2 jars (12 ounces each) mint jelly
1 teaspoon green food coloring
About 4 cups water

2 Place pears in a kettle and add mint jelly, food coloring and enough water to cover pears. Bring to boil, lower heat and simmer for 20 minutes or until pears are tender but still firm. Cool in syrup.

ROSY SPICED APPLES

1 Peel apples, leaving them whole with stems attached.

2 Place apples in a kettle and add sugar, red hots, food coloring

MAKES 12

INGREDIENTS
12 small Granny Smith apples
2 cups sugar
½ cup cinnamon red hots
1 teaspoon red food coloring
About 4 cups water

and enough water to cover apples. Bring to boil, lower heat and simmer for 20 minutes or until apples are tender but still firm. Cool in syrup.

TWIN ROAST TURKEYS WITH TWIN STUFFINGS

1 Remove giblets from turkeys. Sprinkle turkeys inside and out with salt and pepper. Rub with poultry seasoning and garlic powder. Place on racks in roasting pan. Roast in a preheated 350°F oven for 2½ hours or until legs move up and down easily.

2 While turkeys are roasting, prepare stuffings. For sausage onion stuffing, sauté sausage in a 3-quart saucepan, breaking it up with a spoon, until brown and crumbly. Do not pour off fat. Add onions, pepper, celery and butter and sauté for 10 minutes or until vegetables are wilted. Add broth and bring to boil. Simmer for 15 minutes or until vegetables are tender. Add croutons and pecans and stir until liquid is absorbed and stuffing is hot.

3 For couscous stuffing, melt butter in a 3-quart saucepan over medium heat and sauté couscous

MAKES 12 TO 14 SERVINGS

INGREDIENTS
2 turkeys, 10 pounds each, thawed if frozen
Salt and pepper
2 teaspoons poultry seasoning
2 teaspoons garlic powder

SAUSAGE ONION STUFFING
1 pound bulk sausage
2 large onions, chopped
1 green bell pepper, chopped
1 cup chopped celery with leaves
¼ cup butter
3 cups chicken broth
6 cups plain croutons
1 cup coarsely broken pecans

COUSCOUS STUFFING
½ cup butter
2 cups couscous
½ cup pine nuts
½ cup raisins
½ cup finely chopped dried apricots
Grated rind and juice of 2 oranges
4 cups chicken broth
Salt
Spiced Cranberries

and pine nuts until golden brown. Add raisins, apricots, orange rind and juice and chicken broth and stir until liquid is absorbed. Season to taste with salt. Drain drippings from roasting pan. Stir half the drippings into each of the stuffings.

4 Garnish turkey with chicory sprigs. Garnish sausage stuffing with diced red pepper and couscous stuffing with slivered orange rind.

If desired, turkey legs may be decorated with gold foil frills.

NOTE:
For the traditionalists who want a large turkey, prepare as in above recipe, using a 20-pound bird. Roast at 350°F for 5 hours or until leg moves up and down easily.

Serve turkey with Celery and Fresh Tomatoes, Tipsy Pudding and assorted cookies (see Index for recipes).

Page following: Christmas Buffet

GIBLET GRAVY

MAKES 12 TO 14 SERVINGS

INGREDIENTS

Giblets, livers and necks
from 2 turkeys*
6 *cups water*
½ *cup butter*
½ *cup all-purpose flour*
1 *cup beef broth*
⅓ *cup madeira*
Salt and pepper

1 In a 2-quart saucepan, combine giblets, livers, necks and water. Bring to boil, cover and simmer for 1½ hours. Strain broth.

2 Chop giblets, livers and neck meat. Wipe out saucepan. Melt butter in same pan over medium heat and stir in flour. Gradually add turkey broth, beef broth and wine and stir until mixture bubbles and thickens. Simmer for 15 minutes. Stir in chopped giblets, livers and neck meat. Season gravy to taste with salt and pepper.

*For a large turkey, prepare recipe as above using giblets, liver and neck from one turkey.

Opposite: Roast Turkey, page 147

CHRISTMAS GOOSE, DICKENS STYLE

MAKES 10 TO 12 SERVINGS

INGREDIENTS

1 goose, 12 to 14 pounds,
  thawed if frozen
Salt and pepper
Grated rind of 2 oranges

CHESTNUT STUFFING

6 slices bacon, chopped
1 onion, chopped
2 cups sliced celery with leaves
½ cup chopped parsley
1 can (17 ounces) whole
  chestnuts, drained and
  coarsely broken
4 cups cooked wild rice
1 teaspoon crumbled
  dried sage
1 teaspoon crumbled
  dried thyme
1 teaspoon crumbled
  dried marjoram

LIVER TOASTS

½ cup chopped goose fat
1 goose liver
1 truffle, minced
Salt and pepper
10 to 12 Christmas tree shapes
  cut from thinly sliced,
  toasted white bread
Finely chopped
  Italian parsley sprigs

1 Remove giblets from goose. Remove loose fat and reserve for liver toasts. Sprinkle goose inside and out with salt and pepper. Rub with orange rind.

2 For chestnut stuffing, fry bacon in a skillet until crisp. Add onion, celery and parsley and sauté for 5 minutes. Stir in chestnuts, rice and herbs. Season to taste with salt.

3 Stuff goose with mixture. (Do not stuff goose until it is ready to be roasted.) Sew or skewer openings. Place goose breast side up on a rack in a shallow roasting pan. Roast in a preheated 350°F oven for 25 minutes per pound.

4 For liver toasts, fry goose fat in a skillet until pieces are crisp. Add liver and sauté for 5 minutes. Pour contents of skillet into a food processor and puree. Stir in truffle and salt and pepper to taste. Spread mixture thinly on slices of toast. Sprinkle parsley on edges of toast.

5 Place goose on serving platter. Garnish with pine sprigs and sliced blood oranges. Serve with toasts.

GLAZED GAME HENS WITH SPICED CRANBERRIES AND BRUSSELS SPROUTS

MAKES 6 SERVINGS

INGREDIENTS
6 game hens, thawed if frozen
   Salt and pepper
1 can (6 ounces) frozen
   orange juice concentrate,
   undiluted
½ cup cream sherry
1 teaspoon aromatic bitters
1 teaspoon dry mustard

SPICED CRANBERRIES
3 cups cranberries
1 lemon, thinly sliced
1 cup sugar
1 cup water
1 cinnamon stick
4 whole cloves
4 whole allspice
1 whole cardamom seed

BRUSSELS SPROUTS
2 pounds Brussels sprouts,
   cut in half
3 cups chicken broth

1 Remove giblets from hens. Sprinkle hens inside and out with salt and pepper.

2 In a bowl, mix juice concentrate, sherry, bitters and dry mustard. Brush some of mixture over hens. Roast in a preheated 350°F oven for 1 hour, brushing with remaining sherry mixture every 15 minutes.

3 For spiced cranberries, combine cranberries, lemon, sugar, water, cinnamon stick, cloves, allspice and cardamom in a 1½-quart nonaluminum saucepan. Bring to boil, lower heat and simmer for 10 minutes. Cool in syrup, then chill.

4 For Brussels sprouts, combine Brussels sprouts and broth in a 2-quart saucepan. Simmer uncovered, stirring occasionally, for 10 minutes or until sprouts are crisp-tender. (Because they are halved, the sprouts cook quickly with a resulting fresher flavor and firmer texture than if cooked whole.)

5 Place game hens on a large platter and garnish with chicory sprigs, Brussels sprouts and candied cranberries. Serve with Creamed Onions and Peas and Spinach Croustades (see Index for recipes).

Opposite: Glazed Game Hens, page 154

BRACE OF DUCKLINGS WITH RED CABBAGE AND STUFFED GREEN APPLES

1 Remove giblets and sprinkle ducklings inside and out with salt and pepper. Place an orange and a lemon into body cavity of each duckling. Rub outside of birds with sage and thyme. Place on a rack in a shallow roasting pan. Roast in a preheated 350°F oven for 2 hours or until legs move up and down easily.

2 For red cabbage, fry bacon in a 3-quart nonaluminum sauce-pan over medium heat until crisp. Add apples and sauté for 5 minutes. Add cabbage and sauté for 5 minutes. Add cider and vinegar, cover and simmer over low heat for 30 minutes. Season to taste with salt and pepper.

MAKES 6 TO 8 SERVINGS
INGREDIENTS
2 ducklings, thawed if frozen
  Salt and pepper
2 navel oranges,
  cut into wedges
2 lemons, cut into wedges
2 teaspoons crumbled
  dried sage
2 teaspoons crumbled
  dried thyme

RED CABBAGE
4 slices bacon
2 apples, peeled,
  cored and dried
1 head red cabbage,
  cored and shredded
2 cups apple cider
½ cup cider vinegar

STUFFED GREEN APPLES
6 to 8 green apples
1 unpeeled lemon,
  seeded and chopped
1 cup golden raisins
¼ cup chopped
  crystallized ginger
½ cup honey
½ cup chopped walnuts
  Chicory leaves

3 For stuffed apples, slice tops from apples and reserve. Scoop out inside of each apple, leaving a shell ½ inch thick. Discard cores and dice removed apple. In a bowl, mix diced apple with lemon, raisins, ginger, honey and walnuts. Spoon into apples and replace tops.

4 Place ducklings on serving platter and surround with red cabbage and stuffed apples. Garnish with chicory leaves.

Opposite: Brace of Ducklings, page 157

ROAST CHICKEN WITH DRIED FRUIT STUFFING AND HERBED ONION SAUCE

1 Remove giblets and sprinkle chicken inside and out with salt and pepper. In a bowl, mix dried fruit, lemon and cranberries. Stuff chicken with mixture. Sew or skewer opening. Place on a rack in a roasting pan. Roast in a preheated 350°F oven for 2 to 2½ hours or until legs move up and down easily.

2 For sauce, melt butter in a 1-quart saucepan over low heat and sauté onions for 20 minutes or until soft but not brown. Add chicken broth and fines herbes, cover and simmer for 20 minutes. Puree in blender and return to saucepan. Reheat, seasoning to taste with salt and pepper.

MAKES 6 TO 8 SERVINGS

INGREDIENTS
1 roasting chicken,
    7 to 8 pounds,
    thawed if frozen
Salt and pepper
1 pound mixed dried fruit,
    pitted as necessary
1 lemon, thinly sliced
    and seeded
2 cups cranberries

HERBED ONION SAUCE
¼ cup butter
4 large onions, chopped
2 cups chicken broth
1 teaspoon crumbled
    dried fines herbes
    or Herbes de Provence
Sugared red grapes *

3 Serve chicken on a platter surrounded with small clusters of sugared seedless red grapes. Serve sauce separately.

*To sugar grapes, cut grapes into small clusters, wash and pat dry. Brush with egg white beaten only until foamy. Roll in granulated sugar. Let dry at room temperature.

GINGERED CHICKEN BREASTS IN GREEN ONION PASTRY WITH WILD MUSHROOM SAUCE

1 Pound chicken breasts to ¼-inch thickness and sprinkle lightly with salt and pepper.

2 In a skillet, heat oil and sauté remaining filling ingredients for 5 minutes or until vegetables are tender. Cool and divide filling among chicken breasts. Roll up to enclose filling; tie with string. Bake in a preheated 350°F oven for 10 minutes. Cool.

3 In food processor, combine all pastry ingredients except egg and process just until dough forms a ball. Wrap in foil and chill 1 hour.

SERVES 6
INGREDIENTS
6 boned and skinned chicken breast halves
Salt and pepper
FILLING
1 tablespoon peanut oil
3 green onions, sliced
1 tablespoon grated fresh ginger
2 cups chopped raw broccoli
2 tablespoons soy sauce
1 tomato, peeled, seeded and chopped
PASTRY
2½ cups all-purpose flour
½ teaspoon salt
¾ cup cold unsalted butter, cut into ¼-inch-thick slices
¼ cup vegetable shortening
2 green onions, minced
6 to 8 tablespoons ice water
1 egg, well beaten
SAUCE
⅓ cup butter
½ pound fresh wild mushrooms, trimmed and sliced
¼ cup dry sherry
¼ cup all-purpose flour
¾ cup chicken broth
1 cup (½ pint) heavy cream
1 black truffle, shredded

4 Cut dough into 6 pieces. Roll out each piece large enough to enclose a chicken breast. Remove string from chicken and wrap in pastry. Arrange seam side down on greased baking sheet. Brush with egg. Bake in preheated 400°F oven for 15 to 20 minutes or until richly browned.

5 In a saucepan, melt butter and sauté mushrooms over medium heat for 2 to 3 minutes or until wilted. Add sherry and simmer 5 minutes. Sprinkle with flour. Add chicken broth and cream and stir over medium heat until sauce bubbles and thickens. Stir in truffle and season to taste with salt and pepper.

CHICKEN SUPREMES WITH LEMON AND MUSHROOM SAUCE

1 Sprinkle chicken with salt and pepper. Roll in flour, shaking off all excess.

2 In a skillet, melt butter and sauté breasts slowly until brown on all sides and cooked through, about 20 to 25 minutes. Remove chicken and keep warm.

3 Add mushrooms and lemon rind to skillet and sauté over medium heat for 5 minutes. Sprinkle with ⅓ cup flour. Gradually stir in chicken broth, Sauternes,

MAKES 6 SERVINGS

INGREDIENTS
6 large skinless and boneless
  chicken breast halves
Salt and pepper
All-purpose flour
¼ cup butter
1 pound wild or cultivated
  mushrooms, sliced
Slivered rind of 1 lemon
⅓ cup all-purpose flour
2 cups chicken broth
1 cup Sauternes
Pinch each of ground cor-
  iander and cardamom
Fluted mushroom caps
Thin slices of peeled lemon
Paprika

coriander and cardamom. Stir over medium heat until sauce bubbles and thickens, then simmer 10 minutes. Season to taste with salt and pepper.

4 Place chicken on serving plates and top with sauce. Garnish with fluted mushroom caps and thin lemon slices with edges rolled in paprika.

Opposite: Crown Roast of Pork, page 140

SALMON TROUT WITH SHRIMP AND SCALLOP MOUSSELINE

1 Open each salmon and place skin side down.

2 Combine shrimp, scallops, egg whites and cream in food processor and blend until smooth. Divide mixture among salmon, spreading it down the length of each fish. Fold over salmon to enclose filling.

3 Combine shrimp shells, chicken broth, lemon juice and dill in a 10- x 15- x 1-inch jelly roll pan. Place salmon side by side in pan. Cover with foil and bake in a preheated 350°F oven for 30 minutes or until firm to the touch. Carefully remove salmon and set aside. Strain broth.

4 In a 1½-quart saucepan, melt butter over medium heat and

MAKES 6 SERVINGS

INGREDIENTS

6 *salmon trout, bones and heads removed, in one piece with skin*
8 *ounces raw shrimp, shelled and deveined (reserve shells)*
8 *ounces raw scallops*
2 *egg whites*
1 *cup (½ pint) heavy cream*
3 *cups chicken broth Juice of 1 lemon*
¼ *cup chopped fresh dill*
2 *tablespoons butter*
1 *pound mushrooms, sliced*
¼ *cup all-purpose flour*
2 *egg yolks*
6 *cucumber cups Salmon caviar Watercress sprigs*

sauté mushrooms for 5 minutes. Sprinkle with flour. Gradually add strained broth and stir over medium heat until sauce bubbles and thickens.

5 Beat egg yolks in a bowl and beat in some of the hot sauce, then stir this mixture back into remaining sauce. Reheat but do not boil or egg will curdle.

6 Carefully remove skin from both sides of salmon. Return fish to pan, cover with foil and reheat in oven for 10 minutes. Place on serving plates. Top with sauce and garnish with additional cooked shelled and deveined shrimp and sprigs of fresh dill. Serve with cucumber cups filled with salmon caviar.

Opposite: Salmon Trout with Shrimp, page 162

STUFFED FLOUNDER FILLETS WITH SPINACH, PINE NUTS, RED PEPPER AND PEAS

1 Sprinkle flounder with salt and pepper. In a bowl, mix spinach, nuts, ¼ cup of the butter, garlic powder and salt and pepper to taste. Divide mixture among fillets and roll up, enclosing filling.

2 Place in a buttered 9- x 13- x 2-inch pan and brush with remaining butter. Bake in a preheated 350°F oven for 30 to 35 minutes or until flounder is white and opaque.

3 Broil peppers until black on all sides. Place in a plastic bag and cool. Strip off skin, remove seeds and briefly rinse peppers.

MAKES 6 SERVINGS

INGREDIENTS

6 *large flounder fillets*
Salt and pepper
1 *package (10 ounces) frozen chopped spinach, thawed and squeezed dry*
⅓ *cup pine nuts, toasted*
½ *cup melted butter*
½ *teaspoon garlic powder*
3 *red bell peppers*
¼ *cup olive oil*
1 *package (10 ounces) frozen peas*
1 *cup water*
¼ *cup chopped green onions*
6 *tablespoons grated Parmesan cheese*

4 Combine peppers and oil in food processor and puree. Season to taste with salt and pepper.

5 In a small saucepan, simmer peas in water for 5 minutes; drain. Combine in food processor with green onions and puree. Season to taste with salt and pepper.

6 Place flounder on serving plates and top each with some of the red pepper and green pea purees. Dust lightly with cheese.

GRILLED TROUT WITH HERBS AND CAPERS

1 Place 6 of the trout fillets side by side on a heavily oiled 10- x 15- x 1-inch jelly roll pan.

2 Beat remaining ingredients except paprika and spoon half of the mixture over fillets. Top with remaining fillets and remaining oil mixture. Sprinkle with paprika.

MAKES 6 SERVINGS

INGREDIENTS

12 *trout fillets*
1 *cup olive oil*
⅓ *cup fresh lemon juice*
¼ *cup minced parsley*
½ *clove garlic, mashed*
½ *teaspoon salt*
¼ *teaspoon white pepper*
¼ *teaspoon dill seed*
¼ *teaspoon celery seed*
⅓ *cup capers*
 Paprika
 Dill sprigs

3 Broil trout slowly 8 inches from the heat just until firm and opaque. Garnish with dill sprigs.

SCAMPI WITH RED AND GREEN PEPPERS

MAKES 6 SERVINGS

INGREDIENTS
3 pounds jumbo shrimp
½ cup olive oil
3 cloves garlic, minced
½ cup chopped Italian parsley
1 red and 1 green bell pepper,
* seeded and cut into 1-inch*
* squares*
1 teaspoon crumbled
* dried oregano*
Italian bread

1 Shell and devein shrimp; butterfly by cutting shrimp down the backs, not quite all the way through.

2 In a large skillet, heat oil over medium heat and sauté garlic, parsley and peppers for 5 minutes. Add shrimp and oregano and sauté for another 5 to 6 minutes or until shrimp become pink and opaque.

3 Serve with chunks of crusty Italian bread for mopping up the juices.

SALMON STEAKS WITH HERB BUTTER

MAKES 6 SERVINGS

INGREDIENTS
½ cup soft butter
* Grated rind of 1 lemon*
2 tablespoons
* fresh lemon juice*
2 tablespoons chopped parsley
2 tablespoons chopped
* fresh dill*
2 tablespoons
* minced green onions*
1 teaspoon crumbled dried
* summer savory*
6 salmon steaks, 1 inch thick

1 In a bowl, beat butter until fluffy. Stir in lemon rind and juice, parsley, dill, onions and summer savory. With wet hands, shape mixture into a roll 1½ inches in diameter. Wrap in foil and chill.

2 Broil salmon steaks for 10 minutes on each side or until firm and opaque. Place on serving plates.

3 Unwrap butter and cut into 6 rounds. Place 1 round on each salmon steak. Serve garnished with lime slices and sprigs of parsley. Serve with Sweet-Sour Green Beans and Cauliflower with Crumbs and Chartreuse of Vegetables (see Index for recipes). Add a salad of radiccio leaves, endive leaves, and alfalfa sprouts, with a lemon vinaigrette.

Opposite: Scampi with Red and Green Peppers, page 167

BAKED RED SNAPPER WITH CRABMEAT

1 Have snapper boned and head removed; reserve bones and head.

2 In a bowl, mix crabmeat, crumbs, parsley, dill, celery leaves, vegetable juice and salt and pepper to taste. Stuff snapper with mixture and fold over snapper to enclose stuffing. Place in a heavily oiled 9- x 13- x 2-inch pan. Bake in a preheated 350°F oven for 40 to 45 minutes or until snapper is white and opaque.

3 In a 1½-quart saucepan, combine fish bones and head with water, bay leaf and peppercorns. Simmer uncovered for 30 minutes.

MAKES 6 SERVINGS

INGREDIENTS

1 red snapper,
  scaled and cleaned
2 cups flaked crabmeat
2 cups soft breadcrumbs
¼ cup chopped parsley
¼ cup chopped fresh dill
¼ cup chopped celery leaves
1 cup tomato-vegetable juice
  Salt and pepper
3 cups water
1 bay leaf
6 peppercorns
¼ cup soft butter mixed with
  ¼ cup all-purpose flour
½ cup mayonnaise
2 tablespoons tomato paste
  Lime slices
  Watercress sprigs

4 Strain broth and return to saucepan. Add butter-flour mixture and stir over medium heat until sauce bubbles and thickens. Stir in mayonnaise and tomato paste and simmer for 5 minutes.

5 Place snapper on serving platter and surround with lime slices and watercress. Serve sauce separately.

Opposite: Baked Red Snapper with Crabmeat, page 168
Page following: Seafood Buffet

GRILLED LOBSTER WITH MUSSELS

1 Place lobster in cold water to cover in a large kettle or lobster pot. Add salt, cover and bring to boil. Boil for 5 minutes, then drain. Cool.

2 Place mussels in a large kettle and add 1 cup water. Cover tightly and steam until shells open, about 4 to 5 minutes. Discard top shells and leave mussels in bottom shells.

3 In a bowl, mix butter, lemon juice, cheese, crumbs, parsley and dill.

MAKES 6 SERVINGS

INGREDIENTS
6 *lobsters, 1½ pounds each*
2 *tablespoons salt*
4 *dozen mussels, scrubbed, beards removed*
½ *cup melted butter Juice of 2 lemons*
½ *cup grated Parmesan cheese*
3 *cups dry breadcrumbs*
2 *tablespoons minced parsley*
2 *tablespoons minced fresh dill*

4 Turn lobsters on their backs, split lengthwise with a sharp knife and open out. Place lobsters and mussels on baking sheets. Sprinkle cut surfaces of lobsters and top of mussels with crumb mixture. Place under broiler for 8 to 10 minutes or until golden brown, watching carefully to prevent burning. Place each lobster on serving plate and top with a row of mussels. Garnish with lemon slices. Add broccoli, cauliflower and carrots steamed and tossed with herb butter; also a salad of romaine, slivered red, green and yellow peppers and black olives tossed with a mustard salad dressing.

OYSTERS WITH SPINACH, LEEKS AND CHAMPAGNE

1 Scrub and shuck oysters; reserve 24 of the larger shells. Reserve oyster liquor. Set oysters aside.

2 In a large skillet, heat butter and sauté leeks for 5 minutes or until pale golden. Add reserved oyster liquor and champagne and boil for 5 minutes. Stir in cream and simmer, stirring occasionally, until sauce is thickened, about 10 to 15 minutes. Stir in spinach. Season with salt and pepper.

SERVES 6

INGREDIENTS

24 oysters
2 tablespoons butter
1 leek, trimmed, washed and chopped
½ cup champagne
1 cup (½ pint) heavy cream
2 packages (10 ounces each) frozen chopped spinach, cooked and squeezed dry
Salt and pepper
1 cup dry breadcrumbs
3 tablespoons melted butter

3 Spoon spinach mixture into reserved oyster shells and top with oysters. In a bowl, mix crumbs and butter. Sprinkle crumbs over oysters. Bake in a preheated 350°F oven for 15 minutes or until golden brown.

HERB-BAKED CLAMS

SERVES 6

INGREDIENTS
24 cherrystone clams
¼ cup butter
¼ cup minced celery leaves
2 tablespoons minced fresh dill
1 tablespoon chopped fresh
  oregano or 1 teaspoon
  dried
½ pound mushrooms, chopped
1 cup dry breadcrumbs
Salt
½ cup grated Parmesan cheese

1 Scrub clams and open. Reserve 24 of the shells. Drain clams, reserving liquor; chop.

2 In a large skillet, heat butter and sauté celery leaves, dill, oregano and mushrooms over low heat for 10 minutes or until lightly browned. Remove from heat and stir in chopped clams, clam liquor and crumbs. Season to taste with salt. Spoon mixture into reserved shells. Sprinkle top with cheese. Bake in a preheated 350°F oven for 15 minutes or until golden brown.

CRAB-STUFFED JUMBO SHRIMP

SERVES 6

INGREDIENTS
24 jumbo shrimp
1 pound crabmeat
2 green onions, trimmed and
  sliced
⅓ cup chopped celery leaves
Juice of ½ lemon
4 ounces sharp cheddar cheese,
  cut into ½-inch cubes
1 egg

1 Shell shrimp, leaving tail shell attached. Slash shrimp lengthwise along the top, cutting not quite all the way through. Open out shrimp, flatten and arrange cut side up on greased baking sheet.

2 Combine remaining ingredients in food processor and chop finely. Spoon mixture in mounds on top of shrimp. Bake in a preheated 350°F oven for 15 minutes or until shrimp are opaque.

3 Serve Seafood Buffet with champagne, Salmon Mousse, Molded Lime Salad, Wild Rice in Mushroom Caps, Greek Bread and Vienna Egg Bread slices. Desserts should include Austrian Linzer Torte, Italian Cheesecake, Greek Honey Cake and Open-Face Pear Pie, with Viennese Spiced Coffee and Mexican Coffee as beverages (see Index for recipes).

Vegetable Dishes
for Every Palate

*V*egetables once were those green things your
mother made you eat because they were healthy.
Now vegetable sales are soaring since proper cooking and
seasoning has made them look and taste great.

The vegetables in this chapter will please every palate. There are wintry dishes
like potatoes, yams and cabbage, which we have come to associate with traditional
suppers, as well as many lighter dishes and recipes reflecting ethnic influences,
incorporating such flavors as pine nuts and caraway seeds.

It's a nice idea, by the way, to serve an abundance of vegetables at any meal
nowadays; many people no longer eat meat, or eat it sparingly. And if the market
happens to be overflowing with particularly delectable produce on any given day,
why not plan a whole meal around it? This is a delicious way to keep the calorie
count down during the most diet-taxing days of the year.

TWICE-BAKED IDAHO POTATOES

1 Scrub potatoes and bake in a preheated 350°F oven for 1 to 1½ hours or until easily pierced. Cut a thin slice off tops of potatoes. Scoop out interior with a spoon, leaving a shell ½ inch thick.

2 Press potato flesh through a ricer into a bowl. Beat in cream

MAKES 8 SERVINGS

INGREDIENTS
8 large Idaho potatoes
1 package (3 ounces)
   cream cheese
½ cup milk
1 package (10 ounces) frozen
   chopped spinach, thawed
   and squeezed dry
2 tablespoons minced onion
   Salt and pepper
2 cups (8 ounces) grated
   sharp cheddar cheese

cheese and milk. Stir in spinach, onion and salt and pepper to taste.

3 Spoon mixture into potato skins and set on a baking sheet. Sprinkle with cheddar cheese. Bake in a preheated 350°F oven for 15 to 20 minutes or until cheese is melted and lightly browned.

CREAMY WHIPPED SWEET POTATOES OR YAMS

1 Cook potatoes in boiling salted water to cover for 25 to 30 minutes or until easily pierced. Drain and cool slightly. Peel, discarding the dark outer layer of potato.

SERVES 6

INGREDIENTS
6 large sweet potatoes or
   medium yams
¼ cup butter
½ teaspoon ground nutmeg
1 cup (½ pint) sour cream
   Salt

2 Place potatoes in a food processor with remaining ingredients and blend until smooth. Season to taste with salt. Reheat in saucepan until hot.

SWEET POTATOES IN ORANGE SHELLS

1 Scoop out orange halves and reserve shells. Remove membranes from oranges and reserve pulp.

2 In a large saucepan, cook sweet potatoes in boiling salted water to cover for 40 to 45 minutes, or until tender. Drain and peel potatoes; transfer to food pro-

MAKES 8 SERVINGS

INGREDIENTS
4 large navel oranges, halved
2 pounds sweet potatoes
¼ cup butter
¼ cup apricot preserves
Salt

cessor. Add butter and preserves and puree. Fold in orange pulp. Season to taste with salt.

3 Pile potato mixture into reserved orange shells. Bake in a preheated 350°F oven for 15 minutes or until heated through.

YAMS AND APPLES

1 Mix yams and apples. In a large skillet or Dutch oven, melt butter over medium heat. Stir in sugar, cider and spices and simmer for 5 minutes.

MAKES 6 SERVINGS

INGREDIENTS
6 medium yams, cooked, peeled and quartered
3 Granny Smith apples, peeled, cored and quartered
⅓ cup butter
½ cup sugar
1 cup apple cider
½ teaspoon each ground cinnamon, nutmeg and cloves

2 Add yam-apple mixture, cover and simmer, stirring occasionally, until apples are tender but still firm.

SCALLOPED WHITE AND SWEET POTATOES

MAKES 6 SERVINGS

INGREDIENTS
3 Idaho potatoes
3 large sweet potatoes
All-purpose flour
Salt and pepper
About 3 cups milk
½ cup crushed sesame seed
    crackers

1 Peel both kinds of potatoes and cut into paper-thin slices.

2 Layer white and sweet potatoes in a greased 2-quart casserole, sprinkling each layer with a tablespoon of flour and a little salt and pepper. Add enough milk to the casserole to just cover potatoes. Sprinkle top with crumbs. Bake in a preheated 350°F oven for 1½ hours or until potatoes are easily pierced.

TOP-OF-THE-RANGE "BAKED" BEANS

MAKES 6 SERVINGS

INGREDIENTS
2 cups (1 pound) dried navy
    beans
4 ounces salt pork, in one
    piece
24 small white onions, peeled
½ cup maple syrup or molasses
1 teaspoon dry mustard
    Salt and pepper
1 cup chili sauce (optional)

1 In a 3-quart saucepan, combine beans with enough water to cover by 2 inches. Add salt pork and simmer, covered, for 2 hours or until beans are tender, adding more water from time to time to maintain the level of the liquid.

2 When beans are cooked, drain off liquid so beans are just covered. Stir in onions, syrup and mustard. Cover and simmer, stirring occasionally, until liquid is absorbed, about 2 hours. Season to taste with salt and pepper.

For a spicier version, stir 1 cup chili sauce into cooked beans.

STUFFED BABY ARTICHOKES

1 Trim stems and tips of leaves from artichokes. Cook artichokes in boiling salted water with lemon juice for 15 to 20 minutes or until easily pierced. Drain and cool.

2 In a medium bowl, mix crumbs, ham, oregano, garlic, chicken broth and chopped hard-cooked egg whites. Open out

SERVES 6

INGREDIENTS
12 baby artichokes
Juice of 1 lemon
2 cups fine soft breadcrumbs
1 cup ground smoked ham
1½ teaspoons chopped fresh oregano or ½ teaspoon dried
1 teaspoon minced garlic
⅓ cup chicken broth
3 hard-cooked eggs, yolks and whites separated

leaves of artichokes and fill with ham mixture.

3 Place artichokes side by side in a greased 9- x 13-inch baking pan. Bake in a preheated 400°F oven for 15 minutes or until lightly browned. Sieve egg yolks. Arrange artichokes on serving platter and sprinkle with yolks.

ASPARAGUS WITH MINT AND SNOW PEAS

S team asparagus and snow peas for 5 minutes or until tender but still crisp. In a small saucepan, combine remaining ingredients and heat until bubbly. Place vege-

SERVES 6
So expensive but such a treat at Christmas time.

INGREDIENTS
3 pounds fresh asparagus or 3 packages (10 ounces each) frozen asparagus
1 pound snow peas, trimmed
⅓ cup melted butter
2 tablespoons chopped fresh mint
Juice of ½ a lemon

tables on serving platter and spoon butter mixture evenly over top. If desired, garnish with fresh mint sprigs.

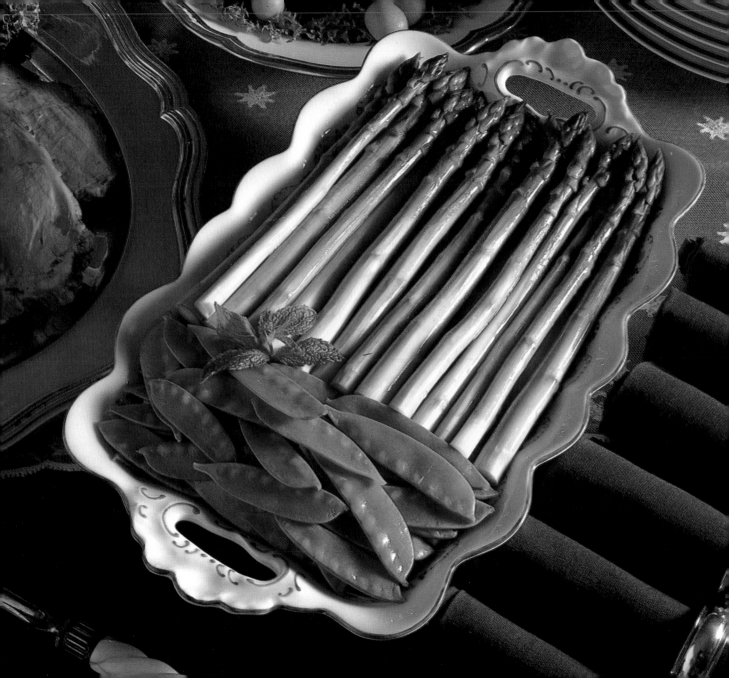

WILD RICE PILAF IN MUSHROOM CAPS

MAKES 6 SERVINGS

INGREDIENTS

¼ cup butter
½ cup chopped onion
½ cup chopped celery
½ cup chopped carrot
12 very large mushrooms
1 cup uncooked wild rice
3 cups chicken broth
2 tomatoes, cored and diced
1 teaspoon crumbled dried
   fines herbes
Salt and pepper
Chopped parsley

1 In a 2-quart saucepan, melt butter over medium heat and sauté onion, celery and carrot for 5 minutes.

2 Remove stems from mushrooms and chop; reserve caps. Add stems to skillet with rice and sauté over low heat for 5 minutes. Add chicken broth, tomatoes and fines herbes. Cover and simmer for 40 to 45 minutes or until rice is tender and liquid is absorbed. Season to taste with salt and pepper.

3 Spoon hot rice mixture into raw mushroom caps. Sprinkle with chopped parsley.

Opposite: Asparagus with Mint and Snow Peas, page 179

CORN CUSTARD WITH SCALLOPED TOMATOES

MAKES 8 SERVINGS

INGREDIENTS

CORN CUSTARD
1 cup cream-style corn
1 cup well-drained kernel corn
2 green onions, sliced
1 green bell pepper, seeded and chopped
4 eggs
1½ cups milk
1 teaspoon salt

SCALLOPED TOMATOES
1 can (1 pound, 3 ounces) tomatoes
1 teaspoon sugar
½ teaspoon crumbled dried basil
¼ cup butter
1 cup soft breadcrumbs

1 For custard, mix cream-style corn, kernel corn, onions and green pepper in a bowl. Beat eggs until foamy. Gradually beat in milk and salt. Pour mixture into a buttered 9-inch square pan. Bake in a preheated 325°F oven for 40 to 45 minutes or until firm to the touch.

2 For scalloped tomatoes, heat tomatoes with sugar and basil in a saucepan.

3 In a small skillet, heat butter with crumbs until crumbs are golden brown and crisp. Cut corn custard into 8 pieces and place on serving plates. Top with hot tomatoes and sprinkle with crisp crumbs.

Opposite: Rum-Glazed Acorn Squash, page 184

RUM-GLAZED ACORN SQUASH

MAKES 6 SERVINGS

INGREDIENTS

3 acorn squash, cut in half
½ cup firmly packed dark brown sugar
½ cup dark rum
6 tablespoons butter

1 Scoop seeds from squash. Place squash cut side down on a greased shallow baking pan. Bake in a preheated 350°F oven for 45 minutes.

2 Remove squash from oven and turn cut side up. Mix brown sugar and rum. Spoon mixture into cavities in squash, adding 1 tablespoon butter to each. Return to oven and bake another 15 minutes or until squash is easily pierced. If desired, serve garnished with Pineapple Carrot Preserves (see Index for recipe).

PINEAPPLE BUTTERNUT SQUASH

MAKES 6 SERVINGS

INGREDIENTS

1 large butternut squash, about 3 pounds
⅓ cup firmly packed light brown sugar
¼ cup butter
1 cup crushed pineapple
Salt

1 Peel squash and cut in half. Remove seeds and cut squash into 1-inch cubes. Place in a 3-quart saucepan and cover with water. Bring to boil, cover and lower heat. Simmer for 40 to 45 minutes or until squash is very tender.

2 Drain squash well. Transfer to food processor and puree. Return squash to saucepan and stir in remaining ingredients, adding salt to taste. Stir over low heat until piping hot.

A CHRISTMAS CORNUCOPIA

BAKED SUCCOTASH

SERVES 6

INGREDIENTS

2 tablespoons butter
6 shallots, chopped
3 green onions, chopped
3 cups well-drained canned
  kernel corn
3 cups well-drained cooked
  baby lima beans
1 cup chicken broth
¼ cup each chopped parsley
  and celery leaves

1 In a large skillet, heat butter and sauté shallots and green onions for 5 minutes or until golden brown. Stir in remaining ingredients.

2 Pour mixture into a 1½-quart casserole. Bake in a preheated 350°F oven for 20 to 25 minutes.

ORANGED CARROTS

MAKES 6 SERVINGS

INGREDIENTS

6 large carrots, scraped and
  cut into ⅓-inch-thick
  rounds
¼ cup butter
¼ cup sugar
3 navel oranges, sectioned
2 tablespoons slivered orange
  rind

1 In a 2-quart saucepan, cover carrots with water and cook for 20 to 25 minutes or until tender; drain.

2 Add butter and sugar and stir over medium heat until carrots are lightly glazed. Just before serving, stir in orange sections and rind.

A CHRISTMAS CORNUCOPIA

SWEET-SOUR GREEN BEANS

MAKES 6 SERVINGS

INGREDIENTS

1½ pounds whole green beans, trimmed
2 onions, cut into rings
6 tablespoons butter
6 tablespoons all-purpose flour
⅓ cup cider vinegar
¼ cup sugar
Salt

1 In a 2-quart saucepan, combine green beans and onions and cover with water. Cover and simmer for 15 to 20 minutes or until beans are just tender. Drain beans and measure cooking liquid, reserving 2½ cups for the sauce.

2 In a 1½-quart nonaluminum saucepan, melt butter over low heat and sauté flour until golden brown, about 15 minutes. Gradually add reserved cooking liquid, vinegar and sugar and stir over medium heat until sauce bubbles and thickens. Season to taste with salt. Add beans to sauce and simmer gently for 10 minutes.

CREAMED ONIONS AND PEAS WITH PEANUTS

MAKES 6 SERVINGS

INGREDIENTS

24 small white onions, peeled
2½ cups chicken broth
¼ cup soft butter mixed with 6 tablespoons all-purpose flour
1 cup (½ pint) sour cream
1 package (10 ounces) frozen peas
Salt and pepper
⅓ cup finely chopped salted peanuts

1 In a 1½-quart saucepan, combine onions and broth. Cover and simmer for 15 minutes or until onions are tender but still firm.

2 Add butter-flour mixture and stir over medium heat until sauce bubbles and thickens. Stir in sour cream, peas and salt and pepper to taste; simmer 5 minutes. Pour into serving bowl and sprinkle with peanuts.

BRAISED LEEKS AND MUSHROOMS

MAKES 6 SERVINGS

INGREDIENTS
6 *large leeks*
1 *pound small button*
mushrooms
2 *cups chicken broth*
2 *tablespoons tomato paste*
2 *tablespoons dry sherry*
3 *tablespoons soft butter*
mixed with 3 tablespoons
all-purpose flour
Salt and pepper
Finely chopped oil-cured
black olives (optional)

1 Trim roots and green leaves from leeks; use the white part only. Cut into 1-inch pieces and wash well to remove sand.

2 In a 2-quart saucepan, combine leeks, mushrooms, broth, tomato paste and sherry. Cover and simmer for 15 minutes or until leeks are tender but still firm.

3 Add butter-flour mixture and stir until sauce bubbles and thickens. Season to taste with salt and pepper. If desired, top with finely chopped olives.

FRESH SPINACH CROUSTADE

MAKES 6 SERVINGS

INGREDIENTS
1 package (17¼ ounces)
   frozen patty shells
1½ *pounds fresh spinach*
2 *tablespoons butter*
2 *green onions, sliced*
¼ *teaspoon crumbled dried*
   rosemary
2 *tablespoons all-purpose flour*
1 *cup milk*
   Salt and pepper
6 *well-drained artichoke*
   bottoms (optional)
2 *tablespoons butter*
   (optional)
6 *red radishes, shredded*
   (optional)

1 Prepare patty shells according to package directions; set aside.

2 Trim stems from spinach and wash leaves well. Melt 2 tablespoons butter in a large saucepan and sauté spinach with onions and rosemary until wilted. Sprinkle with flour. Transfer to food processor and puree. Return to saucepan, add milk and stir over medium heat until mixture thickens. Season to taste with salt and pepper.

3 To serve, place patty shells on serving plates. Spoon spinach over shells.

4 If desired, sauté artichoke bottoms in 2 tablespoons butter over medium heat 5 minutes. Top shell with an artichoke bottom. Fill artichoke bottoms with shredded radishes.

BRAISED CELERY AND TOMATOES WITH ALMONDS

MAKES 6 SERVINGS

INGREDIENTS
1 bunch celery, heart removed and reserved
3 tomatoes, cored and diced
3 tablespoons butter
½ cup dry white wine
¼ teaspoon fennel seeds
¼ teaspoon anise seeds
Salt
½ cup slivered almonds, toasted

1 Cut celery into 1-inch pieces. Chop celery heart and set aside. Mix celery and tomatoes.

2 In a skillet or Dutch oven, melt butter, add celery and tomatoes and sauté over medium heat for 5 minutes. Add wine and seeds, cover tightly and simmer for 20 to 25 minutes or until celery is tender. Season to taste with salt. Serve topped with chopped raw celery heart and slivered almonds.

CHARTREUSE OF VEGETABLES

MAKES 6 SERVINGS

INGREDIENTS
3 carrots, scraped
3 white turnips, peeled
3 stalks celery, cut into 2-inch pieces
3 zucchini, trimmed
2 red bell peppers, seeded
2 leeks, white part only
⅓ cup butter
¼ cup sesame seeds
Salt and pepper

1 Cut all the vegetables into julienne strips; wash leek well to remove sand. Steam separately until crisp-tender; keep warm.

2 In a small skillet, melt butter and sauté seeds until golden.

3 Mound vegetables on serving platter and sprinkle lightly with salt and pepper. Spoon butter and seeds over vegetables.

4 Can also be arranged in groups around Cauliflower with Crumbs.

BROCCOLI WITH GARLIC, PINE NUTS AND MUSHROOMS

1 In a large skillet, heat olive oil and sauté garlic and pine nuts until golden.

MAKES 6 SERVINGS

INGREDIENTS
⅓ cup olive oil
1 clove garlic, minced
½ cup pine nuts
1 bunch broccoli, cut into florets
8 ounces mushrooms, sliced
Juice of 1 lemon
1 cup tomato juice

2 Add remaining ingredients; cover and simmer gently for 10 to 12 minutes or until broccoli is crisp-tender.

BRUSSELS SPROUTS WITH CHEESE CRUMBS

1 In a 2-quart saucepan, cover sprouts with water. Cover and simmer for 15 minutes or until crisp-tender; drain and keep warm.

2 In a skillet, melt butter over low heat. Add crushed crackers and stir until golden brown. Remove from heat and stir in cheese.

MAKES 6 SERVINGS

INGREDIENTS
1½ pounds Brussels sprouts, trimmed and halved
⅓ cup butter
1 cup crushed cheddar cheese crackers
¼ cup grated Parmesan cheese

3 Place sprouts in a serving dish and top with crumbs.

Opposite: Brussels Sprouts with Cheese Crumbs, page 190

GLAZED PARSNIPS

MAKES 6 SERVINGS

INGREDIENTS
6 *medium parsnips, scraped*
3 *tablespoons butter*
2 *Granny Smith apples, peeled,*
   cored and diced
2 *tablespoons honey*
1 *cup apple juice*

1 Cut parsnips into ½-inch-thick slices. In a large skillet, melt butter over medium heat and sauté parsnips and apples for 5 minutes.

2 Add honey and apple juice, cover and simmer for 15 minutes or until parsnips are tender.

STIR-FRIED ZUCCHINI

MAKES 6 SERVINGS

INGREDIENTS
6 *small zucchini, cut into*
   1-inch-thick rounds
3 *tablespoons sesame oil*
6 *green onions, sliced*
   diagonally
2 *tablespoons soy sauce*
½ *cup chicken broth*
½ *cup sliced almonds, toasted*

1 In a skillet, sauté zucchini in oil for 5 minutes.

2 Add onions, soy sauce and chicken broth and stir over medium heat until zucchini is crisp-tender. Serve topped with almonds.

EGGPLANT STEW

MAKES 8 SERVINGS

INGREDIENTS
1 large eggplant
1/3 cup olive oil
2 large onions, sliced
2 cloves garlic, chopped
2 green bell peppers, seeded
    and diced
3 zucchini, diced
3 tomatoes, cored and diced
1/4 cup crumbled dried
    porcini mushrooms
1 cup water
1 teaspoon salt
1 teaspoon crumbled Herbes
    de Provence

1 Cut eggplant in half lengthwise. Scoop out pulp, leaving shells ½ inch thick. Reserve shells to use as serving bowls; chop pulp.

2 In a Dutch oven, heat oil and sauté onions, garlic and peppers over medium heat for 5 minutes. Add remaining ingredients, cover and simmer for 20 to 25 minutes or until thick and stewlike.

3 Spoon eggplant stew into reserved shells and place on serving platter.

CARAWAY CABBAGE

MAKES 6 SERVINGS

INGREDIENTS
1 medium-size green or red
  cabbage, halved
6 strips bacon, chopped
2 onions, chopped
2 green apples, peeled, cored
  and diced
1 teaspoon caraway seeds
1 teaspoon salt
1 teaspoon sugar
3 cups white wine (for green
  cabbage) or red wine (for
  red cabbage)

1 Core and shred cabbage finely. In a Dutch oven, fry bacon until crisp. Remove bacon and reserve.

2 Sauté onions, apples and cabbage in bacon drippings over medium heat for 10 minutes. Add remaining ingredients, cover and simmer for 30 to 35 minutes or until cabbage is tender. Serve sprinkled with reserved crisp bacon pieces.

CAULIFLOWER WITH CRUMBS

MAKES 6 SERVINGS

INGREDIENTS
1 large head cauliflower
½ cup butter
2 cups fine soft breadcrumbs
2 hard-cooked eggs, sieved
¼ cup minced parsley
Juice of 1 lemon
Salt

1 Trim cauliflower and leave whole. Place cauliflower stalk side down in a 3-quart saucepan. Fill pan halfway with water. Cover and simmer for 25 to 30 minutes or until cauliflower is easily pierced but still holds its shape.

2 In a skillet, melt butter over medium heat, add crumbs and stir until crumbs are golden brown. Stir in eggs, parsley, lemon juice and salt to taste.

3 Drain cauliflower and place whole head on serving platter. Cover top with crumb mixture. Cut into wedges to serve.

BEETS IN SOUR CREAM

MAKES 6 SERVINGS

INGREDIENTS
6 large beets
2 tablespoons butter
1 small onion, minced
3 tablespoons all-purpose flour
1½ cups chicken broth
½ cup sour cream
2 tablespoons prepared red horseradish
Salt and pepper
Chopped parsley or tiny beet leaves

1 In a large saucepan, cook beets in boiling salted water, covered, for 40 to 45 minutes or until tender. Drain, peel and cut into julienne strips.

2 In a 1½-quart saucepan, melt butter over medium heat and sauté onions for 5 minutes. Stir in flour. Gradually add chicken broth and stir over medium heat until sauce bubbles and thickens.

3 Stir in sour cream and horseradish. Add beets and season to taste with salt and pepper. Reheat and serve sprinkled with chopped parsley or chopped tiny beet leaves, if available.

SALADS FOR THE SEASON

A great holiday meal, like any great meal, should be orchestrated to please every sense. Salads add crisp texture and piquant flavor. They provide refreshing taste and color. And they are superior sources of vitamins and minerals, since they involve minimal cooking.

Salads can be served as an appetizer, an accompaniment to a festive dinner, to refresh the palate before dessert, or as a light luncheon or snack. There are any number of ways to combine flavors, textures and ingredients—with vegetables, fruit, seafood, meat, poultry—just use your imagination! The possibilities are endless. The recipes included in this section offer many new twists on old favorites—the holidays are one time when you absolutely cannot dispense with old favorites! There are also some ideas for new and different salads to surprise and delight your guests and family—perhaps some combinations that you have not considered before but which will complement your Yuletide menu. All the salads offer plenty of opportunities to add freshness, color, and imagination to your traditional meal.

HOLIDAY MOLDED POTATO SALAD

MAKES 6 TO 8 SERVINGS

INGREDIENTS

6 cups diced cooked potatoes
2 cups thinly sliced celery and
  leaves
½ cup pickle relish
1 red onion, minced
2 tablespoons prepared
  mustard
1 cup mayonnaise
  Salt and pepper
  Chopped parsley
  Tomato wedges, or red
  radish slices and red
  onion rings
  Pickled Beets (see next
  recipe)

1 In a bowl, mix potatoes, celery, relish, onion, mustard and mayonnaise, adding salt and pepper to taste. Line a 1½-quart ring mold with plastic wrap. Press potato salad firmly into mold. Chill several hours. Unmold on serving platter. Garnish top with chopped parsley and fill center with lightly salted tomato wedges.

2 For a Christmas version, line a 2-quart cone-shaped mold with plastic wrap. Fill with salad and press firmly to pack. Chill several hours.

3 Unmold on serving platter and remove plastic wrap. Garnish with radish slices and onion rings. Surround potato salad with Pickled Beets.

SAFFRON RICE SALAD WITH HAM AND TOMATOES

1 In a 2-quart saucepan, melt butter over low heat and sauté saffron for 2 minutes. Add broth and bring to boil. Add rice and salt and simmer, uncovered, for 20 to 25 minutes or until rice is tender and liquid is absorbed.

2 Transfer rice to a bowl and fluff with a fork until cool. Stir in ham, parsley, tomatoes and peas.

MAKES 6 SERVINGS

INGREDIENTS
¼ cup butter
½ teaspoon crumbled saffron
    threads
3 cups chicken broth
1½ cups long-grain rice
½ teaspoon salt
1 cup minced smoked ham
¼ cup chopped parsley
3 tomatoes, cored and diced
1 cup cooked peas

TARRAGON DRESSING
¾ cup olive oil
¼ cup tarragon vinegar
⅓ cup grated Parmesan cheese
    Watercress sprigs

3 For dressing, beat oil, vinegar and cheese in a small bowl until thick. Pour dressing over salad and toss to coat well. Chill. Serve on a bed of watercress. Garnish each serving with a candy cane cut from cucumber skin.

Opposite: Seafood Appetizer Salad in Avocado Halves, page 200;
Pear Appetizer Salad, page 209

SEAFOOD APPETIZER SALAD IN AVOCADO HALVES

1 Brush cut surfaces of avocados with lemon juice to prevent darkening.

2 In a bowl, mix crabmeat and celery. Stir in mayonnaise, chili sauce, vinegar, onion and Worcestershire sauce. Spoon mixture into avocado halves. Chill.

MAKES 6 SERVINGS

INGREDIENTS

3 avocados, halved and seeded
  Lemon juice
2 cups flaked crabmeat
1 cup minced celery
¼ cup mayonnaise
¼ cup chili sauce
1 tablespoon red wine vinegar
1 green onion, minced
½ teaspoon Worcestershire
  sauce
  Chopped cashews
  Leaf lettuce leaves

3 When ready to serve, sprinkle with chopped cashews and place on lettuce leaves on serving plates.

TOMATOES STUFFED WITH ARTICHOKE HEARTS

MAKES 6 SERVINGS

INGREDIENTS
6 *large tomatoes*
6 *pitted black olives, sliced*
6 *ounces feta cheese, crumbled*
1 *package (9 ounces) frozen*
  artichoke hearts, cooked
  and quartered

LEMON HERB DRESSING
½ *cup olive oil*
  Juice of 1 lemon
1 *teaspoon salt*
1 *teaspoon sugar*
1 *teaspoon dry mustard*
1 *teaspoon crumbled*
  dried oregano
1 *teaspoon crumbled*
  dried basil
¼ *cup minced parsley*
  Bibb lettuces, halved

1 Slice tops from tomatoes. Hollow out tomatoes. Drain scooped-out pulp; remove seeds and dice pulp.

2 In a bowl, mix diced tomatoes with olives, cheese and artichoke hearts. Chill.

3 For dressing, beat dressing ingredients in a small bowl until thick. Let stand at room temperature for 1 hour, then beat again.

4 Place tomatoes on serving plates and add Bibb lettuce. Spoon dressing over tomatoes.

MARINATED MIXED BEAN SALAD

MAKES 6 TO 8 SERVINGS

INGREDIENTS
2 cups cooked cut green beans
1 cup each fresh or frozen
   cooked or canned
   chickpeas, kidney beans
   and lima beans
1 red onion, sliced
1 carrot, shredded

ITALIAN DRESSING
1 egg
½ cup chopped parsley
2 tablespoons capers
2 cloves garlic
2 teaspoons anchovy paste
1 cup green olive oil
⅓ cup balsamic vinegar
   Salt
   Shredded escarole leaves

1 In a bowl, combine green beans, chickpeas and beans, onion and carrot.

2 For dressing, combine egg, parsley, capers, garlic, anchovy paste, oil and vinegar in a blender and puree.

3 Pour dressing over salad and season to taste with salt. Chill. Serve on a bed of escarole leaves.

Opposite: Marinated Mixed Bean Salad, page 203

ASSORTED VEGETABLE SALAD

1 Arrange lettuce leaves on a large platter. Place one vegetable on each lettuce leaf. Cover and chill.

2 For dressing, combine dressing ingredients in a small bowl and beat until thick. Let stand at room temperature for 1 hour, then beat again.

MAKES 6 TO 8 SERVINGS

INGREDIENTS
10 Boston lettuce leaves
2 carrots, shredded
2 cooked beets, shredded
4 ounces green beans,
    julienned and cooked
1 red onion, sliced
1 cup cooked peas
2 tomatoes, cored, peeled
    and diced
4 green onions, sliced
2 stalks celery, cut into paper-
    thin diagonal slices
2 zucchini, shredded
1 small celeriac (celery root),
    peeled and shredded

PEPPERCORN DRESSING
1 cup olive or walnut oil
½ cup white wine vinegar
2 teaspoons salt
2 teaspoons sugar
½ teaspoon crumbled
    dried marjoram
½ teaspoon crumbled
    dried chervil
3 tablespoons green
    peppercorns

3 Spoon dressing over vegetables and chill until ready to serve.

MUSHROOM, ARTICHOKE HEART AND SPINACH SALAD

1 In a bowl, mix bacon, eggs, artichoke hearts, mushrooms and spinach. Chill.

2 For dressing, mix dressing ingredients in a small bowl until well blended, adding salt to taste. Chill.

MAKES 6 SERVINGS

INGREDIENTS
8 ounces bacon, cooked
    until crisp
3 hard-cooked eggs, sliced
1 package (9 ounces)
    artichoke hearts,
    cooked and halved
8 ounces mushrooms, sliced
1 pound young spinach,
    stemmed and washed

BLUE CHEESE DRESSING
1 cup mayonnaise
8 ounces blue cheese,
    crumbled
2 tablespoons cider vinegar
2 tablespoons orange juice
    Few drops hot pepper sauce
    Salt

3 When ready to serve, divide salad among serving plates and top with dressing.

PASTA VEGETABLE SALAD

MAKES 6 TO 8 SERVINGS

INGREDIENTS

4 cups cooked rotelli macaroni
   or small pasta shells
1 cup shredded carrots
1 cup sliced celery
1 cup seeded and chopped
   green bell pepper
1 cup cooked peas
1 jar (4 ounces) pimento,
   drained and diced
3 tomatoes, cored and diced
3 green onions, sliced

MUSTARD VINAIGRETTE

1 cup olive oil
⅓ cup thyme vinegar
2 tablespoons Dijon mustard
2 tablespoons catsup
1 teaspoon salt
1 teaspoon sugar
½ teaspoon crumbled
   dried oregano
½ teaspoon crumbled
   dried chervil
1 teaspoon Worcestershire
   sauce

1 In a bowl, mix macaroni, carrots, celery, green pepper, peas, pimento, tomatoes and onions.

2 For vinaigrette, beat dressing ingredients in a small bowl until thick.

3 Pour dressing over salad and toss to coat well. Chill until ready to serve. If desired, garnish with stars cut from red bell peppers.

ONION LOVER'S SALAD

MAKES 6 SERVINGS

INGREDIENTS
2 *Spanish onions, thinly sliced*
3 *green onions, slivered*
1 *leek, white part only, washed*
  well and cut into thin slices
4 *navel oranges, peeled and*
  cut into ½-inch-thick slices

CITRUS DRESSING
6 *tablespoons olive oil*
2 *tablespoons fresh*
  lemon juice
2 *tablespoons orange juice*
1 *clove garlic, mashed*
½ *teaspoon dry mustard*
½ *teaspoon salt*
½ *teaspoon white pepper*
  Pinch of ground cumin

1 In a bowl, mix onions, green onions and leeks. Arrange orange slices on serving plates and top with onion mixture. Chill.

2 For dressing, combine dressing ingredients in a small bowl and beat until thick. Let stand at room temperature for 1 hour, then beat again.

3 Spoon dressing over salad. Chill until ready to serve.

GRAPEFRUIT APPETIZER SALAD

MAKES 6 SERVINGS

INGREDIENTS
3 pink grapefruit, sectioned
  Belgian endive leaves
2 avocados, peeled, seeded
  and cut into cubes

RASPBERRY DRESSING
¾ cup corn oil
¼ cup raspberry vinegar
1 teaspoon salt
1 teaspoon sugar

1 Place grapefruit sections into endive leaves. Arrange like a fan on each serving plate. Add avocado at bottom of fan.

2 For dressing, beat dressing ingredients in a small bowl until thick. Spoon over salad and chill until ready to serve.

PEAR APPETIZER SALAD

MAKES 6 SERVINGS

INGREDIENTS
3 ripe Comice pears, peeled,
  halved and cored
  Lemon juice
3 navel oranges, sectioned
  Shredded leaf lettuce leaves
6 red grapes

GINGER DRESSING
⅓ cup orange juice
⅓ cup honey
1 tablespoon grated
  fresh ginger
1 cup mayonnaise

1 With a sharp knife, cut off rounded blossom end of each pear half so pear halves look like bells; reserve removed pieces. Brush pears with lemon juice to prevent darkening.

2 Place pear "bells" on serving plates and add orange sections and a lettuce leaf at top of plate. Place a red grape at the bottom of pear to resemble clapper. Chill.

3 For dressing, press reserved pear through a sieve into a bowl and stir in remaining dressing ingredients. Chill.

4 When ready to serve, spoon dressing into lettuce cups.

CRANBERRY WINE MOLD

1 In a small nonaluminum saucepan, sprinkle gelatin over 1 cup of the cranberry juice. Let stand until gelatin is softened, about 5 minutes, then stir over low heat until gelatin is dissolved. Pour into a bowl and stir in remaining cranberry juice, port and amaretto. Chill until mixture is syrupy.

2 Fold in relish and apples. Pour mixture into 2 lightly oiled Christmas tree-shaped layer cake pans measuring 10½ x 10 inches at their widest points and 1¼ inches deep. Chill until firm.

MAKES 8 SERVINGS

INGREDIENTS
3 envelopes unflavored gelatin
3 cups cranberry juice
2 cups port wine
½ cup amaretto liqueur
1 jar (14 ounces) cranberry-orange relish
3 tart apples, peeled, cored and chopped

CREAMY RUM DRESSING
1 package (8 ounces) cream cheese, at room temperature
¼ cup sugar
¼ cup dark rum
3 tablespoons fresh lemon juice
½ cup heavy cream, whipped
Orange rind strips (optional)

3 For dressing, beat cream cheese with sugar in a bowl until fluffy. Stir in rum and lemon juice. Fold in whipped cream. Chill.

4 When ready to serve, dip one of the pans into lukewarm water for a few seconds. Tap to loosen and invert onto a serving platter. Spread dressing in a thick layer on top of gelatin. Unmold second layer in the same way as the first and invert onto a lightly moistened baking sheet. Slide gelatin carefully on top of first layer. Chill until ready to serve. If desired, garnish with strips and rounds of orange rind.

MOLDED LIME SALAD

MAKES 6 SERVINGS

INGREDIENTS

1 large package (6 ounces)
   lime gelatin
1½ cups boiling water
2 cups (1 pound) cottage
   cheese, sieved
1 cup shredded unpeeled
   seedless cucumber
1 cup mayonnaise

RUBY DRESSING

¼ cup sugar
1 teaspoon celery seed
½ teaspoon salt
1 teaspoon dry mustard
¼ cup red wine vinegar
1 cup corn oil

Halved cucumber slices or
   spiced apple rings
   (optional)
Leaf lettuce

1 In a heatproof bowl, dissolve gelatin in boiling water; cool. Stir in cottage cheese, cucumber and mayonnaise and chill until syrupy. Stir again and pour into a lightly oiled 1½-quart ring mold. Chill until firm.

2 For dressing, beat sugar, celery seed, salt, mustard, vinegar and oil ingredients in a bowl until well blended. Let stand at room temperature for 1 hour, then beat again.

3 When ready to serve, dip mold into lukewarm water for a few seconds, tap to loosen and invert onto a serving platter. Place a bowl of dressing in the center of the mold. Chill until ready to serve. If desired, garnish with halved cucumber slices or halved spiced apple rings. Fill center with leaf lettuce. Serve dressing on the side.

Opposite: Molded Lime Salad, page 213;
Cranberry Wine Mold, page 211

THE SECOND TIME AROUND

Tempting Treatments for Holiday Leftovers

*A*lthough the word "leftover" usually conjures up an image of overcooked scraps you'd rather not face again, at the holidays—when there is so much good food around—it has a very different image. Tempting overstuffed sandwiches or bubbling, cheese-crusted casseroles just promise more of the very things you couldn't get enough of at last night's dinner.

If, as the song says, "love is lovelier the second time around," then the inevitable leftovers need not be boring and tasteless. Properly prepared, they are the basis for many flavorful dishes for the family and after-holiday guests. And, truth be told, no matter how advanced our tastes or culinary skill might be, who among us can bear to waste expensive food we have lavished such care on? Leftover dishes are an established and endearing feature of the days between Christmas and New Year's. They're economical, easy and very satisfying.

THANK HEAVENS FOR THE EARL OF SANDWICH!
Here are a few quick suggestions for the family favorite.
Spread pumpernickel bread slices with mustard and top with thinly sliced ham and Swiss cheese. Broil until cheese is melted.
Prepare a turkey salad mixture of chopped cooked turkey, chopped celery and mayonnaise. Cover slices of whole wheat toast with very thin slices of peeled tart apple and top with salad and another slice of toast.

Spread rye toast with pickle relish and top with roast beef slices and thinly sliced pickled green tomatoes. Add lettuce and second slice of bread.

Split kaiser rolls and fill with thinly sliced pork. Add green onion pieces and Russian dressing.

Butter whole-grain bread on one side. Top with chicken slices, grated carrot, crushed pineapple and crisp bacon. Top with a second slice of buttered bread.

Split hero rolls and spread with mayonnaise. Top with ham slices, green pepper rings, thin tomato slices and alfalfa sprouts. Drizzle with Italian salad dressing and replace top of roll.

Spread thin slices of turkey with tartar sauce. Top each slice with a few cooked whole green beans. Roll up, enclosing beans. Place rolls into lettuce-lined frankfurter buns.

Mix diced chicken with chopped celery and plain yogurt. Season to taste with curry and stuff into pita bread or taco shells.

Top with chopped peanuts, slivered red pepper and mandarin orange sections.

Spread rye bread with barbecue sauce and cover with roast pork slices. Top with sliced water chestnuts, slivered green onions and slivered snow peas. Drizzle lightly with teriyaki sauce and add a second slice of rye bread.

BEEF PARMESAN

MAKES 6 SERVINGS

INGREDIENTS

1 quart diced cooked potatoes
1 quart diced cooked beef or
  beef and pork
¼ cup butter
2 large onions, sliced
1 can (1 pound) tomatoes,
  undrained
8 ounces mozzarella cheese,
  shredded
½ cup grated Parmesan cheese

1 Mix potatoes and beef and place in a greased 2-quart casserole.

2 In a small skillet, melt butter over medium heat and sauté onions for 5 minutes. Add onions and tomatoes to casserole and stir lightly. Top with cheeses.

3 Bake in a preheated 350°F oven for 20 to 25 minutes or until lightly browned.

BEEF HASHBURGERS

MAKES 6 SERVINGS

INGREDIENTS

3 cups ground cooked beef
  (grind in food processor)
3 cups thick mashed potatoes
1 small onion, minced
⅓ cup chili sauce
  Salt and pepper
  Dry breadcrumbs
3 tablespoons butter
3 tablespoons corn oil
6 slices American cheese
6 onion rolls, split
  Additional chili sauce
  or catsup

1 In a bowl, mix beef, potatoes, onion, chili sauce and salt and pepper to taste. Shape mixture into 6 thick patties.

2 In a large skillet, heat butter and oil. Sauté patties slowly until brown and crusty on both sides.

3 Top patties with cheese slices. Place into rolls. Serve with chili sauce or catsup.

Opposite: Mexican Tacos, page 224; Pork Pasta Sauce, page 223

DEVILED BEEF

MAKES 6 SERVINGS

INGREDIENTS
12 slices cooked beef
6 tablespoons Dijon mustard
1½ cups seasoned dry
    breadcrumbs
¼ cup olive oil

WINE MUSHROOM SAUCE
2 tablespoons butter
4 ounces mushrooms, sliced
¼ cup all-purpose flour
1 cup beef broth
1 cup dry red wine
2 tablespoons fresh
    lemon juice
Salt

1 Spread both sides of the beef slices with a thin layer of mustard. Dip into breadcrumbs, pressing firmly to make crumbs adhere.

2 Brush a baking sheet with 1 tablespoon of the oil. Arrange beef slices on sheet side by side. Drizzle with remaining oil. Bake in a preheated 425°F oven for 12 to 15 minutes or until crusty.

3 For sauce, melt butter in a 1-quart saucepan over medium heat and sauté mushrooms for 5 minutes. Sprinkle with flour. Gradually add broth, wine and lemon juice and stir until sauce bubbles and thickens. Simmer for 5 minutes. Season to taste with salt.

4 Divide beef slices among serving plates and top with sauce.

VEAL PROSCIUTTO

MAKES 6 SERVINGS

INGREDIENTS
6 slices white bread, toasted
  Butter
12 thin slices cooked veal
12 thin slices prosciutto
3 tomatoes, thinly sliced
  Pinch of dried oregano
12 slices fontina cheese
  Purchased caponata
  or olive relish

1 Butter one side of each toast slice. Arrange slices side by side on a baking sheet. Top with veal, prosciutto and tomatoes. Sprinkle with oregano and top with cheese slices.

2 Bake in a preheated 400°F oven for 15 minutes or until cheese melts. Serve with caponata or relish.

VEAL AND CELERY REMOULADE

*I*n a bowl, thoroughly mix all ingredients except spinach, adding salt to taste. Chill. Serve on a bed of spinach leaves.

MAKES 6 SERVINGS

INGREDIENTS
3 cups diced cooked veal
3 cups sliced cooked unpeeled
   new potatoes
1 red onion, chopped
1 cup mayonnaise
¼ cup minced celery
1 clove garlic, crushed
2 tablespoons prepared
   white horseradish
2 tablespoons prepared
   mustard
1 tablespoon balsamic vinegar
Salt
Young spinach leaves

BARBECUED BEEF, LAMB OR VEAL

1 In a 1½-quart nonaluminum saucepan, combine catsup, vinegar and onion and stir over medium heat for 5 minutes. Add meat slices and simmer for 5 minutes.

MAKES 6 SERVINGS

INGREDIENTS
1½ cups catsup
½ cup red wine vinegar
1 small onion, grated
12 thin slices cooked beef,
   lamb or veal
6 hero rolls, split
1 large red onion,
   cut into rings

2 Spoon meat and sauce into hero rolls and top with onion rings.

STIR-FRIED VEAL

MAKES 6 SERVINGS

INGREDIENTS
3 tablespoons cornstarch
3 tablespoons soy sauce
2 tablespoons dry sherry
  or sake
1½ cups chicken broth
¼ cup peanut oil
6 green onions, sliced
2 cloves garlic, chopped
1 cup diagonally sliced celery
1 cup diagonally sliced carrots
4 ounces snow peas, stringed
1 green bell pepper,
  seeded and slivered
1 red bell pepper,
  seeded and slivered
2 tablespoons grated
  fresh ginger
3 cups julienned cooked veal
Salt
Crisp Chinese noodles

1 Mix cornstarch, soy sauce, sherry and broth in a small bowl; set aside.

2 In a wok or Dutch oven, heat oil and stir-fry vegetables and ginger for 5 minutes over high heat. Add veal and stir-fry for another 5 minutes.

3 Add soy sauce mixture and stir until slightly thickened. Season to taste with salt. Serve over crisp Chinese noodles.

LAMB WITH SQUASH

MAKES 6 SERVINGS

INGREDIENTS

3 *large zucchini,*
  halved lengthwise
2 *tablespoons butter*
1 *large onion, chopped*
1 *clove garlic, chopped*
2 *cups ground cooked lamb*
  (grind in food processor)
½ *teaspoon crumbled*
  dried rosemary
1 *egg, well beaten*
¼ *cup catsup*
2 *cups purchased*
  marinara sauce

1 Scoop out zucchini with a spoon, leaving a shell ½ inch thick. Chop zucchini pulp.

2 In a skillet, melt butter over medium heat and sauté onion and garlic for 5 minutes. Add chopped zucchini and sauté for another 5 minutes. Remove from heat and stir in lamb, rosemary, egg and catsup.

3 Stuff zucchini halves with mixture. Place zucchini side by side in a greased 9- x 13- x 2-inch baking pan. Spoon sauce evenly over zucchini.

4 Bake in a preheated 350°F oven for 30 to 35 minutes or until zucchini are easily pierced.

LAMB IN FILO

MAKES 6 SERVINGS

INGREDIENTS

¼ *cup butter*
2 *onions, chopped*
4 *cups ground cooked lamb*
(grind in food processor)
1 *teaspoon crumbled*
dried oregano
1 *package (10 ounces) frozen*
chopped spinach, cooked,
squeezed dry and chopped
1 *cup (4 ounces) crumbled*
feta cheese
1 *can (10½ ounces)*
condensed cream of
mushroom soup, undiluted
1 *package (1 pound) filo*
dough, thawed if frozen
½ *cup melted butter*

1 In skillet, melt ¼ cup butter over medium heat and sauté onions for 5 minutes. Remove from heat. Stir in lamb, oregano, spinach, cheese and soup. Cool.

2 Cut filo dough in half crosswise. Place 2 sheets of the filo dough on work surface and brush with melted butter. Top with 2 more sheets. Repeat until you have a stack of 8 sheets.

3 Place ⅙ of the lamb filling along the long side of the dough, beginning and ending 1½ inches away from short sides. Roll up, turning in ends, to enclose filling.

4 Place on greased baking sheet and brush with more butter. Repeat with remaining dough and filling until you have 6 rolls.

5 Bake in a preheated 375°F oven for 35 to 40 minutes or until brown and crisp.

PORK PASTA SAUCE

MAKES 6 SERVINGS

INGREDIENTS

2 cups finely diced
   cooked pork
4 sweet Italian sausages,
   removed from casing
   and crumbled
1 onion, chopped
1 clove garlic, chopped
1 green bell pepper, seeded
   and chopped
3 cups canned
   crushed tomatoes
1 teaspoon crumbled
   dried oregano
1 teaspoon crumbled
   dried basil
¼ cup grated Romano cheese
   Salt and pepper
1 pound spaghetti,
   cooked and drained
   Grated Parmesan cheese

1 In a 1½-quart saucepan, sauté pork and sausage over medium heat until sausage is brown and crumbly. Add onion, garlic and green pepper and sauté for another 5 minutes.

2 Add tomatoes, oregano, basil and Romano and simmer un-covered, stirring occasionally, for 20 minutes. Season to taste with salt and pepper.

3 Serve sauce over spaghetti. Sprinkle with Parmesan cheese.

MEXICAN BURRITOS OR TACOS

MAKES 4 TO 6 SERVINGS

1 In a skillet, heat lard over medium heat and sauté onion, garlic and bell peppers for 10 minutes. Add pork, raisins, chili powder, cumin and pepper flakes.

2 In a small bowl, mix beef broth and flour until smooth. Add to skillet and stir until thickened.

INGREDIENTS

6 *tablespoons lard*
1 *onion, chopped*
1 *clove garlic, chopped*
1 *red and 1 green bell pepper, seeded and chopped*
2 *cups finely diced cooked pork*
¼ *cup raisins*
1 *tablespoon chili powder*
¼ *teaspoon ground cumin*
1 *teaspoon red pepper flakes*
1 *cup beef broth*
2 *tablespoons all-purpose flour*
 Warm flour tortillas or taco shells
 Shredded cheddar cheese
 Shredded iceberg lettuce
 Chopped tomato

3 Spoon mixture onto flour tortillas and roll up, or spoon into taco shells. Serve topped with cheese, lettuce and tomato. Garnish with orange slices.

SWEET-SOUR PORK OVER ONION SHORTCAKE

1 For shortcake, melt butter in a skillet over medium heat. Sauté onions and parsley for 10 minutes or until very soft but not brown.

2 In a bowl, mix flour, baking powder and salt. Cut in butter until particles are very fine. Add milk and stir until it cleans the bowl.

3 Turn dough out on a floured surface and knead a few times until dough forms a smooth ball. Pat dough out into a 12-inch round on a greased cookie sheet. Spread contents of skillet over top of dough.

4 Bake in a preheated 450°F oven for 15 to 20 minutes or until puffed and brown.

MAKES 8 SERVINGS

INGREDIENTS

Shortcake
3 tablespoons butter
12 small white onions, peeled and sliced
¼ cup minced parsley
2 cups sifted all-purpose flour
2½ teaspoons baking powder
1 teaspoon salt
¼ cup butter
¾ cup milk

SWEET-SOUR PORK
2 tablespoons peanut or sesame oil
1 cup julienned green bell peppers
1 can (1 pound, 4 ounces) pineapple chunks, undrained
½ cup cider vinegar
½ cup sugar
2 tablespoons grated fresh ginger
2 tablespoons soy sauce
3 cups cooked pork cut into 1-inch cubes
1½ cups chicken broth
2 tablespoons cornstarch

5 While shortcake is baking, heat oil in a 1½-quart nonaluminum saucepan and sauté green pepper over medium heat for 5 minutes. Add pineapple chunks, vinegar, sugar, ginger, soy sauce and pork and simmer 5 minutes.

6 Mix chicken broth and cornstarch until smooth, add to saucepan and stir until thickened.

7 Cut shortcake into 8 wedges and place on serving plates. Top with sweet-sour pork.

HAM AND CHICKEN JAMBALAYA

MAKES 6 SERVINGS

INGREDIENTS

¼ cup olive oil
2 onions, chopped
2 cloves garlic, chopped
1 cup chopped celery
1 green bell pepper,
  seeded and chopped
1 cup uncooked
  long-grain rice
3 cups chicken broth
1 can (1 pound) tomatoes,
  undrained
¼ cup tomato paste
6 slices pepperoni, quartered
2 cups diced cooked ham
2 cups diced cooked chicken
  Hot pepper sauce

1 In a 2-quart saucepan, heat olive oil over medium heat and sauté onion, garlic, celery and green pepper for 5 minutes. Add rice and sauté for another 5 minutes.

2 Stir in chicken broth, tomatoes and tomato paste and simmer for 20 minutes or until rice is tender and liquid is absorbed.

3 Stir in pepperoni, ham and chicken and simmer for 5 minutes. Season to taste with hot pepper sauce.

4 Serve with Tomatoes Stuffed with Artichoke Hearts, Marinated Mixed Bean Salad, Italian Panettone, Cheesecake Pie, Apricot Banana Squares and Five Fruit Ice Cream (see Index for recipes).

HAM BREAD-AND-BUTTER CASSEROLE

MAKES 6 SERVINGS

INGREDIENTS
12 slices white bread
12 slices cooked ham
6 slices American cheese
¼ cup melted butter
4 eggs
1½ cups milk
1 teaspoon salt
¼ teaspoon white pepper

1 Make 6 sandwiches using bread, ham and cheese.

2 Spread butter thickly on the bottom of a 9- x 13- x 2-inch baking pan. Place sandwiches side by side in pan.

3 In a bowl, beat eggs with milk, salt and pepper until well blended. Pour mixture evenly over sandwiches.

4 Bake in a preheated 350°F oven for 40 to 45 minutes or until puffed and brown.

HAM GRILLS

MAKES 6 SERVINGS

INGREDIENTS
6 slices canned pineapple
2 cups ground cooked ham
  (grind in food processor)
1 tablespoon Dijon mustard
¼ cup mayonnaise
2 tablespoons pickle relish
6 tablespoons steak sauce
6 cups mashed sweet potatoes,
  heated

1 Place pineapple slices on a greased shallow baking pan. In a bowl, mix ham, mustard, mayonnaise and relish. Spoon mixture in mounds on the pineapple slices. Top each mound with a tablespoon of steak sauce.

2 Bake in a preheated 400°F oven for 15 minutes or until heated through.

3 Make a bed of potatoes on each serving plate and top with pineapple slices.

TURKEY SUPPER SALAD

MAKES 6 SERVINGS

INGREDIENTS

3 cups diced turkey
1 cup sliced celery
1 cup bean sprouts
½ cup sliced water chestnuts
⅓ cup slivered toasted almonds
½ cup sliced stuffed olives
2 cups crumbled
  turkey stuffing
½ cup mayonnaise
½ cup sour cream
  Iceberg lettuce wedges
  Pomegranate seeds or strips
  of red bell pepper

1 In a bowl, mix turkey, celery, sprouts, water chestnuts, almonds, olives, stuffing, mayonnaise and sour cream. Blend well and chill.

2 When ready to serve, place lettuce wedges on serving plates and add turkey salad. Sprinkle with pomegranate seeds or pepper.

228

Opposite: Turkey Frittata, page 230; Stir-Fried Veal, page 220

TURKEY FRITTATA

1 In a large, deep, ovenproof skillet, melt butter over medium heat and sauté onions for 5 minutes. Stir in olives, pimento and turkey.

2 In a bowl, beat eggs with remaining ingredients until well blended. Pour mixture into skillet and cook without stirring until brown on the bottom.

MAKES 6 SERVINGS

INGREDIENTS
¼ cup butter
6 green onions, chopped
½ cup sliced pitted black olives
1 jar (4 ounces) pimento, drained and diced
2 cups diced cooked turkey
12 eggs
2 teaspoons salt
¼ teaspoon pepper
½ cup water
¼ cup minced parsley
Chopped fresh tomatoes
Sliced green onions

3 Place skillet under a broiler and broil until top is golden brown and egg is completely cooked. Cut into wedges to serve. Garnish with chopped salted tomatoes and sliced green onions. If desired, the frittata can be cooled and cut into small squares to serve at room temperature as an hors d'oeuvre. Can also be garnished with a tomato rose and a sprig of chicory.

TURKEY MANICOTTI

1 Cook shells in boiling salted water to cover for 5 minutes. Drain and place in cold water to cover.

2 In a bowl, mix turkey, mayonnaise, onion, celery and egg.

MAKES 6 SERVINGS

INGREDIENTS
12 manicotti shells
2½ cups ground cooked turkey (grind in food processor)
⅓ cup mayonnaise
¼ cup minced onion
¼ cup minced celery
1 egg, well beaten
3 cups purchased mushroom spaghetti sauce
8 ounces mozzarella cheese, shredded

3 Drain manicotti shells well and stuff with turkey mixture. Place side by side in a greased shallow baking pan. Spoon sauce evenly over top. Sprinkle with cheese.

4 Bake in a preheated 350°F oven for 40 to 45 minutes or until cheese is golden brown.

CHICKEN ALMOND ORANGE

MAKES 4 SERVINGS

INGREDIENTS

1 tablespoon butter
½ cup slivered almonds
3 cups diced cooked chicken,
    duck or goose
2 tablespoons cornstarch
1 cup chicken broth
1 can (6 ounces) frozen
    orange juice concentrate,
    undiluted
1 teaspoon molasses
1 teaspoon soy sauce
    Salt and pepper
1 package (6 ounces) wild rice
    and white rice mix

1 In a 1½-quart saucepan, melt butter and sauté almonds until brown. Add chicken.

2 In a bowl, mix cornstarch, broth, juice concentrate, molasses and soy sauce until well blended. Add to saucepan and stir until thickened.

3 Cook rice mix according to package directions until rice is tender. Press hot rice firmly into 4 oiled custard cups. Unmold onto serving plates. Spoon chicken mixture over rice.

CHICKEN PITA PIZZAS

MAKES 6 SERVINGS

INGREDIENTS

6 *pita breads*
  Olive oil
3 *cups purchased pizza*
  or meat sauce
2 *cups finely chopped*
  cooked chicken
½ *cup sliced stuffed olives*
1 *can (4 ounces) sliced*
  mushrooms, drained
1 *pound mozzarella cheese,*
  shredded
  Grated Parmesan cheese
  Red pepper flakes

1 Trim edges of pita bread with scissors and separate each pita into 2 layers. Place pita rounds, rough side up, side by side on a cookie sheet.

2 In a bowl, mix sauce, chicken, olives and mushrooms. Spread mixture thinly on pita breads and sprinkle with mozzarella.

3 Bake in a preheated 425°F oven for 12 to 15 minutes or until cheese is melted.

4 Place 2 pizzas on each serving plate. Serve with grated Parmesan cheese and red pepper flakes.

Chicken Or Turkey Cajun Gumbo

MAKES 6 SERVINGS

INGREDIENTS
½ cup margarine
¼ cup all-purpose flour
1 onion, chopped
1 green bell pepper,
   seeded and chopped
2 stalks celery, chopped
4 cloves garlic, chopped
2 cups sliced fresh
   or frozen okra
1 tablespoon
   Worcestershire sauce
1 tablespoon chili powder
2 cups canned tomatoes,
   undrained
2 cups chicken broth
1 teaspoon gumbo filé
   (powdered sassafras leaves)
4 cups diced cooked chicken or
   turkey
   Salt
   Cooked rice

1 In a 2-quart saucepan, melt margarine, add flour and stir over low heat until mixture is deep brown but not burned. Add onion, pepper, celery, garlic and okra and stir over medium heat for 5 minutes.

2 Add Worcestershire sauce, chili powder, tomatoes, broth and gumbo filé. Cover and simmer, stirring occasionally, for 20 to 25 minutes or until vegetables are tender.

3 Stir in chicken and season to taste with salt. Simmer 5 minutes. Serve in bowls spooned over rice.

BAKED SALMON AND RICE

1 In a bowl, mix rice, salmon, eggs, butter and cream. Season to taste with salt. Pour mixture into a buttered 1½-quart casserole.

MAKES 6 SERVINGS
INGREDIENTS
2 cups cooked brown rice
2 cups flaked cooked salmon
 or other fish
4 hard-cooked eggs, chopped
¼ cup melted butter
1 cup (½ pint) heavy cream
Salt
Chopped parsley
Paprika

2 Bake in a preheated 350°F oven for 30 to 35 minutes or until lightly browned. Sprinkle top with alternating bands of chopped parsley and paprika.

SALMON POT PIE

1 In a bowl, mix salmon and vegetables. In a 1-quart saucepan, melt butter over medium heat and sauté onion for 5 minutes. Sprinkle with flour. Gradually add half-and-half and stir until sauce bubbles and thickens. Stir in lemon juice and hot pepper sauce. Stir sauce into salmon mixture.

MAKES 6 SERVINGS
INGREDIENTS
2 cups flaked cooked
 salmon or other fish
2 cups leftover
 cooked vegetables
¼ cup butter
1 onion, chopped
¼ cup all-purpose flour
2 cups (1 pint) half-and-half
2 tablespoons
 fresh lemon juice
2 drops hot pepper sauce
1 package (7.5 ounces)
 refrigerated biscuit dough
 or 1 package (8 ounces)
 refrigerated crescent
 roll dough

2 Pour into a greased 7- x 11- x 2-inch baking pan. Top with biscuits or with triangles of dough.

3 Bake in a preheated 400°F oven for 30 to 35 minutes or until top is brown and crusty.

WARM AND WONDERFUL LOAVES

Festive Yeast and Quick Breads

*B*read is called the "staff of life" with good
reason. A homemade loaf, fragrant from the oven,
adds so much to a holiday meal. Whether the bread is leavened
with yeast or baking powder, modern ingredients and equipment shorten
preparation time. Yeasts have been improved and no longer require making
sponges, scalding milk or lengthy rising times. Modern ovens preheat in only
15 minutes, saving costly energy. Loaves prepared at home are made of the best
ingredients without additives or preservatives. And best of all, breads can be made
way ahead of time, stored in the freezer and warmed when needed, leaving
the oven free for the family roast.
Whether plain and hearty or filled with sweet fruit and spices, a wonderful-looking
loaf can become a family tradition. All the starred (*) recipes are
suitable for shipping.

VIENNA EGG BRAID

MAKES 2 BRAIDS

INGREDIENTS

2 envelopes active dry yeast
1½ teaspoons salt
1 tablespoon sugar
2 cups lukewarm water
¼ cup vegetable shortening
3 eggs, well beaten
½ teaspoon crumbled saffron
   threads
8 to 9 cups unsifted
   all-purpose flour
1 egg, well beaten

1 In a large bowl, mix yeast with salt, sugar and water. Let stand for 5 minutes or until yeast is dissolved. Add shortening, eggs and saffron. Add half the flour and beat until smooth and shiny. Gradually beat in remaining flour until mixture forms a stiff dough. Knead on a floured surface for 5 minutes or until smooth and elastic.

2 Return dough to washed and dried bowl and grease top. Cover and let rise in a warm place until doubled in bulk, about 1 hour.

3 Punch dough down and cut into 6 pieces. Roll each piece into a 12-inch rope. Braid 3 ropes together, shaping 2 loaves. Pinch ends together and place on ungreased cookie sheets. Brush with egg and let rise in a warm place until doubled in bulk, about 45 minutes.

4 Bake in preheated 400°F oven for 15 minutes. Reduce heat to 375°F and bake an additional 45 minutes or until bread is golden brown. Cool thoroughly before slicing. This is an excellent bread for toast or French toast.

*SWISS SPICED PEAR BREAD

1 Grind dried fruit coarsely and place in a large saucepan. Add lemon peel, Kirsch and enough water to just cover fruit. Cover and simmer 30 minutes.

2 Drain fruit, reserving liquid. Add enough water to liquid to make 4 cups. Place fruit in a bowl and stir in ½ cup butter, sugar, spices and nuts.

3 Heat 1 cup of the liquid to lukewarm. Pour into a very large bowl and stir in yeast. Let stand 5 minutes. Stir in remaining liquid, eggs, salt and enough flour to make a firm dough.

4 Knead dough on a floured surface for 10 minutes or until smooth and elastic. Return to washed and dried bowl, grease top, cover with a damp towel and let rise in a warm place until doubled in bulk, about 1½ hours.

MAKES THREE 9- X 5-INCH LOAVES

INGREDIENTS
1 pound dried pears,
    stemmed and cored
1 pound dried figs, stemmed
½ pound pitted prunes
½ cup chopped
    candied lemon peel
½ cup Kirsch
½ cup butter
½ cup sugar
1 teaspoon ground cinnamon
1 teaspoon ground nutmeg
2 cups coarsely chopped
    toasted hazelnuts
2 envelopes active dry yeast
2 eggs, well beaten
½ teaspoon salt
10 to 12 cups unsifted
    all-purpose flour
½ cup melted butter

5 Remove three 1-cup measures of dough and set aside. Mix fruit mixture into remaining dough; it will be sticky. Divide into 3 equal pieces and shape with floured hands into three 8-inch logs.

6 Roll out each piece of reserved dough on a floured surface to a 10-inch square. Place a log on each piece and wrap with dough, enclosing fruit-nut log completely and sealing ends and edges with a little water. Place each loaf seam side down in a heavily greased 9- x 5- x 3-inch loaf pan. Brush loaves with melted butter. Let rise in a warm place until doubled in bulk, about 1½ hours.

7 Bake in a preheated 350°F oven for 1¼ to 1½ hours or until golden brown. Unmold and cool right side up on racks. Cool thoroughly before slicing. If desired, dust with confectioners' sugar.

Opposite: Swiss Spiced Pear Bread, page 238

*Austrian Gugelhupf

MAKES 1 LARGE RING

INGREDIENTS

1 envelope active dry yeast
¼ cup sugar
½ teaspoon salt
½ cup lukewarm milk
4 eggs, well beaten
¾ cup soft butter
  Grated rind of 2 lemons
3 cups sifted all-purpose flour
2 tablespoons cornstarch
¼ cup chopped
  toasted almonds
¼ cup dried currants
  Confectioners' sugar
  Butter or prune or apricot
  butter (optional)

1 In the large bowl of an electric mixer, combine yeast, sugar, salt and milk. Let stand 5 minutes. Beat in eggs, butter and lemon rind. Add flour and cornstarch and beat until mixture becomes smooth and shiny. Fold in almonds and currants. Cover and let rise in a warm place until doubled in bulk, about 2 hours.

2 Beat dough again briefly. Pour into a well-greased 2½-quart tube or Gugelhupf pan. Let rise in a warm place until doubled in bulk, about 1 hour.

3 Bake in a preheated 375°F oven for 45 to 50 minutes or until richly browned and loaf sounds hollow when thumped. Cool in pan 5 minutes, then unmold upside down onto a rack.

4 When cool, dust lightly with confectioners' sugar. Cut into thin slices and serve as is or spread with butter or prune or apricot butter.

*GERMAN STOLLEN

MAKES 1 LARGE LOAF

INGREDIENTS

2 envelopes active dry yeast
½ cup lukewarm water
½ cup lukewarm milk
½ cup sugar
½ teaspoon salt
2 eggs, well beaten
½ cup soft butter
  Grated rind of 1 lemon
4½ to 5 cups unsifted
  all-purpose flour
½ cup mixed candied fruits
½ cup slivered almonds
¼ cup melted butter

FROSTING

1 cup confectioners' sugar
2 tablespoons fresh
  lemon juice
1 teaspoon vanilla

1 In a large bowl, mix yeast and water. Let stand for 5 minutes. Stir in milk, sugar, salt, eggs, ½ cup butter and lemon rind. Stir in enough flour to make a soft dough.

2 Knead dough on a floured surface for 10 minutes. Return to washed and dried bowl, grease top, cover with a damp towel and let rise in a warm place until doubled in bulk, about 1 hour.

3 Punch dough down and knead in fruit and almonds. Pat dough out into an 8- x 12-inch oval. Fold in half lengthwise and place on a greased baking sheet. Brush with melted butter and let rise in a warm place until doubled in bulk, about 35 to 40 minutes.

4 Bake in a preheated 375°F oven for 30 to 35 minutes or until golden brown.

5 For frosting, combine ingredients in a bowl, and mix until well blended. When stollen is removed from oven, spoon frosting evenly over top. Cool thoroughly on baking sheet before slicing.

*SCOTCH OATMEAL CURRANT BREAD

MAKES ONE 9- X 5-INCH LOAF

INGREDIENTS

1 envelope active dry yeast
¼ cup lukewarm water
1 cup quick-cooking oatmeal
2 tablespoons firmly packed
   dark brown sugar
1 teaspoon salt
1 cup dried currants
4½ to 5 cups unsifted
   all-purpose flour
1 egg white
1 tablespoon water
   Additional quick-cooking
   oatmeal

1 In a large bowl, mix yeast and water. Let stand 5 minutes. Stir in milk, 1 cup oatmeal, brown sugar, salt and currants. Stir in enough flour to make a soft dough. Knead on a floured surface for 8 to 10 minutes or until smooth and elastic. Return to washed and dried bowl, grease top, cover with a damp towel and let rise in a warm place until doubled in bulk, about 1 hour.

2 Punch dough down and let rise again for 30 minutes. Knead again and pat out into a 9 inch-square. Roll up tightly like a jelly roll and place seam side down in a greased 9- x 5- x 3-inch loaf pan.

3 Beat egg white with water until foamy. Brush on top of loaf and sprinkle with oatmeal flakes. Let rise in a warm place until doubled in bulk, about 1 hour.

4 Bake in a preheated 375°F oven for 40 to 45 minutes or until loaf sounds hollow when thumped. Cool in pan 5 minutes, then unmold onto rack right side up. Cool thoroughly before slicing.

*ITALIAN PANETTONE

MAKES ONE 8-INCH ROUND LOAF

INGREDIENTS

1 envelope active dry yeast
½ cup lukewarm water
½ cup lukewarm milk
½ cup melted butter
1 teaspoon ground nutmeg
1 teaspoon salt
½ cup sugar
6 eggs yolks
5½ to 6 cups unsifted
*   all-purpose flour*
½ cup finely chopped mixed
*   candied fruits*
½ cup golden raisins
2 tablespoons melted butter
Warmed honey and colored
*   sprinkles (optional)*

1 In a large bowl, combine yeast and water. Let stand for 5 minutes. Stir in milk, butter, nutmeg, salt, sugar and egg yolks. Stir in enough flour to make a soft dough. Knead on a floured surface for 5 to 6 minutes or until smooth and elastic. Knead in candied fruits and raisins. Return dough to washed and dried bowl and grease top. Cover and let rise in a warm place until doubled in bulk, about 2 hours.

2 Punch dough down and shape into a large, smooth ball. Grease an 8-inch springform pan and tie on a 3-inch-high collar of several thicknesses of heavy-duty foil. Grease foil. Place ball of dough into pan and pat down. Brush with melted butter and cut a small cross, about ½ inch deep, into top of loaf. Let rise in a warm place until doubled in bulk, about 1 hour.

3 Bake in a preheated 325°F oven for 1 to 1¼ hours or until loaf is richly browned and sounds hollow when thumped. Cool in pan, then remove foil and pan sides and bottom.

4 If desired, brush lightly with honey and scatter colored sprinkles over the top. Cut loaf into thin wedges to serve.

5 For a taller loaf, grease a 7-inch springform pan. Line the sides of the pan with a strip of greased brown paper 8 inches wide. Shape dough, slash and let rise as above. Bake in a preheated 400°F oven for 10 minutes. Lower heat to 350°F and bake another 50 minutes. Cool and then remove pan.

*Swedish St. Lucia Ring

MAKES 1 LARGE RING

INGREDIENTS

2 envelopes active dry yeast
½ cup lukewarm water
¾ cup lukewarm milk
¼ cup sugar
½ cup soft butter
½ teaspoon salt
1½ teaspoons ground
    cardamom
    Grated rind of 1 orange
1 egg, well beaten
4 to 4½ cups unsifted
    all-purpose flour
1 egg, well beaten
    Additional sugar

1 In a large bowl, combine yeast and water. Let stand 5 minutes. Stir in milk, ¼ cup sugar, butter, salt, cardamom, orange rind and 1 egg. Stir in enough flour to make a soft dough. Knead dough on a floured surface for 5 minutes or until smooth and elastic. Return to bowl, grease top and cover with a damp towel. Let rise in a warm place until doubled in bulk, about 1 hour.

2 Knead dough again briefly and cut into 3 equal pieces. With the hands, roll each piece into a 24-inch rope. Braid ropes, place on greased baking sheet and bring ends together to form a ring, sealing them well. Brush with beaten egg. Let stand in a warm place until doubled in bulk, about 40 to 45 minutes. Sprinkle lightly with sugar.

3 Bake in a preheated 350°F oven for 35 to 40 minutes or until richly browned. Cool thoroughly on baking sheet before slicing. Traditionally, this bread holds a circle of white candles and is used as a centerpiece.

Opposite: Italian Panettone, page 243

*YUGOSLAVIAN POTECA

MAKES ONE 10-INCH ROUND LOAF

INGREDIENTS
2 envelopes active dry yeast
½ cup lukewarm water
½ cup lukewarm milk
½ cup sugar
½ teaspoon salt
2 eggs, well beaten
½ cup soft butter
   Grated rind of 1 lemon
4½ to 5 cups unsifted
   all-purpose flour
⅓ cup honey
1 cup finely chopped walnuts
⅓ cup butter
⅓ cup heavy cream
1 teaspoon ground cinnamon
1 teaspoon ground nutmeg
1½ cups dried currants
1 egg, well beaten
2 tablespoons sugar

1 In a large bowl, mix yeast and water. Let stand for 5 minutes. Stir in milk, sugar, salt, eggs, ½ cup butter and lemon rind. Stir in enough flour to make a soft dough. Knead on a floured surface for 10 minutes. Return to washed and dried bowl, grease top, cover with a damp towel and let rise in a warm place until doubled in bulk, about 1 hour.

2 While dough is rising, combine all remaining ingredients except egg and sugar in a saucepan and stir over high heat for 1 minute. Cool.

3 Punch dough down and roll out on a floured surface to an 8- by 20-inch rectangle. Spread filling to within 1 inch of the edges. Roll up like a jelly roll, starting at a long side. Stretch rope of dough to 22 inches. Coil seam side down into a heavily greased 10-inch layer cake pan, 2 inches deep. Brush dough with egg and sprinkle with sugar. Let rise in a warm place until doubled in bulk, about 35 to 40 minutes.

4 Bake in a preheated 350°F oven for 45 to 50 minutes or until richly browned. Unmold and turn right side up on a rack. Cool thoroughly before slicing.

Opposite: Assorted Holiday Breads

*SPANISH OR MEXICAN ROSCÓN DE REYES (THREE KINGS' BREAD)

1 In a large bowl, combine yeast and water. Let stand 5 minutes. Stir in milk, salt, butter and eggs. Stir in enough flour to make a soft dough. Mix in nuts and 1 cup candied fruits. Knead on a floured surface for 5 minutes or until smooth and elastic. Return dough to washed and dried bowl, grease top, cover with a damp towel and let rise in a warm place until doubled in bulk, about 1 hour.

2 Knead dough again briefly and shape into a 20-inch rope. Place on a greased baking sheet, bring ends together and pinch to seal. Let rise in a warm place until doubled in bulk, about 35 to 40 minutes.

MAKES 1 LARGE RING

INGREDIENTS
2 envelopes active dry yeast
⅓ cup lukewarm water
½ cup lukewarm milk
½ teaspoon salt
½ cup soft butter
5 eggs, well beaten
4½ to 5 cups unsifted
    all-purpose flour
1 cup chopped Brazil nuts
1 cup chopped mixed
    candied fruits

FROSTING
1 cup confectioners' sugar
2 tablespoons fresh
    lemon juice
1 teaspoon vanilla

3 Bake in a preheated 350°F oven for 40 to 45 minutes or until richly browned.

4 For frosting, mix powdered sugar, lemon juice and vanilla in a bowl and spoon evenly over ring while hot. If desired, sprinkle with mixed candied fruits. Cool thoroughly on baking sheet before slicing.

*FINNISH VIIPURI TWIST

**MAKES 1 LARGE
PRETZEL-SHAPED LOAF**

INGREDIENTS

2 envelopes active dry yeast
2 cups lukewarm water
2 eggs, well beaten
¼ cup melted butter
½ cup sugar
1 teaspoon ground cardamom
½ teaspoon salt
6 to 7 cups unsifted
    all-purpose flour
1 egg, well beaten

1 In a large bowl, combine yeast and water. Let stand 5 minutes. Stir in eggs, butter, sugar, cardamom and salt. Stir in enough flour to make a soft dough. Knead on a floured surface for 5 minutes or until smooth and elastic. Return to washed and dried bowl, grease top, cover with a damp towel and let rise in a warm place until doubled in bulk, about 1 hour.

2 Knead dough again briefly and, with floured hands, shape into a 48-inch rope. Place on a greased baking sheet and twist rope together once, 12 inches from the ends. Curve ends up into a pretzel shape and tuck under, pressing firmly. Brush dough with beaten egg. Let rise in a warm place until doubled in bulk, about 40 to 45 minutes.

3 Bake in a preheated 400°F oven for 40 to 50 minutes or until richly browned. Cool thoroughly on baking sheet before slicing.

*FRENCH POMPE À L'HUILE

MAKES ONE 10-INCH ROUND LOAF

INGREDIENTS
1 envelope active dry yeast
¼ cup lukewarm water
½ teaspoon salt
2 eggs, well beaten
¼ cup sugar
½ cup French olive oil
Grated rind of
1 small orange
2 cups unsifted
all-purpose flour
1 egg, well beaten
Whipped unsalted butter
(optional)

1 In a large bowl, combine yeast and water. Let stand for 5 minutes. Stir in salt, eggs, sugar, oil and orange rind, then flour. Knead dough on a floured surface for 5 to 6 minutes or until smooth and elastic. Return to washed and dried bowl, and grease top, cover with a damp towel and let rise in a warm place until doubled in bulk, about 1 hour.

2 Roll into a 10-inch round and place in a greased 10-inch layer cake pan, 2 inches deep. With a sharp knife, cut a cross ½ inch deep into top of bread. Let rise in a warm place until doubled in bulk, about 35 to 40 minutes.

3 Bake in a preheated 375°F oven for 25 to 30 minutes or until golden brown. Unmold right side up onto a rack. Cool thoroughly before cutting into wedges. If desired, serve spread with whipped unsalted butter.

*NORWEGIAN JULE KAGE

MAKES ONE 9-INCH ROUND LOAF

INGREDIENTS
1 envelope active dry yeast
½ cup lukewarm water
½ teaspoon salt
½ cup sugar
½ cup lukewarm milk
1 egg, well beaten
3 tablespoons vegetable shortening
3½ cups sifted all-purpose flour
1 teaspoon ground cardamom
½ cup raisins
½ cup chopped candied citron
1 egg, well beaten

1 In a large bowl, combine yeast and water. Let stand 5 minutes. Stir in salt, sugar, milk, 1 egg and shortening, then flour and cardamom. Beat until smooth and stir in raisins and citron. Knead dough on a floured surface for 5 to 6 minutes or until smooth and elastic. Return to washed and dried bowl, grease top, cover with a damp towel and let rise in a warm place until doubled in bulk, about 1 hour.

2 Knead again briefly and shape into a smooth ball. Place in a greased 9-inch springform pan and press dough flat. Brush with egg and let rise in a warm place until doubled in bulk, about 35 to 40 minutes.

3 Bake in a preheated 350°F oven for 35 to 40 minutes. Unmold right side up onto a rack. Cool thoroughly before cutting into thin slices.

VARIATION: *BOHEMIAN HOUSKA

MAKES 1 BRAIDED LOAF

INGREDIENTS
Sames as above, plus:
½ cup mixed candied fruits grated rind of 1 lemon
1 cup confectioners' sugar
2 tablespoons fresh lemon juice
1 teaspoon vanilla

1 Prepare Norwegian Jule Kage, omitting citron and adding ½ cup mixed candied fruits and grated rind of 1 lemon. After dough has risen, knead again; cut into 3 equal pieces. With floured hands, roll each piece into a 12-inch rope. Braid the ropes and pinch ends to seal. Place on greased baking sheet. Let rise in a warm place for 35 to 40 minutes or until doubled in bulk. Bake in a preheated 375°F for 35 to 40 minutes or until richly browned.

2 In a small bowl, mix 1 cup confectioners' sugar with 2 tablespoons fresh lemon juice and 1 teaspoon vanilla until smooth. Spoon evenly over hot bread. Cool thoroughly on baking sheet before slicing.

GREEK CHRISTOPSOMO

MAKES 1 LARGE ROUND LOAF

INGREDIENTS

1 envelope active dry yeast
¼ cup lukewarm water
¾ cup lukewarm milk
½ cup sugar
¼ cup melted butter
½ teaspoon salt
2 eggs, well beaten
  Grated rind of 1 orange
4 to 4½ cups unsifted
  all-purpose flour
1 egg, well beaten

1 In a large bowl, combine yeast and water. Let stand for 5 minutes. Stir in milk, sugar, butter, salt, 2 eggs and orange rind. Stir in enough flour to make a soft dough. Knead on a floured surface for 5 to 6 minutes or until smooth and elastic. Return to washed and dried bowl, grease top, cover with a damp towel and let rise in a warm place until doubled in bulk, about 1 hour.

2 Knead again briefly and cut off a piece of dough the size of a baseball. Set aside. Shape remaining dough into a smooth ball about 6 inches in diameter. Place on a greased baking sheet. Cut reserved dough into 2 pieces. Roll each piece into an 8-inch rope. With scissors, make a 2-inch lengthwise cut into the ends of each rope. Brush bread with egg. Place ropes in a cross on top of bread and curl ends outward. Brush with egg. Let rise in a warm place until doubled in bulk, about 1 hour. Brush with egg again.

3 Bake in a preheated 350°F oven for 30 to 35 minutes or until richly browned. Cool thoroughly on rack before cutting into thin wedges.

*HUNGARIAN POPPYSEED BREAD

MAKES ONE 9-INCH TUBE

1 In a small bowl, combine yeast, water and 1 tablespoon sugar. Let stand for 5 minutes.

2 In a large bowl, cream butter until fluffy. Beat in egg yolks, lemon rind, cream, sugar and yeast mixture. Add poppyseeds, almonds and flour and beat until well blended. Fold in egg whites. Pour mixture into a greased and floured 9-inch tube pan. Let rise in a warm place until doubled in bulk, about 1 hour.

INGREDIENTS

2 envelopes active dry yeast
¼ cup lukewarm water
1 tablespoon sugar
1 cup soft butter
8 egg yolks
    Grated rind of 1 lemon
½ cup lukewarm heavy cream
½ cup firmly packed light
    brown sugar
2 cups poppyseeds, ground in
    food processor
½ cup finely chopped
    toasted almonds
3 cups sifted all-purpose flour
5 egg whites, stiffly beaten
    Confectioners' sugar

3 Bake in a preheated 375°F oven for 35 to 40 minutes or until richly browned. Unmold upside down onto a rack to cool. Serve lightly dusted with confectioners' sugar.

*BELGIAN DARK BREAD

MAKES 2 LOAVES

INGREDIENTS
2 envelopes active dry yeast
¼ cup unsweetened
    cocoa powder
1 tablespoon sugar
2 teaspoons salt
1 tablespoon caraway seeds
⅓ cup molasses
2 tablespoons melted butter
2 cups lukewarm beer
3 cups unsifted rye flour
2 cups raisins
3 to 3½ cups unsifted
    all-purpose flour

1 In a large bowl, mix yeast, cocoa, sugar, salt and caraway seeds. Beat in molasses, butter and beer, then rye flour and raisins. Beat in enough all-purpose flour to make a soft dough. Knead dough on a floured surface for 5 to 6 minutes or until smooth and elastic. Return to washed and dried bowl, grease top, cover with a damp towel and let rise in a warm place until doubled in bulk, about 1 hour.

2 Punch dough down and cut in half. Roll each half into an 8- x 15-inch rectangle. Roll up tightly like a jelly roll, starting at a long side. Place rolls seam side down on greased baking sheet. Let rise in a warm place until doubled in bulk, about 35 to 40 minutes. With a sharp knife, cut 3 diagonal slashes into top of each loaf.

3 Bake in a preheated 400°F oven for 30 to 35 minutes or until loaves sound hollow when thumped. Cool thoroughly on racks before slicing.

Opposite: Hungarian Poppyseed Bread, page 253

FAN TAN ROLLS

MAKES 3 DOZEN

INGREDIENTS
2 envelopes active dry yeast
½ teaspoon salt
¼ cup lukewarm water
1 cup lukewarm milk
¼ cup sugar
2 eggs, well beaten
½ cup soft vegetable shortening
5 to 6 cups unsifted
    all-purpose flour
¼ cup melted butter

1 In a large bowl, dissolve yeast and salt in water. Stir in milk, sugar, eggs and shortening. Stir in enough flour to make a stiff dough. Turn dough out on a floured surface and knead for 5 minutes or until smooth and elastic. Return to washed and dried bowl. Grease top, cover and let stand in a warm place until doubled in bulk, about 1 hour.

2 Punch dough down and roll out on a floured surface into a sheet ¼ inch thick. Brush with melted butter. Cut dough into 1-inch-wide strips; cut strips into 1½-inch pieces. Place 7 strips into each of 3 dozen greased muffin cups. Let rise in a warm place until doubled in bulk, about 35 to 40 minutes. Bake in a preheated 350°F oven for 20 to 25 minutes or until golden brown. Serve warm.

3 For crescent rolls, cut dough into 3 pieces. Roll each piece into a 10-inch round. Cut each round into 8 wedges. Brush with melted butter. Roll up wedges, starting at the edge and rolling toward the point. Let rise and bake as above. Makes 32.

4 For cloverleaf rolls, cut dough into 108 pieces. Shape each piece into a smooth ball. Place 3 balls into each muffin cup. Brush with melted butter. Let rise and bake as above. Makes 3 dozen.

MEXICAN SWEET ROLLS

MAKES 30

INGREDIENTS

DOUGH
2 envelopes active dry yeast
½ cup lukewarm water
½ cup lukewarm milk
½ cup sugar
½ teaspoon salt
2 eggs, well beaten
½ cup soft butter
Grated rind of 1 lemon
4½ to 5 cups unsifted
all-purpose flour

FILLING
1 cup sugar
1 cup sifted all-purpose flour
1 teaspoon ground cinnamon
1 cup finely chopped walnuts
½ cup melted butter
2 egg whites, beaten
until frothy

1 In a large bowl, mix yeast and water. Let stand for 5 minutes. Stir in milk, sugar, eggs, ½ cup butter and lemon rind. Stir in enough flour to make a soft dough. Knead on a floured surface until dough is smooth and elastic, about 10 minutes. Return to washed and dried bowl, grease top, cover with a damp towel and let rise in a warm place until doubled in bulk, about 1 hour.

2 For filling, mix sugar, flour, cinnamon, walnuts and butter in a bowl. Fold in egg whites.

3 Punch dough down and cut into 30 pieces. Shape each piece into a smooth ball and arrange on greased baking sheets about 3 inches apart. With floured fingers, flatten to ½-inch thickness. Make an indentation in the center of each round and spoon in some of the filling. Let rise in a warm place until doubled in bulk, about 30 to 35 minutes.

4 Bake in a preheated 375°F oven for 15 to 20 minutes or until golden brown. Cool on racks before serving.

*DUTCH CHEESE LOAF

MAKES ONE 8-INCH ROUND LOAF

INGREDIENTS

1 cup water
¼ cup yellow cornmeal
1 teaspoon salt
¼ cup molasses
1 tablespoon vegetable
   shortening
1 envelope active dry yeast
¼ cup lukewarm water
2 teaspoons caraway seeds
2 to 2½ cups unsifted
   all-purpose flour
8 ounces Edam or
   Gouda cheese,
    cut into ½-inch cubes
Additional cornmeal

1 In a saucepan, combine 1 cup water, ¼ cup cornmeal and salt and stir over medium heat until thick. Remove from heat and stir in molasses and shortening. Cool to lukewarm.

2 In a small bowl, combine yeast and lukewarm water. Let stand for 5 minutes. Stir yeast mixture into lukewarm cornmeal mixture. Beat in caraway seeds and enough flour to make a soft dough. Knead on a floured surface for 5 to 6 minutes or until smooth and elastic. Return to washed and dried bowl, grease top, cover and let rise in a warm place until doubled in bulk, about 1 hour.

3 Flatten dough and sprinkle with cheese. Knead a few times and shape into a ball. Line an 8-inch pie pan with a 12-inch square of foil. Grease foil and sprinkle with cornmeal. Place dough on foil and let rise in a warm place until doubled in bulk, about 35 to 40 minutes.

4 Bake in a preheated 350°F oven for 45 to 50 minutes or until richly browned. Cool thoroughly on rack before cutting into thin wedges.

*Danish No-Knead Christmas Bread

1 In a large bowl, combine yeast and water. Let stand for 5 minutes. Stir in butter, salt, milk and egg. Add flour and beat until mixture is smooth and shiny. Stir in raisins and candied fruits. Let dough stand for 15 minutes, then pour into a greased 9- x 5- x 3-inch loaf pan. Let rise in a warm place until doubled in bulk, about 1 hour.

MAKES ONE 9- X 5-INCH LOAF

INGREDIENTS
1 envelope active dry yeast
¼ cup lukewarm water
¼ cup soft butter
1 teaspoon salt
¾ cup lukewarm milk
1 egg, well beaten
3¼ cups sifted all-purpose flour
1 cup golden raisins
1 cup chopped mixed
   candied fruits

2 Bake in a preheated 350°F oven for 40 to 50 minutes or until richly browned. Unmold and place right side up on rack. Cool thoroughly before slicing.

*Irish Soda Bread

1 In a large bowl, mix flour, salt, sugar, baking soda and caraway seeds. Add buttermilk and raisins and stir only until flour is moistened. Knead dough a few times on a floured surface into a smooth ball. Place on a greased baking sheet. With a sharp knife, cut a cross ½ inch deep on top of loaf.

MAKES 1 ROUND LOAF

INGREDIENTS
4 cups sifted all-purpose flour
1 teaspoon salt
1 tablespoon sugar
1 teaspoon baking soda
1 tablespoon caraway seeds
1½ cups buttermilk
1 cup raisins

2 Bake in a preheated 350°F oven for 40 to 45 minutes or until richly browned. Cool thoroughly on rack before slicing.

*ENGLISH HONEY BREAD

MAKES TWO 8½- X 4½-INCH LOAVES

INGREDIENTS

6 eggs
1 cup sugar
1 cup honey
2 tablespoons corn oil
2 tablespoons
   instant coffee powder
3½ cups sifted all-purpose flour
1½ teaspoons baking powder
1 teaspoon baking soda
1 teaspoon ground cinnamon
1 teaspoon ground allspice
½ teaspoon ground cloves
   Grated rind of 2 lemons
¾ cup raisins
½ cup chopped almonds
2 tablespoons brandy

1 In a large bowl, beat eggs until fluffy. Gradually beat in sugar. Stir in honey, oil and coffee, then stir in flour, baking powder, baking soda, spices and lemon rind. Beat until smooth. Fold in raisins, almonds and brandy.

2 Line 2 greased 8½- x 4½- x 2½-inch loaf pans with brown paper; grease paper. Divide dough between pans.

3 Bake in a preheated 325°F oven for 1 to 1¼ hours or until richly browned and firm to the touch. Cool in pan 5 minutes, then unmold and place right side up on rack. Cool thoroughly before slicing.

*Italian Almond Anise Loaf

1 Place almonds in a skillet and stir over medium heat until golden brown. Cool.

2 In a large bowl, cream butter until fluffy. Gradually beat in sugar. Beat in eggs one at a time, beating well after each addition. Add flour, baking powder, salt, anise seed and almonds and stir only until

MAKES ONE 9- X 5-INCH LOAF

INGREDIENTS
*1 cup chopped blanched
   almonds
½ cup soft butter
1 cup sugar
5 eggs
2¼ cups unsifted
   all-purpose flour
2 teaspoons baking powder
½ teaspoon salt
1 tablespoon anise seed*

blended. Pour mixture into a greased 9- x 5- x 3-inch loaf pan.

3 Bake in a preheated 350°F oven for 50 to 60 minutes or until golden brown. Unmold and place on a rack right side up. Cool thoroughly before cutting into thin slices.

*Midwest Carrot Bread

1 In a large bowl, mix carrots, brown sugar, oil, baking soda and water. Let stand until cool. Stir in eggs. Add flours and baking powder and beat until smooth. Fold in nuts. Pour mixture into a greased 9- x 5- x 3-inch loaf pan.

MAKES ONE 9- X 5-INCH LOAF

INGREDIENTS
*1½ cups shredded raw carrots
1½ cups firmly packed light
   brown sugar
2 tablespoons corn oil
1½ teaspoons baking soda
1½ cups boiling water
3 eggs, well beaten
2 cups unsifted
   all-purpose flour
1¾ cups unsifted
   whole wheat flour
4 teaspoons baking powder
1½ cups chopped walnuts*

2 Bake in a preheated 350°F oven for 1¼ hours or until cake tester inserted in center comes out clean. Unmold and place right side up on rack. Cool thoroughly before slicing.

*PENNSYLVANIA DUTCH APPLE BREAD

MAKES ONE 9- X 5-INCH LOAF

INGREDIENTS

½ cup soft butter
⅔ cup sugar
2 eggs
1½ cups peeled, cored and
    shredded cooking apples
    (Granny Smith, greening
    or Golden Delicious)
1 cup chopped nuts
2 cups sifted all-purpose flour
1 teaspoon baking powder
½ teaspoon baking soda
½ teaspoon salt
1 teaspoon ground mace
1 teaspoon ground nutmeg

1 In a large bowl, cream butter and sugar until fluffy. Stir in eggs one at a time, then stir in apples and nuts. Add remaining ingredients and beat until well blended. Pour mixture into a greased 9- x 5- x 3-inch loaf pan.

2 Bake in a preheated 350°F oven for 50 to 60 minutes or until a cake tester inserted in center comes out clean. Unmold and place right side up on rack. Cool thoroughly before cutting into thick slices.

*INDIAN SQUASH NUT BREAD

MAKES TWO 9- X 5-INCH LOAVES

INGREDIENTS
½ cup butter
½ cup vegetable shortening
2½ cups sugar
4 eggs
2 cups mashed cooked butter-
    nut squash or pumpkin
⅔ cup milk
3½ cups sifted all-purpose flour
1 teaspoon salt
2 teaspoons baking soda
2 teaspoons ground
    cinnamon
2 teaspoons ground nutmeg
½ teaspoon ground cloves
1 cup chopped pecans

1 In a large bowl, cream butter and shortening until fluffy. Gradually blend in sugar. Add eggs one at a time, beating well after each addition. Stir in pumpkin and milk.

2 Mix flour, salt, baking soda and spices. Add flour mixture to batter, and blend well. Fold in pecans. Pour mixture into 2 greased 9- x 5- x 3-inch loaf pans.

3 Bake in a preheated 375°F oven for 1 hour or until a cake tester inserted in center comes out clean. Unmold and place right side up on rack. Cool thoroughly before slicing.

Page following: Assorted Holiday Desserts

TEX-MEX SPOONBREAD

1 In a large bowl, mix corn, cornmeal, eggs, salt, baking soda, milk and lard. Fold in chilies, pimento and half of the cheese.

2 Spread melted butter in a 1½-quart casserole. Pour in batter. Sprinkle with remaining cheese.

MAKES ONE 1½-QUART CASSEROLE

INGREDIENTS

- 1 cup cream-style corn
- 1 cup yellow cornmeal
- 2 eggs, well beaten
- 1 teaspoon salt
- ½ teaspoon baking soda
- ¾ cup milk
- ⅓ cup melted leaf lard
- 1 can (4 ounces) sweet green chilies, drained and diced
- 1 jar (4 ounces) pimento, drained and diced
- 1 cup (4 ounces) shredded sharp cheddar cheese
- 2 tablespoons melted butter

3 Bake in a preheated 400°F oven for 40 minutes or until golden brown. Serve hot, spooned from the casserole.

*NEW ENGLAND OVEN-BAKED BROWN BREAD

1 In a large bowl, mix flours, cornmeal, baking soda and salt. Stir in buttermilk, molasses and raisins. Pour mixture into a greased 9- x 5- x 3-inch loaf pan.

MAKES ONE 9- X 5-INCH LOAF

INGREDIENTS

- 1½ cups unsifted all-purpose flour
- 1½ cups unsifted rye flour
- 1 cup yellow cornmeal
- 1 teaspoon baking soda
- 1 teaspoon salt
- 2 cups buttermilk
- ½ cup molasses
- 1 cup raisins

2 Bake in a preheated 375°F for 50 minutes to 1 hour or until cake tester inserted in center comes out clean. Loosen edges, unmold and place right side up on a rack. Serve warm or cold.

SWEETMEATS

from Around the World
Pies and Ice Cream,
Cakes, Cookies, Candy

"*Visions of sugarplums*" *are the wonderful indulgences
of the season. Just for a few days, diets are forgotten,
soon to be resumed with New Year's resolutions. Rich cakes, buttery cookies
and candies bursting with fruits and nuts are the frills that make the holidays so sinful.
Pretty to look at, with interesting shapes and colors, they add excitement and flavor to
any meal. Pack an assortment in a pretty box or basket when you go visiting, and you
can be sure of a hearty welcome. All the starred (*) recipes are suitable for shipping.*

CHRISTMAS PIES AND "SNOW"

*The quintessential all-American combination—pie and ice cream—is always a favorite,
even at the holiday season. Today ice-cream machines ease the preparation of
homemade ice cream so that you can enjoy that incomparable, old-fashioned flavor.
Prepare ice cream a day or two ahead of time and store in the freezer until
needed. When nostalgia gets the best of us, we drag out the old crank ice cream
machine. Cracked ice and coarse salt are mixed and packed around the
cream can. As my mother used to say, "Crank until you don't care if you
ever eat ice cream, and then it's done!" Carefully wipe off the container
(who wants salty ice cream?) and remove the dasher. In my day, the
container was recapped and stashed in the snow. The ice cream
was incredibly creamy and never too hard—just what a
warm slice of pie calls for!*

BASIC PIE CRUST

1 In a large bowl, mix flour and salt. Cut in shortening with 2 knives or a pastry blender until particles resemble small peas.

MAKES ENOUGH PASTRY FOR ONE 10-INCH DOUBLE-CRUST PIE

INGREDIENTS
*3 cups unsifted
    all-purpose flour
½ teaspoon salt
1 cup vegetable shortening
6 to 8 tablespoons (about)
    ice water*

2 Gradually stir in water with a fork until flour is moistened and large clumps are formed. Knead clumps together a few times until dough forms a smooth ball. Wrap in foil and chill for 30 minutes. Use as directed in recipe.

MINCEMEAT CRANBERRY PIE

1 Prepare pie crust and cut dough in half. Roll out one half on a floured surface to form a round large enough to line the bottom and sides of an ungreased 10-inch pie pan. Fit pastry into pan.

2 In a large bowl, mix mince-meat and remaining ingredients and spread evenly into crust.

MAKES ONE 10-INCH PIE

INGREDIENTS
*1 recipe Basic Pie Crust
    (see above)
3 cups prepared mincemeat
1 cup chopped walnuts
1 jar (14 ounces) cranberry-
    orange relish or 1¾ cups
    homemade cranberry-
    orange relish
1 tablespoon rum*

3 Roll out remaining dough into a circle large enough to cover top of pie. Crimp edges with the tines of a fork and trim neatly. Prick top a few times.

4 Bake in a preheated 400°F oven for 35 to 40 minutes or until richly browned. Cool thoroughly on a rack before cutting into wedges.

APPLE DATE STREUSEL PIE

MAKES ONE 10-INCH PIE

INGREDIENTS
½ *recipe Basic Pie Crust*
(page 268)

FILLING
6 *cups peeled, cored and diced*
   apples (greening, Granny
   Smith or Golden Delicious)
1 *cup chopped pitted dates*
¾ *cup sugar*
¼ *cup molasses*
   Grated rind of 1 orange
2 *teaspoons pumpkin pie spice*

STREUSEL
½ *cup unsifted*
   all-purpose flour
½ *cup sugar*
¼ *cup butter or margarine*
½ *cup chopped pecans*

1 Prepare pie crust and roll out on a floured surface to form a round large enough to line the bottom and sides of an ungreased 10-inch pie pan. Fit pastry into pan. Fold over edges and flute.

2 In a large bowl, mix filling ingredients and place into crust.

3 In a small bowl, mix streusel ingredients with the fingers until crumbly. Sprinkle crumbs evenly over top of filling.

4 Bake in a preheated 425°F oven for 50 to 60 minutes or until apples are easily pierced. Serve warm or cold. Garnish with pitted dates and apple slices.

CHEESE-CRUSTED DEEP-DISH APPLE CRANBERRY PIE

1 Prepare pie crust, mixing cheese with flour, salt and shortening before adding water. Wrap and chill.

2 Mix all filling ingredients in a large bowl and pour into a greased 2-quart shallow casserole.

MAKES ONE 2-QUART CASSEROLE

INGREDIENTS
½ recipe Basic Pie Crust (page 268)
1 cup (4 ounces) grated sharp cheddar cheese

FILLING
8 cups peeled, cored and sliced apples (greening, Granny Smith or Golden Delicious)
1 cup cranberries
1 cup sugar
1 teaspoon ground cinnamon
½ teaspoon ground nutmeg
¼ cup unsifted all-purpose flour
Old-fashioned Vanilla Ice Cream (page 290)

3 Roll out pie crust on a floured surface to form a piece large enough to cover the top of the casserole. Fold edges over casserole to seal and cut a few slashes into crust to allow steam to escape.

4 Bake in a preheated 425°F oven for 50 minutes or until apples are easily pierced. Serve warm spooned into bowls, topped with ice cream.

Opposite: Austrian Linzer Torte, page 310; Eggnog Chiffon Pie, page 272; Lemon-Topped Cheesecake Pie, page 275

EGGNOG CHIFFON PIE

MAKES ONE 9-INCH PIE

INGREDIENTS

CRUST
1½ cups gingersnap cookie
    crumbs
6 tablespoons butter or
    margarine

FILLING
2 envelopes unflavored gelatin
⅓ cup water
2½ cups prepared eggnog
1 cup (½ pint)
    heavy cream, whipped
Freshly grated nutmeg
Additional gingersnap
    crumbs, candied cherries
    and candied papaya

1 In a small bowl, mix crumbs and butter with fingers until well blended. Press mixture firmly and evenly into the bottom and side of an ungreased 9-inch pie pan. Chill.

2 For filling, in a small saucepan, soften gelatin in water for several minutes. Stir over low heat until gelatin is dissolved.

3 In a bowl, mix gelatin and eggnog. Chill just until mixture becomes syrupy. Fold in whipped cream and spoon into crust. Sprinkle lightly with nutmeg. Chill until firm.

4 When ready to serve, spoon a wreath of crumbs on top of pie. Decorate with cherries and a bow cut from thin slices of candied papaya.

BROWNIE PIE WITH COCOA CREAM

MAKES ONE 9-INCH PIE

INGREDIENTS
½ recipe Basic Pie Crust
(page 268)

FILLING
3 ounces unsweetened
    chocolate
½ cup butter
1 cup sugar
3 eggs, well beaten
1 teaspoon vanilla
¾ cup unsifted
    all-purpose flour
½ cup chopped pecans

COCOA CREAM
1 cup (½ pint) heavy cream
⅓ cup sugar
¼ cup unsweetened
    cocoa powder

1 Prepare pie crust and roll out on a floured surface to form a round large enough to cover the bottom and sides of an ungreased 9-inch pie pan. Fit pastry into pan. Fold over edges and flute.

2 For filling, melt chocolate with butter in a saucepan over very low heat. Cool, then stir in sugar, eggs and vanilla. Gradually stir in flour. Fold in pecans. Pour mixture into crust.

3 Bake in a preheated 325°F oven for 30 to 35 minutes or until puffed and firm. Cool on a rack.

4 For cocoa cream, mix cream, sugar and cocoa in a bowl until blended. Cover and chill until pie is ready to serve. Whip cream mixture until thick. To serve, cut pie into wedges and top with cocoa cream.

LEMON-TOPPED CHEESECAKE PIE

1 Prepare pie crust and roll out on a floured surface to form a round large enough to cover the bottom and sides of an ungreased 9-inch pie pan. Fit pastry into pan.

2 For filling, beat cream cheese and sugar in a bowl with an electric mixer until smooth and creamy. Beat in eggs, milk and extracts. Pour mixture into crust.

MAKES ONE 9-INCH PIE

INGREDIENTS
½ recipe Basic Pie Crust
   (page 268)

FILLING
1 package (8 ounces) cream
   cheese, at room temperature
½ cup sugar
2 eggs, well beaten
½ cup milk
½ teaspoon each almond
   and vanilla extract

TOPPING
1 jar lemon curd
   (11¼ ounces)
Julienne strips of lemon rind
   (optional garnish)

3 Bake in a preheated 425°F oven for 10 minutes, then lower heat to 350°F and bake another 20 to 25 minutes or until filling is firm to the touch. Cool, then chill.

4 For topping, place lemon curd in a bowl and stir until creamy. Using a spatula, carefully spread lemon curd over top of pie. If desired, decorate with strips of lemon rind.

*Opposite: Mincemeat Cranberry Pie, page 268;
Bourbon Cider Pie, page 279*

ORANGE RAISIN PEANUT PIE

MAKES ONE 10-INCH PIE

INGREDIENTS
½ recipe Basic Pie Crust
  (page 268)

FILLING
4 eggs, well beaten
¼ teaspoon salt
2 cups dark corn syrup
3 tablespoons melted butter
1 cup coarsely
  chopped peanuts
1 cup raisins
Grated rind of 1 orange

1 Prepare pie crust and roll out on a floured surface to form a round large enough to line the bottom and sides of an ungreased 10-inch pie pan. Fit pastry into pan.

2 For filling, beat eggs with salt and corn syrup in a bowl. Stir in butter, peanuts, raisins and orange rind. Pour mixture into crust.

3 Bake in a preheated 350°F oven for 45 to 50 minutes or until filling is puffed and brown. Cool thoroughly on a rack before cutting into wedges.

Opposite: Open-Face Pear Pie, page 286;
Brownie Pie with Cocoa Cream, page 273

BOURBON CIDER PIE

MAKES ONE 9-INCH PIE

INGREDIENTS

CRUST
*1 cup finely ground pecans
  (grind in food processor)
3 tablespoons sugar*

FILLING
*3 envelopes unflavored gelatin
¾ cup sugar
2 cups apple cider
3 egg yolks
½ cup bourbon
3 egg whites
¼ cup sugar
1 cup (½ pint)
  heavy cream, whipped
Pecan halves
  (optional garnish)*

1 In a bowl, mix pecans and sugar for crust. Press mixture firmly and evenly into a greased 9-inch pie pan. Bake in a preheated 400°F oven for 6 to 8 minutes or until brown. Cool.

2 For filling, mix gelatin, sugar and 1 cup of the cider in a saucepan and stir over low heat until gelatin is dissolved. Beat in egg yolks, remaining cider and bourbon. Chill just until mixture is syrupy.

3 Beat egg whites until stiff. Beat in sugar 1 tablespoon at a time until stiff and glossy. Fold egg whites into bourbon mixture. Fold in whipped cream and spoon into crust.

4 Chill until firm. If desired, garnish pie with pecan halves and curls of candied lemon peel.

Opposite: English Plum Pudding with Hard Sauce, page 312

COCONUT CUSTARD FROZEN PUMPKIN PIE

MAKES ONE 9-INCH PIE

INGREDIENTS

CRUST
2 cups flaked coconut
¼ cup butter or margarine

FILLING
1 quart butter pecan
    ice cream
1 cup canned pumpkin
1 teaspoon ground cinnamon
½ teaspoon ground nutmeg
½ teaspoon ground ginger
¼ cup brandy
    Toasted sliced almonds
    (optional garnish)

1 In a bowl, mix coconut and butter for crust. Press mixture firmly and evenly into a greased 9-inch pie pan. Bake in a pre-heated 300°F oven for 15 to 20 minutes or until golden brown. Cool.

2 For filling, cut ice cream into large chunks and place in a large chilled bowl. Add remaining ingredients and beat with an electric mixer until just blended. Spread evenly in crust and freeze until hard.

3 Wrap frozen pie in foil. If desired, garnish top with toasted sliced almonds.

SWEET POTATO PIE
WITH CARAMEL NUT TOPPING

1 Prepare pie crust and roll out on a floured surface to form a round large enough to line the bottom and sides of an ungreased 9-inch pie pan. Fit pastry into pan. Fold over edges and flute.

2 For filling, mix sweet potatoes, apple butter, light brown sugar and spices in a bowl. Beat eggs and half-and-half into potato mixture. Pour mixture into crust.

MAKES ONE 9-INCH PIE

INGREDIENTS
½ recipe Basic Pie Crust
(page 268)

FILLING
1 cup mashed cooked
*   sweet potatoes*
1 cup apple butter
½ cup firmly packed light
*   brown sugar*
1 teaspoon ground cinnamon
1 teaspoon ground nutmeg
¼ teaspoon ground ginger
3 eggs, well beaten
1 cup half-and-half

TOPPING
1 cup (½ pint) heavy cream
6 tablespoons firmly packed
*   dark brown sugar*
1 teaspoon vanilla
⅓ cup finely chopped
*   toasted walnuts*

3 Bake in a preheated 425°F oven for 15 minutes, then lower heat to 375°F and bake another 20 to 25 minutes or until firm when lightly touched. Cool thoroughly before cutting into wedges.

4 For topping, mix cream with dark brown sugar and vanilla in a bowl. Chill at least 1 hour, then whip until thick. Fold in nuts. Spoon over wedges of pie.

APRICOT BANANA PIE

1 Prepare pie crust and cut in half. Roll out one half on a floured surface to form a round large enough to cover the bottom and sides of a greased 12-inch pizza pan. Fit pastry into pan.

2 For filling, cover pastry with apricot halves and bananas. In a saucepan, mix cornstarch, sugar, reserved apricot liquid, and lemon juice. Stir over medium heat until mixture bubbles and thickens. Stir in butter. Cool and pour over fruit in pizza pan.

3 Roll out remaining pastry on a floured surface to form a round large enough to cover the pan. Place on top of fruit and flute edges together.

4 Bake in a preheated 400°F oven for 35 to 40 minutes or until golden brown.

MAKES ONE 12-INCH PIZZA PAN

INGREDIENTS
1 recipe Basic Pie Crust
(page 268)

FILLING
1 can (1 pound, 13 ounces)
apricot halves, drained,
liquid reserved
4 bananas, cut into
½-inch-thick slices
3 tablespoons cornstarch
½ cup sugar
2 tablespoons
fresh lemon juice
3 tablespoons butter

DOUBLE ORANGE SAUCE
3 tablespoons cornstarch
⅓ cup sugar
1 can (12 ounces) frozen
orange juice concentrate,
undiluted
1 cup orange liqueur

5 For sauce, mix cornstarch and sugar in a saucepan. Gradually stir in orange juice concentrate. Stir over medium heat until sauce bubbles and thickens. Remove from heat and cool to lukewarm. Stir in orange liqueur. Cool pie and serve warm, cut into wedges and topped with sauce.

6 For a European version of this pie, prepare Basic Pie Crust using 3 cups flour. Roll out half the pastry into a rectangle large enough to line the bottom and sides of a greased 10- x 15- x 1-inch jelly roll pan. Fill as above. Roll out remaining pastry into a rectangle large enough to cover pan with an overhang of 1 inch all around. Fold edges together and crimp. Place pan on a baking sheet to catch drips. Prick top with a fork. Brush with beaten egg. Bake at 400°F for 40 to 45 minutes. Cool in pan. Cut into squares and serve dusted with confectioners' sugar. Omit sauce.

Opposite: Bourbon Cider Pie, page 279;
Cheese-Crusted Apple Cranberry Pie, page 270

PINEAPPLE CHESS PIE

MAKES ONE 9-INCH PIE

INGREDIENTS
½ *recipe Basic Pie Crust*
(page 268)

FILLING
½ *cup butter,*
at room temperature
1 *cup sugar*
2 *teaspoons vanilla*
¼ *teaspoon salt*
3 *eggs*
½ *cup sour cream*
1 *can (1 pound, 4 ounces)*
pineapple chunks, drained
1 *tablespoon all-purpose flour*
Sweetened whipped cream
(garnish)

1 Prepare pie crust and roll out on a floured surface to form a round large enough to cover the bottom and sides of an ungreased 9-inch pie pan. Fit pastry into pan; fold over edges and flute.

2 For filling, cream butter, sugar, vanilla and salt in a bowl until fluffy. Beat in eggs one at a time, beating well after each addition. Beat in sour cream.

3 In another bowl, mix 1½ cups of the pineapple chunks with flour; reserve remaining pineapple. Fold pineapple into pie filling. Pour filling into crust.

4 Bake in a preheated 325°F oven for 50 to 60 minutes or until filling is puffed and brown.

5 Cool on a rack and serve garnished with rosettes of sweetened whipped cream topped with remaining pineapple chunks.

Opposite: Assorted Holiday Cakes

OPEN-FACE PEAR PIE

MAKES ONE 10-INCH PIE

INGREDIENTS

EGG PASTRY
2 cups unsifted
    all-purpose flour
Grated rind of 1 lemon
½ teaspoon salt
2 tablespoons sugar
½ cup cold butter
1 egg, well beaten
3 to 4 tablespoons
    fresh lemon juice

FILLING
4 ripe Bartlett pears, peeled,
    halved and cored
2 tablespoons
    fresh lemon juice
1 cup sugar
¼ cup all-purpose flour
3 eggs, well beaten
2 cups (1 pint) sour cream
1½ teaspoons anise seed
Whipped cream
    (optional garnish)

1 For pastry, mix flour, lemon rind, salt and sugar in a bowl. Cut in butter until particles resemble coarse cornmeal. Stir in egg and enough lemon juice to make dough clean the bowl. Knead a few times on a floured surface to form a smooth ball. Wrap and chill for 1 hour.

2 Roll out dough between sheets of waxed paper into a 12-inch round. Peel off one piece of waxed paper. Place dough, waxed paper side up, in an ungreased 10-inch pie pan and remove second piece of paper. Flute edge of pastry.

3 For filling, place pear halves into crust, rounded side up and with tops of pears pointing toward center. Sprinkle with lemon juice. In a bowl, combine remaining ingredients and beat until well blended. Pour mixture evenly over pears.

4 Bake in a preheated 350°F oven for 45 to 50 minutes or until filling is puffed and brown. Cool thoroughly before cutting into wedges. If desired, garnish with rosettes of whipped cream sprinkled lightly with anise seed. If desired, place an unpeeled and cored pear half in center of pie.

RAISIN PIE

MAKES ONE 10-INCH PIE

INGREDIENTS
1 recipe Basic Pie Crust
  (page 268)
Grated rind of 1 orange

FILLING
4 cups raisins
¾ cup sugar
2 cups (1 pint) half-and-half
3 tablespoons
  fresh lemon juice
¼ cup Kirsch

1 Prepare pie crust, adding orange rind to flour before mixing in salt. Roll out half the dough on a floured surface to form a round large enough to cover the bottom and sides of an ungreased 10-inch pie pan. Fit pastry into pan.

2 For filling, grind raisins in food processor and transfer to a large saucepan. Add remaining ingredients and simmer until thickened, about 10 to 15 minutes. Cool to lukewarm, then stir in Kirsch. Spread filling evenly in crust.

3 Roll out remaining pastry to form a round large enough to cover top of pie. Flute edges together.

4 Bake in a preheated 425°F oven for 30 to 35 minutes or until golden brown. Cool thoroughly before cutting into wedges.

PRUNE WHIP PIE

MAKES ONE 9-INCH PIE

INGREDIENTS

CRUST
2 cups graham cracker
   crumbs
⅓ cup sugar
⅓ cup butter or margarine

FILLING
1½ cups prune butter (lekvar)
1 cup finely chopped
   pitted prunes
½ cup chopped walnuts
   Grated rind of 1 orange
2 cups (1 pint)
   heavy cream, whipped
   Slivered orange rind
   (optional garnish)

1 For crust, mix crumbs, sugar and butter in a bowl until well blended. Press mixture firmly and evenly into the bottom and sides of an ungreased 9-inch pie pan. Chill.

2 For filling, mix prune butter, prunes, walnuts and orange rind in a bowl until well blended. Fold in whipped cream. Pile mixture into crust.

3 Chill for several hours. If desired, garnish with slivers of orange rind.

Opposite: Austrian Linzer Torte, page 310

FREEZING ICE CREAM

*T*here are three ways to freeze ice cream—in an ice cube tray, in a hand-cranked or electric machine with ice and salt, or in a modern ice cream maker. If you are making your ice cream in an ice cube tray, freeze it until three-quarters frozen. Scrape into a chilled bowl and beat with an electric mixer until fluffy. Replace in freezer and freeze until hard. Cover tightly when frozen.

If you are using an ice-and-salt machine, use 6 parts cracked ice to 1 part coarse salt. Fill the container only half full, as the ice cream will almost double in volume when churned. If fruits or nuts are to be added, churn for

10 minutes. Wipe off container, open and add fruits or nuts. Reclose and churn again until handle is hard to turn. Remove container, wipe, open lid and remove dasher. Replace lid and place in freezer until ready to serve.

If you are using an electric ice cream maker that does not require ice and salt, follow the manufacturer's directions to get the best results. These "Use and Care" booklets are written by experts to get the best performance from a machine. After the ice cream is made by this kind of a machine, it can be eaten as is or placed into a freezer to harden for future service.

OLD-FASHIONED VANILLA ICE CREAM

1 In a blender, beat eggs well, then beat with sugar.

2 Heat milk with vanilla beans and seeds to boiling. Strain milk; while hot, add to eggs with blender running. Pour into a bowl and chill. Stir in heavy cream. Freeze as desired (see "Freezing Ice Cream," page 290).

MAKES ABOUT 2 QUARTS

INGREDIENTS

2 *eggs*
¾ *cup sugar*
2 *cups milk*
2 *vanilla beans, halved
   lengthwise, seeds scraped*
3 *cups (1½ pints)
   heavy cream*

Variations:

CANDY CANE ICE CREAM
When vanilla ice cream is frozen, fold in 1 cup finely crushed candy canes. Keep in freezer until ready to serve.

HOT PUDDING SUNDAE
Scoop vanilla ice cream into serving dishes. Prepare a rich chocolate pudding. When it is hot and thickened, spoon it over the cold ice cream and sprinkle with chopped salted peanuts.

Opposite: Assorted Holiday Desserts

DOUBLE CHOCOLATE ICE CREAM

1 In a saucepan, combine sugar, flour, milk and coffee. Stir over medium heat until mixture thickens slightly.

2 Beat eggs in a large bowl until foamy. Gradually beat in hot milk mixture, then melted chocolate; cool. Stir in heavy cream and vanilla. Freeze as desired (see "Freezing Ice Cream," page 290).

MAKES ABOUT 2 QUARTS

INGREDIENTS

¾ *cup sugar*
2 *teaspoons all-purpose flour*
1 *cup milk*
2 *tablespoons instant coffee*
2 *eggs*
3 *squares (3 ounces) unsweetened chocolate, melted*
4 *cups (2 pints) heavy cream*
2 *teaspoons vanilla*
1 *package (6 ounces) chocolate mini-chips*
1 *cup coarsely broken chocolate cookies*

3 When ice cream is half-frozen, fold in mini-chips and cookies. Freeze until hard; store in freezer until ready to serve.

Variation:
ROCKY ROAD ICE CREAM
Omit chocolate cookies. Add 1 cup miniature marshmallows and ½ cup chopped toasted almonds to half-frozen ice cream.

GINGERBREAD ICE CREAM

MAKES ABOUT 2½ QUARTS

1 In a blender, combine brown sugar, molasses, coffee, eggs and half-and-half and blend until sugar is dissolved. Stir mixture into heavy cream. Freeze as desired (see "Freezing Ice Cream," page 290).

2 When ice cream is half-frozen, stir in ginger. Freeze until hard; store in freezer until ready to serve.

INGREDIENTS
1½ cups firmly packed
    dark brown sugar
½ cup molasses
½ cup cold strong coffee
2 eggs
2 cups (1 pint) half-and-half
6 cups (1½ quarts)
    heavy cream
⅓ cup minced
    crystallized ginger
Hot applesauce
(optional topping)

3 If desired, top each serving with hot applesauce.

PUMPKIN PIE ICE CREAM

MAKES ABOUT 2 QUARTS

INGREDIENTS

4 egg yolks
2 cups milk
1 can (1 pound)
  pumpkin pie filling
3 cups (1½ pints)
  heavy cream
1 tablespoon rum flavoring
½ cup dried currants
Warm maple syrup or
  heated mincemeat
  (optional topping)

1 In the top of a double boiler set over simmering water, beat egg yolks and milk until well blended. Stir until mixture thickens slightly and coats a spoon.

2 In a large bowl, mix pie filling and heavy cream. Gradually beat in hot milk and rum flavoring. Chill several hours. Freeze as desired (see "Freezing Ice Cream," page 290).

3 When ice cream is half-frozen, stir in currants. Freeze until hard; store in freezer until ready to serve.

4 If desired, top each serving with warm maple syrup or mincemeat.

MAPLE WALNUT ICE CREAM

MAKES ABOUT 3 QUARTS

INGREDIENTS
1 cup pure maple syrup
2 eggs
2 cups (1 pint) half-and-half
1 cup sugar
2 teaspoons maple flavoring
6 cups (1½ quarts)
*   heavy cream*
1 cup chopped walnuts
Toasted coconut and toasted
*   walnuts (optional toppings)*

1 In a blender, combine syrup, eggs, half-and-half, sugar and flavoring and blend until sugar is dissolved. Stir mixture into heavy cream. Freeze as desired (see "Freezing Ice Cream," page 290).

2 When ice cream is half-frozen, stir in walnuts. Freeze until hard; store in freezer until ready to serve.

3 If desired, top each serving with toasted coconut and walnuts.

CRÈME DE MENTHE SHERBET

MAKES ABOUT 1½ QUARTS

INGREDIENTS
1 cup green crème de menthe
1 cup fresh lemon juice
2 cups water
4 egg whites
½ cup sugar

1 In a bowl, mix crème de menthe, lemon juice and water. Pour into a freezer container and freeze until three-quarters frozen.

2 Beat egg whites in a bowl until stiff. Beat in sugar 1 table-spoon at a time until mixture is stiff and glossy.

3 Scrape frozen mixture into a bowl and beat with an electric mixer until slushy. Fold in beaten egg whites. Return to container and freeze until hard.

295

PEAR GINGER SORBET

1 In food processor, combine pears, sugar and marmalade and puree. Pour into a freezer container and freeze until hard.

MAKES ABOUT 2 QUARTS

INGREDIENTS
- 6 *large ripe Comice pears, peeled, cored and diced*
- 1 *cup sugar*
- ½ *cup ginger marmalade Chestnuts in rum syrup (optional topping)*

2 When ready to serve, place chunks of the sorbet in food processor and chop finely. Spoon into serving dishes and, if desired, top with chestnuts in rum syrup.

MELON CHAMPAGNE SORBET

1 In food processor, combine all ingredients except melon balls and puree. Pour into a freezer container and freeze until hard.

MAKES ABOUT 2 QUARTS

INGREDIENTS
- 2 *quarts diced peeled honeydew or casaba melon*
- 1 *cup sugar*
- 1 *cup champagne Melon balls (garnish)*

2 When ready to serve, place chunks of the sorbet into a food processor and chop finely. Spoon into serving dishes and garnish with melon balls.

EASY LEMON SHERBET

1 Pour milk into a freezer container and freeze until half-frozen. Scrape into a bowl and beat with an electric beater until thick, fluffy and doubled in volume. Stir in lemonade concentrate and honey. Pour into freezer container and freeze until hard.

MAKES ABOUT 2 QUARTS

INGREDIENTS
*2 cans (14½ ounces each)
evaporated milk
2 cans (6 ounces each)
frozen pink lemonade
concentrate, undiluted
½ cup honey
Spiced crabapples (optional
garnish)*

2 If desired, garnish each serving with spiced crabapples.

QUICK RASPBERRY SHERBET

1 Drain raspberries into a bowl. Transfer raspberries to a food mill and press pulp into juice (food mill will remove all the seeds).

2 In a small saucepan, sprinkle gelatin over water and let stand until softened, about 5 minutes, then stir over low heat until gelatin

MAKES ABOUT 1½ QUARTS

INGREDIENTS
*2 packages (10 ounces each)
frozen raspberries in syrup
1 envelope unflavored gelatin
1 cup water
2 cups (1 pint) heavy cream*

is dissolved. Stir gelatin mixture into raspberry puree. Chill until the consistency of unbeaten egg whites.

3 Whip cream and fold into raspberry mixture. Pour into freezer container and freeze until hard.

GRAPEFRUIT CAMPARI SHERBET

1 Reserve 6 of the grapefruit sections for garnish. In a bowl, mix remaining grapefruit sections, grape juice, sugar and Campari until sugar is dissolved. Place in a freezer container and freeze until three-quarters frozen.

2 In a bowl, beat egg whites until stiff. Beat in sugar 1 tablespoon at a time until mixture is stiff and glossy.

MAKES ABOUT 1 QUART

INGREDIENTS
4 pink grapefruit, divided into sections
1 cup white grape juice
½ cup sugar
½ cup Campari
2 egg whites
¼ cup sugar

3 Scrape grapefruit mixture into a bowl and beat with an electric beater until fluffy. Fold in egg whites. Return to freezer and freeze until hard.

4 Serve garnished with reserved grapefruit sections.

COFFEE ANISETTE GRANITA

1 In a bowl, mix all ingredients except cream and stir until sugar is dissolved. Pour into a shallow freezer container and freeze, stirring granita every 30 minutes until mixture is frozen into granules.

MAKES ABOUT 2 QUARTS

INGREDIENTS
4 cups cold strong coffee
½ cup sugar
½ cup anisette
Grated rind of 1 lemon
Heavy cream

2 Spoon granita into serving dishes and serve drizzled with a little heavy cream.

SWISS CHOCOLATE CUPCAKES

MAKES 2 DOZEN

INGREDIENTS

2/3 cup soft butter
1 1/2 cups sugar
3 eggs
1/2 cup unsweetened
  cocoa powder
2 teaspoons vanilla
2 cups sifted all-purpose flour
1 teaspoon baking soda
1/2 teaspoon salt
1 cup milk
1 cup seedless raspberry
  preserves

FROSTING

3 cups sifted confectioners'
  sugar
Pinch of salt
1/4 cup unsweetened cocoa
  powder
1 egg yolk
1/3 cup soft butter
2 teaspoons rum
1/3 cup (about) hot water

1 In a large bowl, cream butter until fluffy. Blend in sugar. Add eggs one at a time, beating well after each addition. Stir in cocoa and vanilla.

2 Mix flour, baking soda and salt. Alternately add dry ingredients and milk to butter mixture, beginning and ending with the dry ingredients.

3 Line muffin pans with cupcake papers and fill with butter. Bake in a preheated 350°F oven for 25 to 30 minutes or until firm to the touch. Cool cupcakes on rack.

4 With a sharp knife, cut a cone-shaped section from each cupcake. Spoon preserves into cupcake and replace cone-shaped section.

5 For frosting, sift confectioners' sugar, salt and cocoa into a bowl. Stir in egg yolk, butter and rum. Gradually beat in hot water until frosting is of spreading consistency. Spread frosting on tops of cupcakes.

6 For those who are willing to pay the price, garnish cupcakes with fresh raspberries.

DANISH FROSTED CHOCOLATE ORANGE CAKE

MAKES ONE 9-INCH LAYER CAKE

INGREDIENTS

CAKE
3 cups sifted all-purpose flour
¾ cup Dutch cocoa powder
1 tablespoon baking powder
Grated rind of 4 oranges
2 cups (1 pound) soft unsalted
   butter
2 cups sugar
4 eggs
¾ cup lukewarm water
¾ cup milk

FILLING
1½ cups apricot preserves

FROSTING
¼ cup vegetable shortening
4 squares (4 ounces)
   unsweetened chocolate,
   melted and cooled
3 cups sifted confectioners'
   sugar
2 teaspoons vanilla
6 to 7 tablespoons milk
½ cup sliced almonds

1 For cake, sift flour, cocoa and baking powder twice. Stir in orange rind and set aside.

2 In the large bowl of an electric mixer, cream butter until very fluffy. Gradually beat in sugar. Add eggs one at a time, beating well after each addition.

3 Mix water and milk. Alternately add dry ingredients and milk mixture to butter, beginning and ending with dry ingredients. Spread mixture into 2 greased and floured 9-inch cake pans, 2 inches deep.

4 Bake in a preheated 350°F oven for 40 to 45 minutes or until firm to the touch in the center. Cool cakes in pans 5 minutes, then unmold on racks and cool completely.

5 Cut each layer into 2 layers. Sandwich with preserves and place cake on serving platter.

6 For frosting, combine shortening, chocolate, confectioners' sugar and vanilla in a bowl. Beat in enough milk to give frosting a spreading consistency. Spread frosting on sides and top of cake. Press almonds onto sides of cake.

Opposite: Danish Frosted Chocolate Orange Cake, page 301

FRENCH BÛCHE DE NOËL

1 For cake, grease a 10- x 15- x 1-inch jelly roll pan and line with waxed paper. Grease paper.

2 Preheat oven to 350°F. Sift flour with salt and half the sugar 3 times.

3 In a large bowl, beat egg whites until stiff. Beat in remaining sugar 1 tablespoon at a time until mixture is stiff and glossy.

4 In a small bowl, beat egg yolks with vanilla until thick and lemon-colored. Fold egg yolks into egg whites. Fold in flour in 4 portions. Spread batter evenly in prepared pan.

5 Bake for 15 minutes or until cake springs back when lightly

MAKES ONE 10-INCH-LONG ROLL

INGREDIENTS

CAKE
1 cup sifted all-purpose flour
¼ teaspoon salt
1⅓ cups sugar
4 eggs, separated
1 teaspoon vanilla

MOCHA BUTTERCREAM
1 cup soft butter
12 squares (12 ounces) semisweet chocolate, melted and cooled
2 egg yolks
1 teaspoon vanilla
1 tablespoon brandy
2 teaspoons instant coffee

touched. Dust a towel with confectioners' sugar and unmold cake onto towel. Trim off crisp edges with a sharp knife and roll up cake in towel, starting at a short side. Cool on rack in towel. For buttercream, cream butter in a medium bowl until fluffy. Add cooled chocolate, egg yolks, vanilla, brandy and coffee and beat until smooth and well blended.

6 Unroll cooled cake. Spread half the frosting on cake and reroll. Place on serving platter. Leave whole or, with a sharp knife, cut off the ends on a diagonal. Place cut-off pieces on either side of the log to resemble sawed-off branches. Spread entire roll and branches with remaining frosting. Run the tines of a fork lengthwise down log to imitate bark. Chill.

7 To prepare meringue mushrooms, beat egg whites with lemon juice until stiff. Gradually beat in sugar until mixture is stiff and glossy.

8 Place meringue in a pastry bag fitted with a large (#4) round tip, reserving 2 tablespoons of the meringue. Press out on foil-lined baking sheets, making 2-inch-high pointed mounds for stems and rounded discs for caps. If rounded caps have points, tap them down with a finger dipped in confectioners' sugar.

MERINGUE MUSHROOMS
2 egg whites
1 teaspoon lemon juice
²/₃ cup sugar
Unsweetened cocoa powder

9 Bake mushrooms in a preheated 200°F oven for 1 hour or until hard to the touch. Remove from foil and, with the tip of a sharp knife, cut a small hole in the bottom of each cap. Dip tips of stems into reserved meringue and press into hole in cap. Let dry at room temperature.

10 When ready to serve, dust tops of mushrooms with cocoa and place around log. Garnish with stems and leaves cut from green-tinted marzipan and candied cherries. If desired, decorate with tiny artificial birds and with green-tinted coconut resembling moss.

GREEK HONEY NUT CAKE
(AMYGDALOPITA)

1 For syrup, combine honey, sugar and water in a saucepan. Bring to boil, lower heat and simmer for 5 minutes. Cool and stir in lemon juice. Set aside.

2 For cake, cream butter with sugar in a large bowl until fluffy. Add eggs one at a time, beating well after each addition.

3 Sift flour with baking powder and spices. Add dry ingredients and milk alternately to butter mixture, beginning and ending with dry ingredients. Fold in orange rind and almonds.

MAKES ONE 8-INCH SQUARE CAKE

INGREDIENTS

SYRUP
1 cup honey
⅓ cup sugar
1 cup water
1 tablespoon fresh lemon juice

CAKE
½ cup soft butter
⅔ cup sugar
3 eggs
1 cup sifted all-purpose flour
1½ teaspoons baking powder
1 teaspoon ground cinnamon
½ teaspoon ground nutmeg
½ teaspoon ground cloves
¼ cup milk
Grated rind of 1 orange
4 ounces blanched almonds,
   ground (in food processor)

4 Pour batter into a greased and floured 8-inch square baking pan. Bake in a preheated 350°F oven for 30 to 35 minutes or until tester inserted in center comes out clean.

5 Remove cake from oven. With a knife, cut cake in pan into diamonds. Place pan on a rack and pour cold syrup over hot cake. Let stand until syrup is absorbed. Chill until ready to serve.

Opposite: Assorted Christmas Cookies

*Ukrainian Medivnyk (Christmas Honey Cake)

1 In a large bowl, cream butter until fluffy. Gradually beat in sugar and egg yolks. Stir in honey and sour cream. Beat in flour, baking powder, baking soda, spices and salt. Fold in walnuts and vanilla, then egg whites. Pour batter into a greased and floured 10- x 4-inch tube pan.

2 Bake in a preheated 350°F oven for 1 hour or until top springs back when lightly touched. Cool in pan for 10 minutes, then loosen edges and unmold cake on a rack to cool completely. Place cake upside down on serving platter.

MAKES ONE 10-INCH TUBE CAKE

INGREDIENTS
1 cup soft butter
1 cup firmly packed light
    brown sugar
6 egg yolks
1 cup honey
1 cup (½ pint) sour cream
3¼ cups sifted all-purpose flour
2 teaspoons baking powder
2 teaspoons baking soda
1 teaspoon ground nutmeg
1 teaspoon ground cinnamon
¼ teaspoon salt
1 cup chopped walnuts
1 teaspoon vanilla
6 egg whites, stiffly beaten

FROSTING
1½ cups confectioners' sugar
2 tablespoons (about) fresh
    lemon juice

3 For frosting, mix confectioners' sugar with lemon juice until the consistency of heavy cream. Spoon over top of cake, allowing excess to drip down the sides.

4 If desired, decorate with candy poinsettias: use large red and small green gumdrops. Roll out large gumdrops on sugared surface into thin sheet. Cut with scissors into poinsettia-shaped leaves. Arrange on top of cake and fill centers with finely chopped green gumdrops.

NOTE:
If desired, batter may be baked in a 2-quart fancy mold or in small, individual molds.

Opposite: Ukrainian Medivnyk, page 306

KENTUCKY BOURBON CAKE

MAKES ONE 10-INCH TUBE CAKE

INGREDIENTS

4 cups sifted all-purpose flour
2 teaspoons baking powder
½ teaspoon salt
1 cup soft butter
1 pound confectioners' sugar,
  sifted
2 teaspoons vanilla
6 eggs
¾ cup bourbon
2 cups chopped pecans
1 cup bourbon
  confectioners' sugar

1 Sift flour with baking powder and salt.

2 In a large bowl, cream butter until very fluffy and almost white. Gradually beat in 1 pound confectioners' sugar. Stir in vanilla. Add eggs one at a time, beating well after each addition. Add dry ingredients alternately with ¾ cup bourbon, beginning and ending with dry ingredients. Fold in pecans. Pour mixture into a greased and floured 10- x 4-inch tube pan.

3 Bake in a preheated 325°F oven for 1½ hours or until firm to the touch. Cool cake in pan 15 minutes, then unmold on rack.

4 While cake is warm, spoon 1 cup bourbon slowly over, allowing it to soak in. Cool thoroughly before slicing. Serve dusted with confectioners' sugar.

ITALIAN RICOTTA CHEESECAKE WITH AMARETTO SAUCE

1 For pastry, mix flour and salt in a large bowl. Cut in butter until particles resemble coarse cornmeal. Add lemon rind, egg yolk and enough ice water to make dough clean the bowl. Knead dough a few times on a floured surface, cover and chill for 30 minutes.

2 Place dough in an ungreased 9-inch springform pan and pat out to cover the bottom and 2 inches up the sides. Chill.

3 For filling, beat eggs and egg white in a large bowl until foamy. Gradually beat in sugar until thick and creamy. Blend in remaining ingredients and pour into crust.

MAKES ONE 9-INCH ROUND CAKE

INGREDIENTS

PASTRY

1½ cups unsifted
    all-purpose flour
¼ teaspoon salt
½ cup cold butter, thinly sliced
    Grated rind of 1 lemon
1 egg yolk
2 tablespoons (about) ice water

FILLING

5 eggs
1 egg white
1⅓ cups sugar
2 pounds ricotta
    Grated rind of 2 lemons
⅓ cup all-purpose flour
1 tablespoon vanilla
½ teaspoon salt

AMARETTO SAUCE

3 tablespoons cornstarch
½ cup amaretto liqueur
½ cup marsala
1 cup water
1 can (12 ounces) frozen
    orange juice concentrate,
    undiluted
1 can (11 ounces) mandarin
    oranges, drained

---

4 Bake in a preheated 350°F oven for 1 hour or until filling feels firm in the center. Cool in pan on rack for 1 hour, then remove sides. Cool completely on rack, then chill until ready to serve.

5 For sauce, mix cornstarch with amaretto in a saucepan until smooth. Add remaining ingredients except mandarin oranges and stir over low heat until sauce bubbles and thickens. Remove from heat, cover and cool. Fold in oranges. Chill. Garnish cake with additional mandarin oranges.

6 When ready to serve, cut wedges of cheesecake and serve topped with sauce.

AUSTRIAN LINZER TORTE

MAKES ONE 10-INCH TORTE

1 In a large bowl, cut butter into flour until particles resemble coarse cornmeal. Add sugar, almonds, lemon rind and juice, spices and egg yolks and stir until dough cleans the bowl. Knead a few times on a floured surface until a smooth ball. Wrap and chill for 1 hour.

2 Pat half the dough into an even layer on the bottom of an ungreased 10-inch springform pan. Brush edges of dough with egg. Shape remaining dough into ½-inch-thick ropes, including one 33-inch-long rope to go around the outer edge.

INGREDIENTS
1 cup cold butter, thinly sliced
2¼ cups unsifted all-purpose
    flour
1 cup superfine sugar
1¼ cups finely chopped
    unblanched almonds
    (chop in food processor)
Grated rind and juice of
    ½ lemon
¼ teaspoon each ground
    cinnamon, cloves
    and nutmeg
4 egg yolks
1 egg, well beaten
1 cup apricot or raspberry
    preserves
¼ cup sliced almonds

3 Spread preserves evenly over dough in pan. Arrange ropes in a lattice over top of preserves. Fit long rope of dough around edge. Brush with egg. Sprinkle edge with almonds.

4 Bake in a preheated 400°F oven for 10 minutes, then lower heat to 325°F and bake for another 30 minutes, or until richly browned. Cool in pan. Loosen edges and remove sides of pan to serve.

310

*ENGLISH DARK FRUITCAKE WITH HARD ICING

1 In a large bowl, mix candied fruit, raisins, pecans and brandy. Cover and let stand at room temperature overnight.

2 In a large bowl, cream butter and blend in brown sugar. Add eggs and yolks one at a time, beating well after each addition. Stir in flour, baking soda, salt and spices until well blended. Fold in fruits and nuts.

3 Line a greased 10-inch angel food cake pan with brown paper; grease paper. Fill with cake mixture. Cover top loosely with foil and crimp edges to pan.

MAKES ONE 10-INCH TUBE CAKE

INGREDIENTS

7 *cups (3½ pounds) chopped mixed candied fruits*
1 *cup raisins or dried currants*
2 *cups coarsely broken pecans*
1½ *cups brandy*
1 *cup soft butter*
1½ *cups firmly packed dark brown sugar*
4 *eggs*
2 *egg yolks*
3 *cups unsifted all-purpose flour*
1 *teaspoon baking soda*
½ *teaspoon salt*
1 *teaspoon each ground allspice, cinnamon, ginger, cloves, nutmeg*

HARD ICING

2 *egg whites*
1 *pound confectioners' sugar, sifted*

4 Bake in a preheated 275°F oven for 4 hours. Remove foil and raise heat to 325°F. Bake another 30 minutes or until richly browned. Cool cake thoroughly in pan. Remove pan and strip off brown paper.

5 For icing, beat egg whites with half the confectioners' sugar in a small bowl until well blended. Gradually beat in remaining sugar, beating until mixture holds stiff peaks.

6 Spread icing on top of cake, making peaks. Garnish with candied cherries and leaves cut from angelica. Let dry until hard at room temperature. Wrap cake loosely in foil and store in a cool, dry place. Age at least 2 weeks before serving.

*ENGLISH PLUM PUDDING WITH BRANDY HARD SAUCE

1 In a large bowl, mix milk, molasses and baking soda. Stir in suet, brown sugar and eggs. Blend in flour, spices and salt. Fold in almonds, raisins, figs, dates and brandy.

2 Spoon mixture into 2 greased and floured heatproof bowls, 7 inches across and 4 inches deep. Cover top with a double thickness of waxed paper, tied on with string.

3 English plum puddings are usually steamed, but for the sake of convenience these will be oven-steamed. Stand bowl in pans with water coming halfway up the sides and bake in a preheated 300°F oven for 2½ hours. Cool to lukewarm, remove waxed paper and remove puddings from bowls. Wrap and store in a cool, dry place until ready to serve.

MAKES 2 PUDDINGS

INGREDIENTS

⅔ cup milk
1 cup molasses
2 teaspoons baking soda
⅔ cup ground suet
½ cup firmly packed
　　dark brown sugar
2 eggs, well beaten
4 cups sifted all-purpose flour
½ teaspoon ground cloves
½ teaspoon ground cinnamon
½ teaspoon salt
½ cup chopped blanched
　　almonds
2 cups raisins or dried
　　currants
½ pound figs, stemmed and
　　finely chopped
½ pound pitted dates, finely
　　chopped
½ cup brandy

BRANDY HARD SAUCE

1½ cups firmly packed
　　light brown sugar
½ cup soft butter
⅓ cup heavy cream
2 tablespoons brandy

4 For hard sauce, cream brown sugar with butter until fluffy. Gradually beat in cream and brandy. Chill.

5 Unwrap puddings and return to bowls. Cover tops with foil and reheat in a 300°F oven for 30 minutes. Turn out onto serving platter and cut a hole 1 inch wide and 1 inch deep in top of pudding. Surround mold with cooked, dried, mixed fruits. Fill hole with warmed brandy and spoon some over the entire pudding. Set aflame. When flames die, cut pudding into serving pieces and top with hard sauce.

Opposite: English Plum Pudding, page 312

*New England Steamed Pudding

MAKES 6 TO 8 SERVINGS

INGREDIENTS

3 cups soft breadcrumbs
1 cup milk
½ cup melted vegetable
  shortening
1 cup orange marmalade
1 cup unsifted all-purpose
  flour
1 teaspoon baking soda
½ teaspoon salt
2 teaspoons ground
  cinnamon
½ teaspoon ground nutmeg
½ teaspoon ground cardamom
1 cup dried currants

SPICED CREAM

1 cup (½ pint) heavy cream
2 tablespoons confectioners'
  sugar
½ teaspoon ground cinnamon
½ teaspoon ground nutmeg
Grated rind of 1 orange

1 Place a rack (or a tunafish can with top and bottom removed) into the bottom of a large kettle. Add enough water to kettle to come halfway up the sides of a 1-quart pudding mold or heatproof bowl. Remove mold, cover kettle and bring water to boil.

2 In a large bowl, soak breadcrumbs in milk for 10 minutes. Stir in remaining pudding ingredients until well blended. Place mixture in the heavily greased 1-quart mold or bowl. Cover with buttered foil.

3 Wearing oven mitts, place mold into boiling water in kettle. Cover kettle and steam pudding for 3 hours, adding boiling water from time to time to keep up the level of the water. Remove mold from water, dry and uncover. Loosen edges of pudding and unmold on serving platter. Serve surrounded with Spiced Cranberries.

4 For spiced cream, whip cream with confectioners' sugar and spices until thick. Fold in orange rind.

5 Spoon hot pudding into serving bowls and top with cream. If you are shipping this pudding, cool it thoroughly and wrap in foil before packing. The spiced cream is perishable, so include the recipe for the cream and let the recipients prepare the sauce.

TIPSY PUDDING

SERVES 6 TO 8

INGREDIENTS

3 packages (3 ounces each)
   ladyfingers
1 cup cream sherry
1 jar (12 ounces) raspberry
   preserves
6 egg yolks
⅓ cup sugar
3 cups milk, scalded
2 teaspoons vanilla
1 cup (½ pint) heavy cream
¼ cup confectioners' sugar
   Mixed candied fruits

1 Place half the ladyfingers into a 2-quart decorative glass bowl. Sprinkle with half the sherry. Spread with half the preserves.

2 In a glass or enamel saucepan, beat egg yolks with sugar. Gradually beat in milk. Stir constantly over very low heat until mixture coats a spoon. Cool to lukewarm.

3 Pour half the custard into the bowl. Repeat layers, ending with custard. Chill several hours.

4 When ready to serve, whip cream with confectioners' sugar until stiff. Spoon around outer edge of bowl. Garnish cream with candied fruits. Spoon into bowls to serve.

APRICOT RUM SAVARIN

MAKES ONE 9-INCH RING

INGREDIENTS
1 envelope active dry yeast
½ teaspoon salt
1 tablespoon sugar
½ cup lukewarm milk
4 eggs, well beaten
⅔ cup soft butter
2 cups unsifted all-purpose
 flour

SYRUP
½ cup sugar
¾ cup orange juice
½ cup dark rum

GLAZE
½ cup sieved apricot preserves
3 tablespoons dark rum

1 In a large bowl, mix yeast, salt, sugar and milk until yeast is dissolved. Add eggs, butter and flour and beat on high speed until smooth and shiny. Cover bowl and let dough rise in a warm place until doubled in bulk, about 1 hour.

2 Beat dough again and pour into a well-greased 9-inch ring mold. Let rise to within ½ inch of top of mold. Bake in a preheated 400°F oven for 30 to 35 minutes or until golden brown and firm to the touch.

3 Unmold savarin on serving plate. In a saucepan, heat sugar and orange juice to boiling. Lower heat and simmer for 10 minutes. Remove from heat and stir in rum. Spoon syrup evenly over savarin, allowing it to soak in.

4 In a small saucepan, heat preserves and rum until bubbly. Brush apricot mixture over entire savarin. Fill center with Rum Poached Fruit. Serve topped with whipped cream.

*ALABAMA PEANUT PIE COOKIES

MAKES ONE 10- X 15-INCH PAN

INGREDIENTS

2 cups unsifted
  all-purpose flour
½ cup sifted
  confectioners' sugar
1 cup cold butter, thinly sliced
6 eggs
1½ cups firmly packed
  light brown sugar
1 cup dark corn syrup
¼ cup melted butter
2 teaspoons vanilla
3 cups shelled
  unsalted peanuts

1 In a bowl, mix flour and confectioners' sugar. Add sliced butter and mix with the fingers until crumbly. Press crumbs firmly and evenly into a greased 10- x 15-inch jelly roll pan.

2 Beat eggs until foamy. Beat in brown sugar, corn syrup, melted butter and vanilla.

3 Chop peanuts coarsely in food processor and fold into egg mixture. Pour into pan and spread evenly.

4 Bake in a preheated 350°F oven for 40 minutes or until filling is set. Cool in pan, then cut into 2-inch squares.

*CALIFORNIA GRANOLA BARS

MAKES 35

INGREDIENTS

1½ cups walnuts
½ cup dried apples
½ cup dried apricots
6 cups quick-cooking
  oatmeal
¾ cup unsalted butter
½ cup honey
½ cup firmly packed
  light brown sugar
1 teaspoon ground
  cinnamon
1 teaspoon vanilla
¼ teaspoon salt

1 Place nuts, apples and apricots in a food processor and chop finely. Transfer to a large bowl and add oatmeal.

2 In a saucepan, combine butter, honey, sugar and cinnamon and bring to boil; boil for 1 minute. Stir into oatmeal mixture with vanilla and salt. Press mixture firmly and evenly into a greased 10- x 15- x 1-inch jelly roll pan.

3 Bake in a preheated 350°F oven for 15 minutes or until golden brown. Cool in pan and cut into 35 1½- x 3-inch bars. Store in an airtight container in a cool, dry place.

*MIDWEST FROSTED CARROT BARS

MAKES ONE 9- X 13- X 2-INCH PAN

INGREDIENTS
2 eggs
1 cup sugar
3/4 cup corn oil
1 cup sifted
  all-purpose flour
1 teaspoon baking soda
2 teaspoons ground
  cinnamon
1/4 teaspoon salt
1 1/2 cups finely grated
  raw carrots (about 4)
1 cup raisins
1 cup chopped walnuts

FROSTING
1 package (3 ounces)
  cream cheese
2 tablespoons milk
2 1/2 cups sifted
  confectioners' sugar
1 teaspoon vanilla
2 tablespoons (about) milk

1 In a large bowl, beat eggs until foamy. Gradually beat in sugar. Stir in oil, flour, baking soda, cinnamon, salt and carrots. When well blended, stir in raisins and nuts. Spread evenly into greased 9- x 13- x 2-inch baking pan.

2 Bake in a preheated 350°F oven for 25 to 30 minutes or until firm to the touch. Cool in pan on rack.

3 For frosting, beat cream cheese with milk in a bowl until well blended. Stir in confectioners' sugar and vanilla. Add enough milk to make frosting a good spreading consistency. Spread over top of cooled bars. Cut into rectangles, squares, diamonds, or triangles.

BRAZILIAN LACE WAFERS

1 In a bowl, cream butter and blend in brown sugar and water. Stir in flour, cinnamon and nuts. Shape mixture into 60 balls. Place 6 at a time on greased baking sheets, 2 inches apart.

MAKES 60 COOKIES

INGREDIENTS
¼ cup soft butter
1½ cups firmly packed
   light brown sugar
2 tablespoons water
1 cup sifted all-purpose flour
1 teaspoon ground
   cinnamon
1½ cups finely chopped
   Brazil nuts

2 Bake in a preheated 325°F oven for 15 minutes or until cookies are spread thin and browned on the edges. Let cool 30 seconds, then remove from baking sheets with a pancake turner and cool on racks. Store in an airtight container in a cool, dry place. These cookies have a candy-like texture.

*CHRISTMAS PINWHEEL COOKIES

1 In a large bowl, cream butter until fluffy. Beat in sugar and sour cream. Stir in flour, baking soda and salt. Knead dough a few times on a floured surface until a smooth ball. Wrap and chill for 2 hours.

2 Cut dough into 4 pieces. Roll each piece on a floured surface into a 14- x 7-inch rectangle. Sprinkle each of the 4 rectangles with half a box of gelatin; you will have 2 red

MAKES ABOUT 8 DOZEN

INGREDIENTS
1½ cups soft butter
1 cup sugar
1 cup (½ pint) sour cream
4 cups sifted all-purpose flour
1 teaspoon baking soda
¼ teaspoon salt
1 package (3 ounces)
   strawberry gelatin
1 package (3 ounces)
   lime gelatin

and 2 green pieces. Roll up each piece starting at a long edge. Wrap and chill 2 hours. Cut into ¼-inch-thick slices and place on greased baking sheets.

3 Bake in a preheated 325°F oven for 10 to 12 minutes or until golden brown. Cool on racks. Store in an airtight container in a cool, dry place.

Opposite: Assorted Christmas Cookies

*CANADIAN HONEY DROPS

MAKES 4½ DOZEN SANDWICH COOKIES

INGREDIENTS

¾ cup soft butter
¾ cup vegetable shortening
1½ cups firmly packed
    light brown sugar
3 eggs
½ cup honey
1½ teaspoons vanilla
5 cups sifted all-purpose flour
4 teaspoons baking soda
1 can (14 ounces) sweetened
    chestnut puree (chestnut
    spread) or 1 jar
    (13 ounces) hazelnut
    spread
Confectioners' sugar

1 In a large bowl, cream butter and shortening. Blend in brown sugar. Add eggs one at a time, beating well after each addition. Stir in honey and vanilla, then flour and baking soda. Cover and chill dough overnight.

2 Shape dough into 1-inch balls. Place on ungreased baking sheets.

3 Bake in a preheated 350°F oven for 10 to 12 minutes or until firm to the touch. Cool on racks. Sandwich 2 cookies together with chestnut spread. Dust with confectioners' sugar. Store at room temperature.

*DANISH ALMOND RINGS

MAKES 30 COOKIES

INGREDIENTS
1 pound almond paste
1 egg white
1 cup confectioners' sugar
6 tablespoons sugar
1 tablespoon all-purpose flour
¼ teaspoon baking powder

FROSTING
2 cups sifted confectioners'
sugar
4 to 6 tablespoons milk

1 Break almond paste into small pieces and place in a large bowl. Add egg white, sugars, flour and baking powder and knead with hands until well blended. Cut mixture into 30 pieces and roll each into a 4-inch rope.

2 Line baking sheets with foil; grease foil. Place ropes on prepared baking sheets and shape into rings.

3 Bake in a preheated 300°F oven for 15 to 20 minutes or until pale brown. Cool on baking sheets. Carefully remove rings from foil and place on racks.

4 For frosting, mix confectioners' sugar and milk in a small bowl until smooth. With a teaspoon, drizzle frosting back and forth over rings. If desired, sprinkle with colored sugar or sprinkles. Let dry at room temperature, then store in an airtight container in a cool, dry place.

*DUTCH SPECULAAS

1 In a large bowl, cream butter until fluffy. Stir in confectioners' sugar. Beat in 1 egg, lemon rind and spices. Stir in flour and baking powder. Knead dough a few times on a floured surface until a smooth ball.

2 Roll out to ⅛-inch thickness and cut with a Christmas tree-

MAKES ABOUT 4 DOZEN COOKIES, DEPENDING ON SIZE

INGREDIENTS
½ cup soft butter
1 cup confectioners' sugar
1 egg
    Grated rind of 1 lemon
½ teaspoon ground cinnamon
½ teaspoon ground mace
2¼ cups sifted all-purpose flour
½ teaspoon baking powder
1 egg, well beaten
    Sliced almonds

shaped cookie cutter. Place on greased baking sheets. Brush with egg and sprinkle with almonds.

3 Bake in a preheated 350°F oven for 15 minutes or until firm. Cool on rack. Store in an airtight container in a cool, dry place.

FRENCH TUILES

1 In a large bowl, stir egg whites with sugar and salt until sugar is dissolved. Stir in butter, shortening, flour and almonds. Drop mixture by level measuring tablespoons onto greased baking sheets; drop only 6 on a sheet and place mounds 5 inches apart to allow for spreading.

2 Bake in a preheated 350°F oven for 8 to 10 minutes or until

MAKES ABOUT 5 DOZEN COOKIES

INGREDIENTS
¾ cup unbeaten egg whites
    (about 3)
1½ cups sugar
¼ teaspoon salt
½ cup lukewarm melted butter
½ cup lukewarm melted
    vegetable shortening
1 cup sifted all-purpose flour
¾ cup finely chopped
    blanched almonds

brown on the edges. Let stand for 30 seconds, then remove with a pancake turner and place on a rolling pin to shape cookie into a curve. Cool. Repeat with remaining dough. Cool cookies thoroughly before storing in airtight containers in a cool, dry place.

3 If cookies become too hard to curve, return to oven and warm until soft.

*BERLINER KRAENZE

1 In a large bowl, cream shortening and butter until fluffy. Stir in sugar, lemon rind and eggs, then flour.

2 Cut dough into 72 pieces and roll each piece into a 6-inch rope. Shape into a circle and tie a single knot, leaving ends free. Place on greased baking sheets.

MAKES ABOUT 6 DOZEN COOKIES

INGREDIENTS
1 cup vegetable shortening
½ cup soft butter
1 cup sugar
Grated rind of 2 lemons
2 eggs
4 cup unsifted
all-purpose flour
1 egg white
2 tablespoons sugar
Candied cherries, citron and
angelica (optional)

3 In a small bowl, beat egg whites until stiff. Gradually beat in sugar until stiff and glossy. Brush some of this mixture on each cookie. If desired, decorate with cherries, citron and/or angelica.

4 Bake in a preheated 400°F oven for 10 to 12 minutes or until firm but not brown. Cool on rack and store in an airtight container in a cool, dry place.

*GERMAN PFEFFERNUESSE

1 In a large bowl, cream butter with sugar and molasses. Mix remaining ingredients and blend into butter mixture. Shape into 1-inch balls and place 1½ inches apart on greased baking sheets.

MAKES ABOUT 7 DOZEN COOKIES

INGREDIENTS
1 cup soft butter
1 cup sugar
1 cup molasses
1 teaspoon baking soda
½ teaspoon salt
1 teaspoon each ground cloves,
ginger and cinnamon
½ teaspoon black pepper
3½ cups sifted all-purpose flour
Confectioners' sugar

2 Bake in a preheated 350°F for 12 to 15 minutes or until firm to the touch. Roll while warm in confectioners' sugar. Cool on racks, then roll in sugar again. Store in an airtight container in a cool, dry place.

*GERMAN LEBKUCHEN

1 Bring honey to boil and pour into a bowl. Stir in brown sugar, egg, lemon juice, spices, orange peel and walnuts. Mix flour and baking soda and stir into honey mixture. Cover and chill dough overnight.

2 Knead dough a few times on a floured surface and roll out to ¼-inch thickness. Cut into 1½- x 2½-inch rectangles. Place on greased baking sheets, 1 inch apart.

MAKES ABOUT 6 DOZEN COOKIES

INGREDIENTS

COOKIES
1 cup honey
¾ cup firmly packed light
   brown sugar
1 egg, well beaten
1 tablespoon lemon juice
1 teaspoon each ground
   cinnamon, cloves, allspice
   and nutmeg
⅓ cup minced candied orange
   peel
⅓ cup minced walnuts
3 cups unsifted all-purpose
   flour
½ teaspoon baking soda

GLAZE
1 cup sugar
½ cup water
¼ cup confectioners' sugar

3 Bake in a preheated 400°F oven for 10 to 12 minutes or until firm to the touch.

4 For glaze, boil sugar and water in a saucepan for 5 minutes. Remove from heat and stir in confectioners' sugar. Brush glaze over hot cookies. Cool cookies on racks and store in an airtight container in a cool, dry place. This is a hard cookie that softens after storage.

Opposite: Assorted Christmas Candies

GERMAN ZIMTSTERNE

**MAKES ABOUT 5 DOZEN COOKIES,
DEPENDING ON SIZE**

INGREDIENTS
4 egg whites
4 cups unsifted confectioners'
   sugar
4 cups unblanched ground
   almonds (grind in food
   processor)
1 tablespoon lemon juice
1½ tablespoons ground
   cinnamon
½ teaspoon ground mace
   Additional confectioners'
   sugar

1 In a large bowl, beat egg whites until stiff. Beat in 4 cups confectioners' sugar 3 tablespoons at a time, beating well after each addition until mixture is stiff and glossy. Remove 1⅓ cups of this mixture and set aside.

2 Beat almonds, lemon juice and spices into remaining egg white mixture. Cover with a towel and let stand for 1 hour; mixture will become firm.

3 Sprinkle a board with confectioners' sugar. Briefly knead dough on board to a smooth ball. Sprinkle board and rolling pin with confectioners' sugar. Roll out dough to ½-inch thickness. Cut out cookies with sugared star-shaped cutter. Place on greased and floured baking sheets. Brush each cookie with reserved egg white mixture.

4 Bake in a preheated 275°F oven for 15 minutes or until firm to the touch but not brown. Cool on racks and store in an airtight container in a cool, dry place.

VIENNESE VANILLEKIPFERL

MAKES 4½ DOZEN COOKIES

INGREDIENTS

1 vanilla bean
2 cups confectioners' sugar
1½ cups walnuts
½ cup soft butter
½ cup vegetable shortening
⅔ cup sugar
1½ teaspoons vanilla
*2½ cups unsifted all-purpose
  flour*

1 To prepare vanilla sugar, cut vanilla bean in half lengthwise and scrape out seeds. Mix seeds and vanilla bean with confectioners' sugar and store in a tightly covered jar for 1 week.

2 Finely grind walnuts in food processor.

3 In a bowl, cream butter and shortening with sugar. Stir in vanilla and walnuts. Stir in flour and then knead.

4 Divide dough into 54 equal pieces. Shape each piece into a 3-inch log with tapering ends. Place on greased baking sheets and curve ends, shaping crescents.

5 Bake in a preheated 325°F oven for about 20 minutes or until lightly browned. Cool cookies completely on baking sheets. Remove carefully (they are fragile) and roll in vanilla sugar. Store in an airtight container in a cool, dry place.

*GREEK KOURAMBIEDES

1 In a large bowl, cream butter until fluffy and almost white. Stir in ½ cup confectioners' sugar, egg yolks, vanilla and cognac, then flour and baking powder.

2 Shape dough into ¾-inch balls. Place on greased baking sheets and press a whole clove into the center of each.

MAKES ABOUT 50 COOKIES

INGREDIENTS
1 cup soft butter
½ cup confectioners' sugar
2 egg yolks
2 teaspoons vanilla
2 tablespoons cognac
2½ cups unsifted all-purpose flour
1 teaspoon baking soda
Whole cloves
Additional confectioners' sugar

3 Bake in a preheated 350°F oven for 10 to 12 minutes or until firm to the touch. Cool on racks and sprinkle lightly with confectioners' sugar.

This dough can also be shaped into crescents, pears or S-shapes. If this is done, omit whole cloves and add ½ teaspoon ground cloves to the dough along with the flour.

*GREEK SESAME SEED COOKIES

1 In a large bowl, cream butter and stir in sugar. Beat in eggs, ⅓ cup sesame seeds and water. Stir in flour, baking powder and salt. Knead dough a few times until a smooth ball.

2 Roll out dough, one-quarter at a time, on a floured surface to ⅛-inch thickness. Cut into ¾- x 2½-inch pieces. Twist each strip once

MAKES ABOUT 9 DOZEN

INGREDIENTS
1 cup soft butter
2 cups sugar
2 eggs
⅓ cup toasted sesame seeds
¼ cup water
4 cups unsifted all-purpose flour
2 teaspoons baking powder
¼ teaspoon salt
2 egg whites, lightly beaten
About ½ cup additional sesame seeds

to shape into a bow and place on greased baking sheets. Brush tops with egg white and sprinkle with sesame seeds.

3 Bake in a preheated 350°F oven for 8 to 10 minutes or until golden brown. Cool on racks and store in an airtight container in a cool, dry place.

Opposite: Assorted Christmas Cookies

*HUNGARIAN HUSSAR'S KISSES

MAKES 5 DOZEN COOKIES

INGREDIENTS

1⅓ cups soft unsalted butter
⅔ cup sugar
2 eggs
2 egg yolks
3 cups sifted all-purpose flour
1 cup finely ground walnuts
  (grind in food processor)
1 egg, well beaten
1 cup seedless raspberry or
  apricot preserves

1 In a large bowl, cream butter and sugar until fluffy. Stir in 2 eggs and egg yolks. Stir in flour and half the walnuts.

2 Cut dough into 60 pieces and roll each piece into a small ball. Place on greased baking sheets and press a hollow in center of each. Brush with egg and sprinkle with remaining walnuts.

3 Bake in a preheated 350°F oven for 15 minutes or until golden. Fill centers of hot cookies with jam. Place on racks to cool. Store in an airtight container in a cool, dry place.

NORWEGIAN SPRITZ

MAKES ABOUT 8 DOZEN COOKIES, DEPENDING ON SIZE AND SHAPE

INGREDIENTS

½ cup soft butter
½ cup vegetable shortening
1 cup sugar
2 eggs
1 teaspoon each almond and
  vanilla extracts
3 cups sifted all-purpose flour
½ teaspoon salt

1 In a bowl, cream butter, shortening and sugar. Beat in eggs and extracts. Stir in flour and salt. Place dough into a cookie press and press out on ungreased baking sheets in desired shapes and sizes.

2 Bake in a preheated 400°F oven for 7 to 10 minutes or until golden brown. Decorate as desired with candied cherries, candied fruits, or melted chocolate, or drizzle with a frosting made of confectioners' sugar mixed with fresh lemon juice and sprinkle with colored sugar or sprinkles.

3 Dough may be pressed out of the cookie press using strip cookie disc; cut into 2-inch lengths and bake as above. Sandwich cookies with currant jelly or sieved apricot preserves; dip ends into melted chocolate and then into chocolate sprinkles.

*ITALIAN AMARETTI

MAKES 6 DOZEN MACAROONS

INGREDIENTS
2 egg whites
½ teaspoon salt
1 cup sugar
2 cups blanched whole
*   almonds*
1 teaspoon each almond and
*   vanilla extracts*
Confectioners' sugar

1 In a bowl, beat egg whites and salt until stiff. Beat in sugar 1 tablespoon at a time until mixture is stiff and glossy.

2 Grind almonds to a fine powder in food processor. Fold almonds and extracts into egg whites.

3 Line baking sheets with pieces of cooking parchment or foil. Grease and dust lightly with flour. Drop almond mixture in olive-size mounds on baking sheets. Sift confectioners' sugar lightly over tops. Let stand for 2 hours.

4 Bake in a preheated 300°F oven for 15 to 20 minutes or until golden brown. Let stand on baking sheets for 5 minutes, then remove and cool on racks. Store in an airtight container in a cool, dry place.

Variation:
For a festive touch, drizzle cookies with 4 squares (4 ounces) semisweet chocolate melted with 3 tablespoons vegetable shortening over warm water; sprinkle with nonpareils.

*SCOTCH SHORTBREAD

**MAKES THREE 7-INCH CIRCLES,
48 WEDGES**

INGREDIENTS
1½ *cups soft butter*
¾ *cup firmly packed dark
    brown sugar*
4 *cups sifted all-purpose flour*
1 *tablespoon ground ginger*
½ *teaspoon salt*

1 In a large bowl, cream butter and brown sugar. Stir in flour, ginger and salt. Knead dough a few times on a floured surface until a smooth ball.

2 Cut dough into 3 pieces. Place pieces on ungreased baking sheets and pat out to 7-inch circles. With a sharp knife, cut each circle into 16 wedges.

3 Bake in a preheated 300°F oven for 25 to 30 minutes or until pale brown and firm to the touch. Cool on baking sheets, then separate shortbread into wedges. Store in an airtight container in a cool, dry place.

This dough can also be rolled to ½-inch thickness and cut into shapes with small cookie cutters.

Page following: Assorted Christmas Cookies

*SERBIAN HARD COOKIES

MAKES 3 DOZEN

INGREDIENTS

3 eggs
1½ cups sugar
2½ cups sifted all-purpose flour
2 teaspoons ground cinnamon
¾ cup finely chopped hazelnuts
⅓ cup minced candied lemon peel
2 tablespoons fresh lemon juice

FROSTING

2 cups sifted confectioners' sugar
¼ cup fresh lemon juice

1 In a large bowl, beat eggs and sugar until thick. Stir in flour, cinnamon, hazelnuts, lemon peel and lemon juice. Knead dough a few times on a floured surface until a smooth ball. Return to bowl, cover and let stand at room temperature overnight.

2 Roll out dough on a floured surface in ¼-inch thickness. Cut into 3- x ½-inch strips. Place on greased and floured baking sheets.

3 Bake in a preheated 350°F oven for 30 minutes or until golden brown.

4 Meanwhile, prepare frosting by mixing confectioners' sugar and lemon juice until smooth. Remove cookies from oven and frost while hot. Cool on racks and store in an airtight container in a cool, dry place.

*SPANISH GALLETAS

MAKES 5 DOZEN COOKIES

INGREDIENTS

4 eggs
1 cup sugar
¾ cup soft butter
1 cup sugar
*2 tablespoons ground
    cinnamon*
4 cups sifted all-purpose flour
¼ teaspoon salt
*1 egg, well beaten
    Additional sugar*

1 With an electric mixer, beat eggs with 1 cup sugar for 10 minutes.

2 In another bowl, beat butter with 1 cup sugar for 5 minutes. Mix butter mixture into egg mixture. Stir in cinnamon, flour and salt, blending well. (Dough will be sticky.)

3 Shape dough with moistened fingers into logs about 2½ inches long. Place on greased and floured baking sheets, 2 inches apart. Brush cookies with egg and sprinkle with sugar.

4 Bake in a preheated 350°F oven for 10 minutes or until golden brown. Cool on racks. Store in an airtight container in a cool, dry place.

SWEDISH SANDBAKELSER

**MAKES 2 TO 3 DOZEN
DEPENDING ON SIZE**

INGREDIENTS
⅓ cup slivered almonds
½ cup soft butter
½ cup sugar
1 egg white
2 teaspoons vanilla
1⅓ cups sifted all-purpose flour
   Confectioners' sugar

1 Grind almonds in food processor.

2 In a bowl, cream butter and sugar until fluffy. Stir in egg white, vanilla and nuts, then flour. Cover dough and chill for 2 hours.

3 Press dough ⅛-inch thick in bottom and sides of small sandbakelser forms. Place on baking sheets.

4 Bake in preheated 350°F oven for 10 to 12 minutes or until golden brown. Cool 5 minutes, then remove from pans. Serve upside down, sprinkled with confectioners' sugar; alternatively, fill at the last minute with lemon curd or vanilla pudding and serve as tiny tartlets.

*SWEDISH TOSCAS

MAKES 2 DOZEN TARTLETS

INGREDIENTS
3/4 cup soft butter
1/2 cup sugar
2 cups unsifted
  all-purpose flour

FILLING
2/3 cup slivered almonds
1/2 cup sugar
3 tablespoons butter
3 tablespoons heavy cream
4 teaspoons all-purpose flour

1 In a small bowl, cream butter and sugar. Stir in flour. Knead on a floured surface a few times until a smooth ball.

2 Cut dough into 24 pieces. Press evenly into mini-muffin pans or 2-inch tartlet pans.

3 For filling, combine ingredients in a saucepan and bring to boil. Cool and spoon into dough-lined pans.

4 Bake in a preheated 350°F oven for 10 to 15 minutes or until golden brown. Cool 5 minutes, then remove tartlets from pan. Cool on rack. Store in an airtight container in a cool, dry place.

*EASY FOOLPROOF FUDGE

MAKES ONE 9-INCH SQUARE PAN

INGREDIENTS
4 cups sugar
1 can (14½ ounces)
    evaporated milk
1 cup butter
1 jar (7 ounces) marshmallow
    creme
1 package (12 ounces)
    semisweet chocolate chips
2 cups coarsely broken
    walnuts
2 teaspoons vanilla

1 In a 3-quart saucepan, combine sugar, milk, and butter and boil until mixture reaches 236°F on a candy thermometer (soft ball stage). Remove from heat and stir in remaining ingredients. Stir until chocolate is melted and mixture is well blended.

2 Spread evenly into a buttered 9-inch square pan and cool until firm.

3 Cut candy into pieces of desired sizes. Store in an airtight container in a cool, dry place.

*GEORGIA SPICED PECANS

MAKES ABOUT 1¼ POUNDS

INGREDIENTS
1 cup sugar
2 teaspoons ground
    cinnamon
6 tablespoons milk
1 teaspoon vanilla extract
3 cups (12 ounces)
    pecan halves

1 In a 2-quart saucepan, combine sugar, cinnamon and milk and boil until mixture reaches 238°F on a candy thermometer (soft ball stage). Add vanilla and pecans and stir until mixture becomes creamy.

2 Spread in a thin layer on a buttered baking sheet, separating pecans into individual pieces. Cool, then store in an airtight container in a cool, dry place.

*MEXICAN PENUCHE

MAKES 1¾ POUNDS

INGREDIENTS

3 cups firmly packed dark
   brown sugar
¼ cup light corn syrup
1 cup milk
1 square (1 ounce) unsweetened chocolate, grated
1 tablespoon butter
1 teaspoon vanilla
1 teaspoon ground cinnamon
1½ cups coarsely broken
   walnuts

1 In a 3-quart saucepan, combine brown sugar, corn syrup, milk, chocolate and butter and bring to boil. Boil until mixture reaches 238°F on a candy thermometer (soft ball stage). Remove from heat and let stand 10 minutes.

2 Add vanilla, cinnamon and walnuts, and stir vigorously until mixture loses its gloss. Pour into a buttered 9- x 9-inch square pan and let stand until hardened.

3 Cut into 1-inch squares. Store in an airtight container in a cool, dry place.

*NAPA VALLEY GRAPE WALNUTS

MAKES ABOUT 1 POUND

INGREDIENTS

1 cup sugar
½ cup grape juice
2 cups walnut halves

1 In a 1½-quart saucepan, bring sugar and grape juice to boil. Continue to boil without stirring until mixture reaches 248°F on candy thermometer (firm ball stage).

2 Place walnuts in a bowl and pour hot syrup over them. Stir until mixture becomes thick and creamy.

3 Spread out thinly on a buttered baking sheet. Let candy stand until hard.

4 Break into individual pieces. Store in an airtight container in a cool, dry place.

*NEW ORLEANS PRALINES

★★★★★★

MAKES 12

INGREDIENTS
48 pecan halves
3 cups firmly packed light
   brown sugar
1 cup half-and-half
3 tablespoons light corn syrup
⅓ cup butter
2 teaspoons vanilla

1 Line 2 baking sheets with foil. Place groups of 4 pecans on foil, making 6 clusters on each baking sheet.

2 In a 3-quart saucepan, combine brown sugar, half-and-half, syrup and butter and boil until mixture reaches 238°F on a candy thermometer (soft ball stage). Remove from heat and cool to 110°F.

3 Beat until mixture just starts to thicken. Working quickly and using a large spoon, drop sugar mixture over pecan clusters, allowing it to spread into a thin patty 3½ inches in diameter. If sugar mixture hardens too quickly, stir in 1 to 2 teaspoons hot water to soften.

4 Cool pralines, then layer in an airtight container between sheets of waxed paper. Store in a cool, dry place.

*VERMONT MAPLE CONFECTION

MAKES 64 PIECES

INGREDIENTS
4 cups pure maple syrup
2 tablespoons light corn syrup
1½ cups half-and-half
2 teaspoons vanilla
1½ cups chopped walnuts

1 In a 3-quart saucepan, boil syrups and half-and-half without stirring until mixture registers 236°F on a candy thermometer (soft ball stage). Remove from heat and cool to 110°F.

2 Beat with an electric mixer at low speed for 10 minutes or until thickened. Stir in vanilla and nuts. Pour into a buttered 8-inch square pan and cool until firm.

3 Cut candy into 1-inch squares. Store in an airtight container in a cool, dry place.

UKRAINIAN DRIED FRUIT CANDY

MAKES ONE 8-INCH SQUARE PAN

INGREDIENTS
½ pound each pitted prunes, pitted dates, raisins and blanched almonds
2 tablespoons honey
4 squares (4 ounces) semisweet chocolate
36 whole unblanched almonds

1 In food processor, combine fruits and ½ pound almonds and chop coarsely. Scrape mixture into a bowl and stir in honey.

2 Line an 8-inch square pan with foil and oil lightly. Press fruit mixture evenly into bottom of pan.

3 Melt chocolate over hot water; spread over fruit layer. Press almonds in rows into chocolate. Chill until chocolate hardens.

4 Use foil to remove candy from pan. With a sharp knife, cut into pieces between almonds. Store in a covered container in a cool, dry place.

*ITALIAN TORRONE (CREMONA NOUGAT)

1 Line the bottom and sides of an ungreased 8-inch square pan with wafers, cutting them to fit with a sharp serrated knife.

2 Bring honey to boil in a saucepan; continue to boil until honey reaches 290°F on a candy thermometer.

3 In a large bowl, beat egg whites until stiff. Gradually beat in a thin stream of hot honey.

MAKES 32 PIECES

INGREDIENTS
*1 package Ostia nougat wafers
  (sold in Italian and
  specialty food shops)
1 cup honey
3 egg whites
1⅓ cups sugar
⅔ cup water
2 teaspoons vanilla
1 cup toasted whole blanched
  almonds or hazelnuts*

4 In another saucepan, combine sugar and water and boil until mixture reaches 290°F on a candy thermometer. Gradually beat this syrup into egg white mixture. Beat in vanilla. Fold in almonds.

5 Pour mixture into lined pan and cover top with more wafers. Cover with waxed paper and top with a weight. Let stand at room temperature for 12 hours.

6 Remove block of nougat from pan and cut with an oiled knife into 1- x 2-inch pieces. Wrap each piece in plastic wrap and store in a cool, dry place.

*CHRISTMAS CANDY

1 In a 2-quart saucepan, combine sugar, half-and-half, corn syrup and salt and boil until mixture reaches 236°F on a candy thermometer (soft ball stage). Remove from heat and stir in vanilla. Cool for 5 minutes.

2 Beat with an electric mixer at low speed for 5 minutes. Stir in remaining ingredients.

MAKES 64 PIECES

INGREDIENTS

1½ cups sugar
¾ cup half-and-half
½ cup light corn syrup
¼ teaspoon salt
1 teaspoon vanilla
½ cup diced candied green pineapple
½ cup halved candied cherries
1 cup chopped Brazil nuts
1½ cups pecan halves

3 Line a 9-inch square pan with foil and oil lightly. Pour candy mixture into pan and chill until firm.

4 Use foil to pull candy out of pan. Cut into 64 squares. Store in an airtight container in a cool, dry place.

TRUFFLES

1 Melt chocolate in the top part of a double boiler over hot water. In a saucepan, heat cream and half-and-half until just simmering. Remove from heat and cool to lukewarm. Stir cream into chocolate. Stir in vanilla. Cool.

MAKES 3 DOZEN

INGREDIENTS

1½ pounds semisweet chocolate
⅓ cup heavy cream
⅓ cup half-and-half
1 teaspoon vanilla
½ cup finely chopped walnuts or pecans
½ cup flaked coconut

2 Beat mixture with an electric mixer until light and fluffy. Chill until firm. Scoop by teaspoons and roll with hands into small balls. Roll half the balls in nuts and half in coconut. Refrigerate until ready to serve.

*MARZIPAN FRUITS

1 In a saucepan, combine half-and-half, flour and almond paste and stir over medium heat until mixture becomes thick and forms a ball. Transfer to a bowl and cool.

2 Add confectioners' sugar and knead until smooth and malleable. Tint marzipan with food coloring and shape as desired.

Strawberries—tint red, shape into strawberries. Brush with egg white beaten until foamy, then roll in red sugar. Tint some more marzipan green and roll into a thin sheet. With scissors, cut hulls and stems and press on top of strawberries.

Pears—tint yellow and shape into pears. Use a whole clove pointed end up for the stem and pointed side in for the blossom end. Paint a brush on the side of the pear using Egg Yolk Paint (see page 53).

Peaches—tint orange and shape into peaches, making a groove at one side for split in peach. Tint some more marzipan green and roll into a thin sheet. Cut leaves and stems for peaches. Paint a blush on the peach using Egg Yolk Paint (see page 53).

Bananas—tint yellow and shape into bananas. Use Egg Yolk Paint (see page 53) tinted green for the ends of the bananas. Mix cocoa with water and, using a fine brush, paint flecks and lines on bananas.

Apples—tint green and shape into apples. Use a whole clove pointed end up for the stem. Paint on blush using Egg Yolk Paint (see page 53). Tint some more marzipan green and roll into a thin sheet. Cut leaves and press next to stem on apple.

Grapes—tint green and shape into grapes. Using egg white beaten until foamy to "glue" them together, shape grapes into bunches. Tint some more marzipan deep green and roll into a thin sheet. Shape into long, curly tendrils and grape leaves. Make veins on leaves using a toothpick.

MAKES 1¾ POUNDS

INGREDIENTS
1⅓ cups half-and-half
1 cup unsifted all-purpose flour
1 can (8 ounces) almond paste, broken into small pieces
1 pound confectioners' sugar, sifted

PECAN ROLLS

MAKES 32

INGREDIENTS
28 caramels
¼ cup half-and-half
2 tablespoons butter
2 cups confectioners' sugar
2 cups pecan halves

1 In a 1½-quart saucepan, heat caramels with half-and-half and butter over low heat until melted. Stir in confectioners' sugar and pecans. Shape mixture into a roll 16 inches long. Wrap roll in buttered waxed paper. Chill several hours.

2 With a sharp knife, cut roll into ½-inch slices. Store in an airtight container in a cool, dry place.

NO-COOK AFTER DINNER MINTS

MAKES 3 DOZEN

INGREDIENTS
1 egg white
2 teaspoons half-and-half
1 teaspoon peppermint extract
¼ teaspoon salt
1 pound confectioners' sugar
¼ cup butter, melted
 Food coloring
 Royal Icing (see Cookie and
 Candy House), optional

1 In a bowl, mix egg white, half-and-half, peppermint extract, salt and half the confectioners' sugar. Stir in butter, desired food coloring and enough of the remaining sugar to make a mixture that can be kneaded. Shape mixture into ¾-inch balls. Place on waxed paper and pat into 1-inch rounds.

2 If desired, mints can be decorated with rosettes and leaves of Royal Icing tinted to the desired color with food coloring. Let dry at room temperature for several hours. Store in an airtight container in a cool, dry place.

Beverages
of All Kinds

*I*t has long been one of our most time-honored
traditions to join friends in toasting the holidays and
the coming year with a drink. Whether it's a casual invitation to
"Join us for drinks," or a more formal cocktail party/buffet, the holiday
season is a time for toasting, for celebrating, or just plain socializing. Many
casual Yuletide parties consist of nothing more than drinks and savory tidbits—a
time to enjoy the warmth of being with old friends, the excitement of meeting new
people, and the anticipation of a brand new year.

This section contains recipes for the traditional Eggnog, Wassail Bowl and Holiday
Champagne Punch. Serve these in your best crystal punch bowl with assorted hors
d'oeuvres and snacks for a perfect holiday get-together. You will also find recipes for
individual drinks, warm or cold, rich or low-calorie. Just remember—keep the
alcohol level low for at least an hour before departure (and, of course, always offer
juices, soft drinks, coffee, and other nonalcoholic choices) to prevent accidents on
the way home. Keep the holiday season festive—and safe!

EGGNOG

MAKES ABOUT 1 GALLON

INGREDIENTS

12 eggs
1 cup sugar
1 cup milk
2 cups brandy or dark rum
6 cups (1½ quarts) heavy
  cream
Freshly grated nutmeg

1 In a large bowl, beat eggs until very thick and creamy. Gradually beat in sugar. Blend in milk and brandy.

2 Whip cream in another bowl until it holds soft peaks. Stir whipped cream into egg mixture. Chill until ready to serve.

3 When ready to serve, stir again and ladle into punch cups. Top each serving with a dusting of nutmeg.

WASSAIL BOWL

MAKES 25 PUNCH-CUP SERVINGS

INGREDIENTS

12 small red apples
6 whole cloves
6 whole allspice berries
½ teaspoon ground cardamom
2 cinnamon sticks
1-inch piece peeled fresh ginger
2 liters ale
1 bottle (750 ml) dry sherry
6 eggs

1 Bake apples whole in a preheated 350°F oven for 20 minutes or until they are tender but still hold their shape.

2 In a large saucepan, combine spices and 1 liter of the ale. Bring to boil, lower heat and simmer for 10 minutes. Strain and return liquid to saucepan. Stir in remaining ale and sherry and bring just to simmer.

3 In a 4-quart punchbowl, beat eggs until thick and lemon-colored. Gradually beat in hot ale mixture. Float baked apples on top. Serve warm in punch cups.

Opposite: Eggnog, page 350

MULLED WINE OR CIDER

1 In a large nonaluminum saucepan, combine cranberry juice, sugar, peels and spices. Bring to boil, lower heat and simmer for 10 minutes. Strain and return liquid to saucepan. Stir in wine or cider and reheat but do not boil.

MAKES 15 PUNCH-CUP SERVINGS

INGREDIENTS
1 quart cranberry juice
½ cup sugar*
  Peel from 1 orange and 1 lemon
1 cinnamon stick
6 whole cloves
6 whole allspice berries
1 bottle (750 ml) burgundy or port or 1 quart apple cider
  Orange slices studded with whole cloves*

2 Ladle into heatproof cups and serve topped with orange slices.

*If using cider, substitute firmly packed light brown sugar. Use lemon slices instead of orange slices.

HOT BUTTERED RUM LEMONADE

*I*n a heatproof mug, stir confectioners' sugar, lemon juice and rum until sugar is dissolved. Fill mug with boiling water. Top with butter and nutmeg. Serve at once.

MAKES 1 SERVING

INGREDIENTS
2 tablespoons confectioners' sugar
¼ cup fresh lemon juice
¼ cup dark rum
  Boiling water
1 tablespoon cold butter
  Freshly grated nutmeg

FOR THE HOLIDAY TOAST

CRANBERRY RUM DRINK

1 In a large nonaluminum saucepan, bring cranberry-raspberry drink and sugar to boil. Remove from heat and stir in rum.

MAKES 6 TO 8 SERVINGS

INGREDIENTS
1 *quart cranberry-raspberry drink*
⅓ *cup sugar*
2 *cups dark rum*
Lemon slices
Cinnamon sticks

2 Ladle into heatproof mugs and serve at once, top with lemon slice and a cinnamon stick.

KIR OR KIR ROYALE

*P*lace crème de cassis into a white wine glass. Fill glass with white wine or champagne and stir gently. Serve at once. If made with white

MAKES 1 SERVING

INGREDIENTS
2 *tablespoons crème de cassis (blackcurrant liqueur)*
Chilled white wine or champagne

wine, this Burgundian specialty is called Kir; if made with champagne it is Kir Royale.

MIMOSA

1 Just before serving, stir champagne slowly into orange juice. Stir in Triple Sec. Pour into glasses and garnish with orange slices.

SERVES 8

INGREDIENTS
4 *cups chilled champagne*
4 *cups chilled fresh orange juice*
⅓ *cup Triple Sec*
Halved orange slices

Page following: Assorted Holiday Drinks

BRANDY MILK POSSET

1 In a large saucepan, heat milk with lemon rind and almond extract until steaming.

2 Gradually beat hot milk into egg whites. Stir in cognac and peach brandy.

MAKES 6 SERVINGS

INGREDIENTS
1 quart milk
1 teaspoon grated lemon rind
½ teaspoon almond extract
2 egg whites, stiffly beaten
½ cup cognac
1 cup peach brandy

3 Ladle into heatproof mugs and serve at once.

HOLIDAY CHAMPAGNE PUNCH

*I*n a 3-quart bowl, mix rums, fruit juices and sugar. Chill. When ready to serve, slowly stir in champagne. Garnish with orange and lemon slices. Ladle into punch glasses.

SERVES 12

INGREDIENTS
½ cup light rum
½ cup dark rum
½ cup fresh lemon juice
1 cup fresh orange juice
1 cup pineapple juice
½ cup sugar
2 bottles (750 ml each)
    champagne, chilled
Orange and lemon slices

SWEDISH GLÖGG

1 In a saucepan, combine water, sugar, peel, cardamom, cloves, almonds, raisins and prunes. Cover and simmer for 20 minutes. Remove from heat and pour into a heatproof bowl.

MAKES ABOUT 20 SERVINGS

INGREDIENTS

1 cup water
⅓ cup sugar
Peel of 1 orange
3 cardamom seeds
8 whole cloves
⅓ cup blanched whole
  almonds
½ cup raisins
1 cup pitted prunes
2 bottles (750 ml each) port
2 cups aquavit

2 Stir in wine and aquavit. Serve in heatproof mugs with some of the fruit and almonds.

NEW ORLEANS SAZERAC

1 In a small pitcher, stir sugar, water, Pernod and bitters until sugar is dissolved. Stir in bourbon.

MAKES 6 SERVINGS

INGREDIENTS

1 tablespoon superfine sugar
1 tablespoon water
2 tablespoons Pernod
1 teaspoon aromatic bitters
1½ cups bourbon
Crushed ice
Lemon twists

2 Fill cocktail glasses with crushed ice. Add bourbon mixture. Serve with short straws and a lemon twist.

CAJUN YELLOWBIRD

1 In a small pitcher, mix liqueur, rum and juices.

MAKES 6 SERVINGS

INGREDIENTS
¾ cup banana liqueur
¾ cup light rum
1 tablespoon fresh lemon juice
2 tablespoons pineapple juice
2 tablespoons orange juice
Crushed ice
Orange slices and pineapple chunks

2 Fill cocktail glasses with crushed ice and add rum mixture. Serve with short straws, garnishing each glass with an orange slice and a pineapple chunk.

ORANGE SANGAREE

1 In a nonaluminum saucepan, combine orange juice, lemon juice, sugar and spices and simmer for 5 minutes. Cool, strain and chill.

MAKES 6 SERVINGS

INGREDIENTS
1½ cups orange juice
¾ cups fresh lemon juice
¾ cup sugar
6 whole cloves
12 whole allspice berries
1 bottle (750 ml) red Bordeaux
Ice cubes
Chilled champagne
Orange slices

2 Divide mixture among 6 tall glasses. Add red wine and 2 ice cubes to each glass. Fill glasses with chilled champagne. Add orange slices and serve.

SYLLABUB

1 In a 3-quart punchbowl, mix Sauternes, lemon rind and juice, and sugar. Stir until sugar is dissolved. Stir in milk and heavy cream.

MAKES 16 PUNCH-CUP SERVINGS

INGREDIENTS
2 cups Sauternes
    Grated rind and juice of
    2 lemons
1½ cups sugar
2 cups milk
3 cups (1½ pints) heavy
    cream
4 egg whites
⅓ cup sugar
    Freshly grated nutmeg

2 In another bowl, beat egg whites until stiff. Gradually add sugar, beating until mixture is stiff and glossy. Spoon meringue in mounds on top of punch. Sprinkle with nutmeg. Serve at once in punch cups.

ALMOND MOCHA

1 In a saucepan, whisk coffee, sugar, amaretto, cinnamon and milk. Bring to boil, then pour into heatproof mugs.

MAKES 6 SERVINGS

INGREDIENTS
3 cups strong coffee
3 tablespoons sugar
1¼ cups amaretto liqueur
1½ teaspoons ground
    cinnamon
2 cups milk
1 cup (½ pint) heavy cream
1 tablespoon confectioners'
    sugar
2 tablespoons raspberry
    liqueur

2 Whip cream with confectioners' sugar until thick. Fold in raspberry liqueur. Spoon on top of hot mocha and serve at once with long spoons.

CHRISTMAS PUNCH

MAKES 6 SERVINGS

INGREDIENTS
1 cup tequila
6 tablespoons fresh lime juice
½ cup grenadine
3 cups crushed ice
Lime slices
6 tablespoons green crème de menthe

1 In a blender, combine tequila, lime juice, grenadine and crushed ice and blend well.

2 Pour into cocktail glasses. Garnish with a lime slice. Serve crème de menthe in a cordial glass. Pour over cocktail and sip through a straw.

MEXICAN COFFEE

MAKES 6 SERVINGS

INGREDIENTS
3 cups strong hot coffee
1 teaspoon ground cinnamon
3 cups milk
6 tablespoons sugar
1½ pints chocolate ice cream

1 In a saucepan, combine coffee, cinnamon, milk and sugar and bring to boil.

2 Pour into large heatproof mugs. Top with ice cream and serve at once with spoons.

TEA NECTAR

1 In a nonaluminum saucepan, combine all ingredients and bring to boil. Lower heat and simmer for 5 minutes.

MAKES 6 SERVINGS

INGREDIENTS
3 cups apricot nectar
1½ cups pineapple juice
1 teaspoon ground cinnamon
1 lemon, sliced
12 whole cloves
1 tablespoon instant tea

2 Strain into heatproof mugs and serve at once.

BRAZILIAN COFFEE

1 In a large saucepan, combine chocolate, sugar and milk and whisk over low heat until chocolate is melted. Remove from heat and stir in vanilla and liqueur.

MAKES 6 SERVINGS

INGREDIENTS
3 squares (3 ounces)
   unsweetened chocolate
⅓ cup sugar
6 cups milk
1 teaspoon vanilla
½ cup coffee liqueur
   Cinnamon sticks

2 Pour into heatproof mugs and add cinnamon sticks. Serve at once.

VIENNESE SPICED COFFEE

MAKES 6 SERVINGS

INGREDIENTS
4 cups strong coffee
½ cup cognac
2 tablespoons syrup from
  spiced crab apples
1 cup (½ pint) heavy cream,
  whipped to soft peaks
Ground cinnamon

1 In a saucepan, heat coffee with cognac and syrup until steaming but not boiling.

2 Pour into large coffeecups and top with cream. Dust cream with cinnamon and serve at once.

BANANA THICK SHAKE

MAKES 6 SERVINGS

INGREDIENTS
3 cups milk
3 ripe bananas, peeled
  and sliced
⅓ cup honey
1 teaspoon vanilla
1 pint vanilla ice cream,
  softened

1 In a blender, combine all ingredients except ice cream and process until smooth. Beat mixture into ice cream.

2 Pour into tall glasses and serve with wide straws.

CONVERSION TABLES

The cup and spoon measures given in the book are U.S. Customary (cup = 235 ml; 1 tablespoon = 15 ml.) Use these tables when working with British Imperial or Metric kitchen utensils.

LIQUID MEASURES

The Imperial pint is larger than the U.S. pint; therefore note the following when measuring liquid ingredients.

U.S.	IMPERIAL
1 cup = 8 fluid ounces	1 cup = 10 fluid ounces
½ cup = 4 fluid ounces	½ cup = 5 fluid ounces
1 tablespoon = ¾ fluid ounce	1 tablespoon = 1 fluid ounce

U.S. MEASURE	METRIC*	IMPERIAL*
1 quart (4 cups)	950 mL	1½ pints + 4 tablespoons
1 pint (2 cups)	450 mL	¾ pint
1 cup	236 mL	¼ pint + 6 tablespoons
1 tablespoon	15 mL	1 + tablespoon
1 teaspoon	5 mL	1 teaspoon

Note that exact quantities are not always given. Differences are more crucial when dealing with large quantities. For teaspoon and tablespoon measures, simply use scant or generous quantities, or for more accurate conversions, rely upon metric.

SOLID MEASURES

Outside the U.S., cooks measure more items by weight. Here are approximate equivalents for basic items in this book.*

	U.S. CUSTOMARY	METRIC	IMPERIAL
Beans (dried, raw)	1 cup	225g	8 ounces
Butter	1 cup	225g	8 ounces
	½ cup	115g	4 ounces
	¼ cup	60g	2 ounces
	1 tablespoon	15g	½ ounce
Cheese (grated)	1 cup	115g	4 ounces
Coconut (shredded)	½ cup	60g	2 ounces
Fruit (chopped)	1 cup	225g	8 ounces

To avoid awkward measurements, some conversions are not exact.

	U.S. CUSTOMARY	METRIC	IMPERIAL
Herbs (chopped)	¼ cup	7g	¼ ounce
Mushrooms (chopped)	1 cup	70g	2½ ounces
Nut Meats (chopped)	1 cup	115g	4 ounces
Pasta (dried, raw)	1 cup	225g	8 ounces
Peas (shelled)	1 cup	225g	8 ounces
Raisins (and other dried fruits)	1 cup	175g	6 ounces
Rice (uncooked)	1 cup	225g	8 ounces
(cooked)	3 cups	225g	8 ounces
Spinach (cooked)	½ cup	285g	10 ounces
Vegetables (chopped raw: onion, celery)	1 cup	115g	4 ounces

DRY MEASURES

The following items are measured by weight outside of the U.S. These items are variable, especially the flour, depending on individual variety of flour and moisture. American cup measurements on following items are loosely packed, flour is measured directly from package (presifted).

	U.S. CUSTOMARY	METRIC	IMPERIAL
Flour (all-purpose)	1 cup	150g	5 ounces
	½ cup	70g	2½ ounces
Cornmeal	1 cup	175g	6 ounces
Sugar (granulated)	1 cup	190g	6½ ounces
	½ cup	85g	3 ounces
	¼ cup	40g	1¾ ounces
(powdered)	1 cup	80g	2⅔ ounces
	½ cup	40g	1⅓ ounces
	¼ cup	20g	¾ ounce
(brown)	1 cup	160g	5⅓ ounces
	⅓ cup	80g	2⅔ ounces
	¼ cup	40g	1⅓ ounces

OVEN TEMPERATURES

Gas Mark	¼	2	4	6	8
Fahrenheit	225°	300°	350°	400°	450°
Celsius	110°	150°	180°	200°	230°

INDEX

Almond
- Anise Loaf, Italian, 261
- Mocha (Beverage), 359
- Rings, Danish, 323

Amaretti, Italian (Cookies), 334

Appetizers, 84-109
- Brie Cheese Fondue, Easy, 101
- Carpaccio, 104
- Caviar, Three, Mosaic, 100
- Cheese Platter, how to arrange, 84
- Cranberries, Pickled, 108
- Cream Cheese Chutney Snacks, 100
- Crudités with Curry Herb Dip, 93
- Eggs, Spicy Deviled, 99
- Endive Stuffed with Goat Cheese and Grapes, 99
- Grapefruit Salad, 209
- Liver Pâté Wreath, 106
- Mozzarella, Smoked, with Tapenade, 101
- Mushrooms and Cauliflower à la Grecque, 67
- Pasta Shells Stuffed with Crabmeat Salad, 95
- Pâté Maison, 64
- Pear Salad, 209
- Pine Cone Blue Cheese, 102
- Polpette (Italian Meatballs), 105
- Quick and Easy, 84-90
- Salmon Mousse, 98
- Seafood Salad in Avocado, 200
- Sesame Chicken Wings, 108
- Shrimp Pâté, 67
- Shrimp, Pickled, and Olives with Christmas Cheese Balls, 94
- Smoked Salmon and Sturgeon with Horseradish Cream, 104
- Sweetbreads and Oysters Creamed, in Toast Cups, 109

Apple(s)
- Bread, Pennsylvania Dutch, 262
- Cranberry Cheese-Crusted Pie, 270
- Date Streusel Pie, 269
- Pecan Chutney, 78
- Rosy Spiced, 146
- and Yams, 177

Apricot Banana Pie, 283
Apricot Rum Savarin, 316
Artichokes, Baby, Stuffed, 179
Asparagus and Snow Peas, 179

Austrian Gugelhupf, 240
Austrian Linzer Torte, 310

Banana Apricot Pie, 283
Banana, Thick Shake, 362
Barbecued Beef, Lamb or Veal, 219
Bean(s)
- "Baked," Top-of-the-Range, 178
- Black, Soup, 113
- Salad, Marinated, Mixed, 203

Beef
- Carpaccio, 104
- Dijon Shell of, 129
- Filets, Spicy, 129
- Rib Roast, with Horseradish Sauce and Yorkshire Pudding, 127
- Steak Tartare, Bite-Size, 90
- Toasts, 86

Beef, Cooked (Leftover)
- Barbecued, 219
- Deviled, 218
- Hashburgers, 217
- Parmesan, 217

Beets in Sour Cream, 195
Belgian Dark Bread, 255
Berliner Kraenze (Cookies), 325
Beverage Table (Bar), Setting, 32

Beverages, 350-62
- Almond Mocha, 359
- Banana Thick Shake, 362
- Brandy Milk Posset, 356
- Cajun Yellowbird, 358
- Champagne Punch, Holiday, 356
- Coffee. See Coffee
- Cranberry Cordial, 83
- Cranberry Rum Drink, 353
- Eggnog, 350
- Glögg, Swedish, 357
- Hot Buttered Rum Lemonade, 352
- Kir or Kir Royale, 353
- Mimosa, 353
- Mulled Wine or Cider, 352
- Orange Sangaree, 358
- Punch, Christmas, 360
- Sazerac, New Orleans, 357
- Syllabub, 359
- Tea Nectar, 361
- Wassail Bowl, 350

Black Bean Soup, 113
Blue Cheese Pine Cone, 102

Bohemian Houska (Bread), 251
Bolognese Sauce for Pasta, Sausage and Meat, 68
Bourbon Cake, Kentucky, 308
Bourbon Cider Pie, 279
Brace of Ducklings with Red Cabbage and Stuffed Green Apples, 157
Brandied Cheese, 90
Brandied Pears, 79
Brandy Milk Posset, 356
Brazilian Coffee, 361
Brazilian Lace Wafers, 320

Bread, 237-66. See also Rolls
- Almond Anise Loaf, Italian, 261
- Apple, Pennsylvania Dutch, 262
- Belgian Dark, 255
- Brown, New England, 266
- Carrot, Midwest, 261
- Cheese Loaf, Dutch, 258
- Christopsomo, Greek, 252
- Cranberry Orange, 74
- Egg, Vienna, 237
- Gugelhupf, Austrian, 240
- Honey, English, 260
- Jule Kage, Norwegian, 251; Bohemian Houska, 251
- No-Knead, Danish, 259
- Oatmeal Currant, Scotch, 242
- Panettone, Italian, 243
- Pompe a l'Huile, French, 250
- Poppyseed, Hungarian, 253
- Poteca, Yugoslavian, 246
- Roscón de Reyes (Three Kings'), Spanish or Mexican, 248
- Sculpture Dough, 59
- Soda, Irish, 259
- Spiced Pear, Swiss, 238
- Spoonbread, Tex-Mex, 266
- Squash Nut, Indian, 263
- St. Lucia Ring, Swedish, 245
- Stollen, German, 241
- Viipuri Twist, Finnish, 249

Brie Cheese Fondue, Easy, 101
Broccoli with Garlic, Pine Nuts and Mushrooms, 190
Brown Bread, New England Oven-Baked, 266
Brownie Pie with Cocoa Cream, 273
Brussels Sprouts with Cheese Crumbs, 190
Bûche de Noël, French, 302

Buffet Table, Setting 31
Burritos, Mexican, 224
Butter, Herb and Garlic, 69

Cabbage, Caraway, 194
Café au Lait, Spiced Mix, 82
Cajun Yellowbird (Beverage), 358

Cake, 299-311 (Starred (*) Cakes Can Be Shipped)
- Apricot Rum Savarin, 316
- Bourbon, Kentucky, 308
- Bûche de Noël, French, 302
- Cheesecake, Italian Ricotta, 309
- Chocolate Orange, Danish, 301
- Cupcakes, Chocolate, Swiss, 299
- *Fruitcake, Dark, with Hard Icing, English, 311
- Honey Nut, Greek, 305
- *Honey, Ukrainian, 306
- Linzer Torte, Austrian, 310

Canadian Honey Drops, 322
Candy. See also Confections
- Cane Cookies, 55
- Christmas, 346
- and Cookie House, 56

Caraway Cabbage, 194
Carpaccio, 104

Carrot(s)
- Bars, Frosted, Midwest, 319
- Bread, Midwest, 261
- Oranged, 185
- Pineapple Preserves, 78

Cauliflower with Crumbs, 195
Cauliflower and Mushrooms à la Grecque, 67
Caviar Potatoes, 85
Caviar, Three, Mosaic, 100
Celery and Leek Soup, Cream of, 113
Celery and Tomatoes Braised, 189
Cereal Wreath, 60
Champagne Melon Sorbet, 296
Champagne Punch, Holiday, 356
Chartreuse of Vegetables, 189

Cheese
- Balls, Pickled Shrimp and Olives with, 94
- Blue Cheese Pine Cone, 102
- Brie, Fondue, Easy, 101
- Cream, and Chutney Snacks, 100
- —Crusted Apple Cranberry Pie, 270

Goat, Endive Stuffed with, 99
Loaf, Dutch, 258
Nut Snacks, 89
Platter, how to arrange, 84
Sauce, All-Purpose, for Pasta,
    Vegetables, Chicken or Fish, 69
Cheesecake, Italian Ricotta with
    Amaretto Sauce, 309
Cheesecake Pie, Lemon-Topped, 275
Chestnut Herb and Sausage Soup, 124
Chicken
    Breasts, Gingered in Green Onion
        Pastry, 159
    Roast, with Dried Fruit Stuffing and
        Herbed Onion Rice, 158
    Supremes with Lemon and Mushroom
        Sauce, 160
    Wings, Sesame, 108
Chicken, Cooked (Leftover)
    Almond Orange, 231
    Cajun Gumbo, 233
    and Ham Jambalaya, 226
    Pita Pizzas, 232
Children's Recipes, 53-62
    Bread Sculpture Dough, 59
    Candy Cane Cookies, 55
    Cereal Wreath, 60
    Cookie and Candy House, 56
    Cutout Cookies, 53
    Gingerbread House, 58
    Popcorn Balls, 59
    Santa's Pillows, 62
    Snowballs, 62
    Sparkling Marshmallows, 60
Chocolate
    Cupcakes, Swiss, 299
    –Dipped Dried Fruits and Raisin Nut
        Clusters, 81
    Ice Cream, Double, 292
    Orange Cake, Frosted, Danish, 301
Christmas
    about, 5-8
    Candles, 39-40
    Customs Around the World, 12-19
    Decorations, 20-26
    Gift Wrapping, 34-36
    Stockings, about making, 37-38
    Table Settings, 27-33
    Tree Ornaments, 40-51
    Tree, The Story of the, 8-11
    Wreath, about making, 38-39
Chutney, Apple Pecan, 78
Cider, Mulled, 352
Clams Herb-Baked, 174

Coconut Custard Frozen Pumpkin Pie, 280
Coffee
    Anisette Granita, 298
    Brazilian, 361
    Liqueur, 83
    Mexican, 360
    Viennese Spiced, 362
Cognac Balls, 82
Compote Rum Dried Fruit, 77
Confections, 341-48 (Starred (*)
    Confections Can Be Shipped)
    *Christmas Candy, 346
    Dried Fruit Candy, Ukrainian, 344
    *Fudge, Easy Foolproof, 341
    *Maple, Vermont, 344
    *Marzipan Fruits, 347
    Mints, No-Cook, After Dinner, 348
    Pecan Rolls, 348
    *Pecans, Spiced, Georgia, 341
    *Penuche, Mexican, 342
    Pralines, New Orleans, 343
    *Torrone, Italian (Cremona
        Nougat), 345
    Truffles, 346
    *Walnuts, Grape, Napa Valley, 342
Cookie(s), 317-40
    Almond Rings, Danish, 323
    Amaretti, Italian, 334
    Berliner Kraenze, 325
    Candy Cane, 55
    and Candy House, 56
    Carrot Bars, Frosted, Midwest, 319
    Cognac Balls, 82
    Cutout, 53
    Galletas, Spanish, 338
    Granola Bars, California, 318
    Honey Drops, Canadian, 322
    Hussar's Kisses, Hungarian, 332
    Kourambiedes, Greek, 330
    Lace Wafers, Brazilian, 320
    Lebkuchen, German, 326
    Peanut Pie, Alabama, 317
    Pfeffernuesse, German, 325
    Pinwheel, 320
    Sandbakelser, Swedish, 339
    Serbian, Hard, 337
    Sesame Seed, Greek, 330
    Shortbread Scotch, 335
    Speculaas, Dutch, 324
    Spritz, Norwegian, 333
    Toscas, Swedish (Tartlets), 340
    Tuiles, French, 324
    Vanillekipferl, Viennese, 329
    Zimtsterne, German, 328

Corn Custard with Scalloped Tomatoes, 182
Crab and Scallop Soup, 120
Crab-Stuffed Jumbo Shrimp, 174
Crabmeat Salad, Pasta Shells Stuffed with, 95
Cranberry(ies)
    Cordial, 83
    Mincemeat Pie, 268
    Orange Bread with Cointreau Butter, 74
    Pickled, 108
    Raspberry Sauce, 77
    Rum Drink, 353
    Wine Mold, 211
Cream Cheese and Chutney Snacks, 100
Crème de Menthe Sherbet, 295
Crudités with Curry Herb Dip, 93
Crunch Chunks (Tidbit), 89
Crusted Double Lamp Chops, 142
Cupcakes, Swiss Chocolate, 299
Cutout Cookies, 53

Danish
    Almond Rings, 323
    Frosted Chocolate Orange Cake, 301
    No-Knead Christmas Bread, 259
Date Nut Dips, 85
Decorations. See Christmas
Dessert (Coffee) Table, Setting, 33
Deviled Beef, 218
Deviled Eggs, Spicy, 99
Dijon Shell of Beef, 129
Ducklings Brace of, with Red Cabbage
    and Stuffed Green Apples, 157
Dutch Cheese Loaf, 258
Dutch Speculaas, 324

Eggnog, 350
Eggnog Chiffon Pie, 272
Eggplant Stew, 193
Eggs, Spicy Deviled, 99
Endive Stuffed with Goat Cheese
    and Grapes, 99
English
    Fruitcake with Hard Icing, 311
    Honey Bread, 260
    Plum Pudding with Brandy Hard
        Sauce, 312

Family Table, Setting, 30
Fan Tan Rolls, 256
Finnish Viipuri Twist (Bread), 249
Fish. See Name of Fish
Flavored Vinegars, 72
Flounder Fillets Stuffed with Spinach,
    Pine Nuts, Red Pepper and Peas, 164

Fondue Brie Cheese, Easy, 101
French
    Bûche de Noël, 302
    Pompe a l'Huile (Bread), 250
    Tuiles, 324
Frozen Pumpkin Pie, Coconut
    Custard, 280
Fruit(s). See also Name of Fruit
    Compote, Rum Dried, 77
    Dried, Chocolate-Dipped, and
        Raisin Nut Clusters, 81
    Dried, Ukrainian Candy, 344
    Soup, Swedish, 120
Fruitcake, Dark, with Hard Icing,
    English, 311
Fudge, Easy Foolproof, 341

Galletas, Spanish (Cookies), 338
Game Hens Glazed with Spiced
    Cranberries, 154
German
    Lebkuchen, 326
    Pfeffernuesse, 325
    Stollen, 241
    Zimtsterne (Cookies), 328
Giblet Gravy, 150
Gift Wrapping, 34-36
Gifts from the Kitchen, 64-83. See Also
    Bread; Cake; Cookies; Pudding
Gingerbread House, 58
Gingerbread Ice Cream, 293
Gingered Chicken Breasts in Green Onion
    Pastry with Wild Mushroom Sauce, 159
Glögg, Swedish, 357
Goose, Dickens Style Christmas, 153
Gorgonzola Crisps, 90
Granita, Coffee Anisette, 298
Granola Bars, California, 318
Grape Grills, 85
Grapefruit Appetizer Salad, 209
Grapefruit Campari Sherbet, 298
Gravy, Giblet, 150
Greek
    Christopsomo (Bread), 252
    Honey Nut Cake (Amygdalopita), 305
    Kourambiedes (Cookies), 330
    Sesame Seed Cookies, 330
Green Beans, Sweet-Sour, 186
Guelhupf, Austrian, 240
Gumbo, Cajun, Chicken or Turkey, 233

Ham
    Bread-and-Butter Casserole, 227
    and Chicken Jambalaya, 226

Grills, 227
  Spiced with Minted Peas, 145
Herb
  -Baked Clams, 174
  and Garlic Butter, 69
  and Spice Blends, 71
Honey
  Bread, English, 260
  Cake, Ukrainian Medivnyk, 306
  Drops, Canadian, 322
  Nut Cake, Greek, 305
Hot Buttered Rum Lemonade, 352
Hungarian Poppyseed Bread, 253
Hussar's Kisses, Hungarian (Cookies), 332

Ice Cream, 290-98. *See also* Granita;
  Sherbet; Sorbet
  Banana Thick Shake, 362
  Chocolate, Double, 292
  Gingerbread, 293
  Maple Walnut, 295
  Pumpkin, 294
  Vanilla, Old-Fashioned, 290
Indian Squash Nut Bread, 263
Irish Soda Bread, 259
Italian
  Almond Anise Loaf, 261
  Amaretti, 334
  Cheesecake, Ricotta, with Amaretto
    Sauce, 309
  Meatballs (Polpette), 105
  Melon, 85
  Panettone, 243
  Torrone (Cremona Nougat), 345

Jule Kage, Norwegian, 251

Kir or Kir Royale, 353
Kourambiedes, Greek, 330

Lace Wafers, Brazilian, 320
Lamb
  Chops, Crusted Double, 142
  Leg of, with Bombay Sauce, 143
  Rack of, Marinated, 141
Lamb, Cooked (Leftover)
  Barbecued, 219
  in Filo, 222
  with Squash, 221
Lebkuchen, German, 326
Leek and Celery Soup, Cream of, 113
Leeks and Mushrooms, Braised, 187
Leftover(s), 217-34
  Sandwiches, 214-15

Lemon Sherbet, Easy, 297
Lemon-Topped Cheesecake Pie, 275
Lemonade, Hot Buttered Rum, 352
Lime Salad, Molded, 213
Linzer Torte, Austrian, 310
Liqueur, Coffee, 83
Liver Pâté Wreath, 106
Lobster Grilled with Mussels, 172
Lychees Chinoise, 89

Manicotti, Turkey, 230
Maple Confection, Vermont, 344
Maple Walnut Ice Cream, 295
Marinated Mixed Bean Salad, 203
Marinated Rack of Lamb, 141
Marshmallows, Sparkling, 60
Marzipan Fruits, 347
Meatballs, Italian (Polpette), 105
Melon Champagne Sorbet, 296
Melon, Italian, 85
Mexican
  Burritos or Tacos, 224
  Coffee, 360
  Penuche, 342
  Pork, 86
  Roscón de Reyes (Three Kings'
    Bread), 248
  Sweet Rolls, 257
Mimosa (Beverage), 353
Mincemeat Cranberry Pie, 268
Minestrone, 112
Minted Peas, 146
Mints, No-Cook After Dinner, 348
Mozzarella Melts, 90
Mozzarella, Smoked, with Tapenade, 101
Mulled Wine or Cider, 352
Mushroom(s). *See also* Wild Mushrooms
  Artichoke and Spinach Salad, 205
  and Cauliflower à la Grecque, 67
  and Leeks, Braised, 187
  and Seafood Soup, Quick, 115
Mustard Blends, 72

New England Oven-Baked Brown Bread, 266
New England Steamed Pudding, 314
New Orleans Pralines, 343
New Orleans Sazerac (Beverage), 357
Norwegian Jule Kage (Bread), 251
Norwegian Spritz, 333

Oatmeal Currant Bread, Scotch, 242
Olive Dunks, Stuffed, 86
Onion(s)
  Dainties, 89

Lover's Salad, 208
  and Peas Creamed with Peanuts, 186
  Soup with Cheese Custard, 114
Orange Raisin Peanut Pie, 276
Orange Sangaree (Beverage), 358
Oranged Carrots, 185
Oriental Broils, 86
Ornaments, Christmas Tree, 40-51
Oyster(s)
  with Spinach, Leeks and
    Champagne, 173
  Stew, 121
  and Sweetbreads Creamed, in
    Toast Cups, 109

Panettone, Italian, 243
Parsnips, Glazed, 192
Party Snacks, 84-109. *See also* Appetizers
Pasta
  Sauce, Pork, 223
  Sausage and Meat Bolognese Sauce
    for, 68
  Shells Stuffed with Crabmeat Salad, 95
  Turkey Manicotti, 230
  Vegetable Salad, 207
Pâté
  Liver, Wreath, 106
  Maison, 64
  Shrimp, 67
Peanut Pie Cookies, Alabama, 317
Pear(s)
  Appetizer Salad, 209
  Brandied, 79
  Bread, Swiss Spiced, 238
  Ginger Sorbet, 296
  Pie, Open-Face, 286
Peas, Minted, 146
Peas and Onions Creamed with
  Peanuts, 186
Pecan(s)
  Apple Chutney, 78
  Georgia Spiced, 341
  Rolls, 348
Pennsylvania Dutch Apple Bread, 262
Penuche, Mexican, 342
Pepper Relish, Red and Green, 75
Pfeffernuesse, German, 325
Pickled Cranberries, 108
Pickled Shrimp and Olives with Christmas
  Cheese Balls, 94
Pie, 268-88
  Apple Cranberry Deep-Dish
    Cheese-Crusted, 270
  Apple Date Streusel, 269

Bourbon Cider, 279
Brownie with Cocoa Cream, 273
Cheesecake, Lemon-Topped, 275
Coconut Custard Frozen Pumpkin, 280
Crust, Basic, 268
Eggnog Chiffon, 272
Mincemeat Cranberry, 268
Orange Raisin Peanut, 276
Pear, Open-Face, 286
Pineapple Chess, 284
Prune Whip, 288
Raisin, 287
Sweet Potato with Caramel Nut
  Topping, 281
Pilaf, Wild Rice in Mushroom Caps, 181
Pine Cone Blue Cheese, 102
Pineapple
  Butternut Squash, 184
  Carrot Preserves, 78
  Chess Pie, 284
Pinwheel Cookies, 320
Pizzas, Chicken Pita, 232
Plum Pudding with Brandy Hard
  Sauce, English, 312
Polpette (Italian Meatballs), 105
Popcorn Balls, 59
Poppyseed Bread, Hungarian, 253
Pork
  Crown Roast of, Apple, Apricot and
    Rice Stuffing, 140
  Mexican, 86
Pork, Cooked (Leftover)
  Pasta Sauce, 223
  Sweet-Sour on Onion Shortcake, 225
Potato(es). *See also* Sweet Potatoes
  Salad, Holiday Molded, 197
  Twice-Baked, Idaho, 176
  White and Sweet, Scalloped, 178
Pralines, New Orleans, 343
Preserves, Pineapple Carrot, 78
Prune Whip Pie, 288
Pudding, 312-15 (Starred (*) Puddings
  Can Be Shipped)
  *Plum with Brandy Hard Sauce, 312
  *Steamed, New England, 314
  Tipsy, 315
Pumpkin
  Ice Cream, 294
  Pie, Frozen, Coconut Custard, 280
  or Squash Soup, 116
Punch, Christmas, 360
Punch, Holiday Champagne, 356

Quick and Easy Appetizers, 85-90

Raisin Pie, 287
Raspberry Sherbet, Quick, 297
Red Snapper Baked with Crabmeat, 168
Red and Green Soup, 119
Relish, Red and Green Pepper, 75
Rib Roast, Standing, with Horseradish
    Sauce and Yorkshire Pudding, 127
Rice. *See also* Wild Rice Saffron,
    Salad with Ham and Tomatoes, 198
    and Salmon, Baked, 234
Rolls, Fan Tan, 256
Rolls, Sweet, Mexican, 257
Rum Dried Fruit Compote, 77
Rum-Glazed Acorn Squash, 184

Salad, 197-213
    Crabmeat, Pasta Shells Stuffed with, 95
    Cranberry Wine Mold, 211
    Grapefruit Appetizer, 209
    Marinated Mixed Bean, 203
    Molded Lime, 213
    Mushroom, Artichoke Heart
        and Spinach, 205
    Onion Lover's, 208
    Pasta Vegetable, 207
    Pear Appetizer, 209
    Potato, Holiday Molded, 197
    Saffron Rice with Ham and
        Tomatoes, 198
    Seafood Appetizer in Avocado
        Halves, 200
    Tomatoes Stuffed with Artichoke
        Hearts, 201
    Turkey Supper, 228
    Veal and Celery Remoulade, 219
    Vegetables, Assorted, 204
Salmon
    Mousse, 98
    Smoked, Horseradish Cream, 104
    Steaks with Herb Butter, 167
    Trout with Shrimp and
        Scallop Mousseline, 162
Salmon, Cooked (Leftovers)
    Pot Pie, 234
    and Rice, Baked, 234
Sandbakelser, Swedish (Cookies), 339
Sandwiches
    Leftover, 214-15
    Souffléd, 86
    Waffled, 86
Santa's Pillows, 62
Sauce
    Cheese, All-Purpose, for Pasta,
        Vegetables, Chicken or Fish, 69

Cranberry Raspberry, 77
    for Pasta, 68
Sausage and Meat Bolognese Sauce
    for Pasta, 68
Savarin, Apricot Rum, 316
Scallop and Crab Soup, 120
Scampi, Red and Green Peppers, 167
Scotch Oatmeal Currant Bread, 242
Scotch Shortbread, 335
Seafood
    Appetizer Salad in Avocado Halves, 200
    and Mushroom Soup, Quick, 115
    Orgy, 89
Serbian Hard Cookies, 337
Sesame Chicken Wings, 108
Sesame Seed Cookies, Greek, 330
Sherbet
    Crème de Menthe, 295
    Grapefruit Campari, 298
    Lemon, Easy, 297
    Raspberry, Quick, 297
Shortbread, Scotch, 335
Shrimp
    Jumbo, Crab-Stuffed, 174
    Pâté, 67
    Pickled, and Olives with Christmas
        Cheese Balls, 94
    Scampi with Red and Green
        Peppers, 167
Smoked Salmon with Horseradish
    Cream, 104
Snowballs, 62
Soda Bread, Irish, 259
Sorbet, Melon Champagne, 296
Sorbet, Pear Ginger, 296
Soup, 112-24
    Black Bean, 113
    Chestnut, Herb and Sausage, 124
    Crab and Scallop, 120
    Cream of Celery and Leek, 113
    Minestrone, 112
    Mushroom and Seafood, Quick, 115
    Onion with Cheese Custard, 114
    Oyster Stew, 121
    Pumpkin or Squash, 116
    Red and Green, 119
    Swedish Fruit, 120
    Turkey Giblet, 123
    Wild Mushroom Broth, 116
Spanish Galletas, 338
Spanish Roscón de Reyes (Three
    Kings' Bread), 248
Sparkling Marshmallows, 60
Speculaas, Dutch, 324
Spice and Herb Blends, 71

Spiced (Spicy)
    Apples, Rosy, 146
    Beef Filets, 129
    Café au Lait Mix, 82
    Glazed Ham with Minted Peas, 145
Spinach Croustade, Fresh, 188
Spinach, Mushroom and Artichoke
    Heart Salad, 205
Spoonbread, Tex-Mex, 266
Spritz, Norwegian, 333
Squash
    Butternut, Pineapple, 184
    Nut Bread, Indian, 263
    or Pumpkin Soup, 116
    Rum-Glazed Acorn, 184
Steak Tartare, Bite-Size, 90
Stir-Fried Veal, 220
Stir-Fried Zucchini, 192
Stollen, German, 241
Sturgeon with Horseradish Cream, 104
Succotash, Baked, 185
Swedish
    Fruit Soup, 120
    Glögg, 357
    St. Lucia Ring, 245
    Sandbakelser, 339
    Toscas (Tartlets), 340
Sweet Potato(es). *See also* Potatoes
    in Orange Shells, 177
    Pie with Caramel Nut Topping, 281
    and White Potatoes, Scalloped, 178
    Yams and Apples, 177
    or Yams, Creamy Whipped, 176
Sweet-Sour Green Beans, 186
Sweet-Sour Pork over Onion
    Shortcake, 225
Sweetbreads and Oysters, Creamed in
    Toast Cups, 109
Swiss Chocolate Cupcakes, 299
Swiss Spiced Pear Bread, 238
Syllabub (Beverage), 359

Table Decorations and Settings, 27-33
Tacos, Mexican, 224
Tartlets, Swedish Toscas, 340
Tea Nectar, 361
Tex-Mex Spoonbread, 266
Tipsy Pudding, 315
Tomatoes
    and Celery, Braised with Almonds, 189
    Scalloped, Corn Custard with, 182
    Stuffed, 89
    Stuffed with Artichoke Hearts, 201
Top-of-the-Range "Baked" Beans, 178
Torrone, Italian (Cremona Nougat), 345

Trout with Herbs and Capers, 165
Truffles, 346
Tuiles, French, 324
Turkey
    Giblet Soup, 123
    with Twin Stuffings, 147
Turkey, Cooked (Leftover)
    Cajun Gumbo, 233
    Frittata, 230
    Manicotti, 230
    Supper Salad, 228
Twice-Baked Idaho Potatoes, 176

Ukrainian Dried Fruit Candy, 344
Ukrainian Honey Cake (Medivnyk), 306

Vanilla Ice Cream, Old-Fashioned, 290
Veal
    Chops Braised with Sage and
        Proscuitto, 132
    Chops with Sun-Dried Tomatoes, Capers
        and Cream Sauce, 137
    Galantine, Hot, 135
    Roast with Eggplant, Peppers, 131
Veal, Cooked (Leftover)
    Barbecued, 219
    and Celery Remoulade, 219
    Stir-Fried, 220
    Prosciutto, 218
Vegetable, 176-95. *See also*
        Name of Vegetable
    Chartreuse of, 189
    Pasta Salad, 207
    Salad, Assorted, 204
Vermont Maple Confection, 344
Vienna Egg Bread, 237
Viennese Spiced Coffee, 362
Viennese Vanillekipferl (Cookies), 329
Viipuri Twist, Finnish, 249
Vinegars, Flavored, 72

Walnuts, Grape, Napa Valley, 342
Wassail Bowl, 350
White and Sweet Potatoes, Scalloped, 178
Wild Mushroom Broth, 116
Wild Rice Pilaf in Mushroom Caps, 181
Wine, Mulled, 352
Wreath, Cereal, 60
Wreath, Christmas, about making, 38-39

Yams. *See* Sweet Potatoes
Yugoslavian Poteca (Bread), 246

Zucchini, Stir-Fried, 192